How to GROW VEGETABLES Organically

How to GROW VEGETABLES Organically

by JEFF COX & the Editors
of *Rodale's Organic Gardening*® Magazine

 Rodale Press, Emmaus, Pennsylvania

Printed in the United States of America on recycled paper containing a high percentage of de-inked fiber.

Book Design by Lisa L. Gatti
Illustrations by Sally J. Bensusen and John Carlance
Contributors: Anna Carr, Jeff Cox, Tony DeCrosta, Mark Kane, Michael Lafavore, John Meeker, Jerry Minnich, Suzanne Nelson, Jack Ruttle, and Warren Schultz.

Library of Congress Cataloging-in-Publication Data

Cox, Jeff, 1940–
    How to grow vegetables organically / Jeff Cox and the editors of
  Rodale's organic gardening.
        p.   cm.
    Bibliography: p.
    Includes index.
    ISBN 0–87857–683–5
    1. Vegetable gardening. 2. Organic gardening. 3. Container
gardening. I. Rodale's organic gardening. II. Title.
SB324.3.C69   1988
635'.0484––dc19   87–25265
                                                CIP

2 4 6 8 10 9 7 5 3 1   hardcover

To the dedicated researchers and growers whose work made this book possible.

CONTENTS

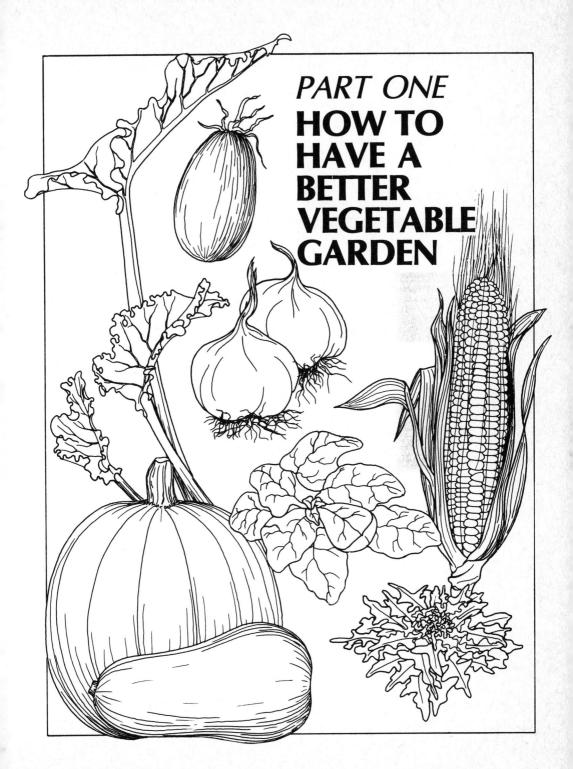

PART ONE
HOW TO HAVE A BETTER VEGETABLE GARDEN

CHAPTER 1

GARDEN PLANNING

── SOME BASIC CONSIDERATIONS ──

A well thought-out garden plan can enable you to make the most efficient use of your garden space. Whatever you reap from your garden will directly reflect how much effort has gone into it, both during the initial planning process and later on, as the growing season progresses.

Long before the shovel slides into your garden soil and a single seed is sown, you should already have a clear vision of what your garden is going to look like. A good place to start is to ask yourself the following questions.

HOW MUCH SPACE AND TIME DO YOU WANT TO DEVOTE?

You may have 1,000 square feet at your disposal, but that doesn't mean you should immediately plan to plant the entire area; that may be more of an investment in time than you are ready to make. There's no way around it—gardening does take time, if you want to do it well. There are ways to cut down on maintenance, but the truth of the matter is that every square foot of garden is going to require your attention at some point in the course of preparing the soil, planting seeds, mulching, watering, and so on throughout the season. If the time you can spend on a garden is limited, keep this in mind as you plan the dimensions. It's better to err on the small side the first year than to prepare a larger area only to watch it become overgrown and unkempt due to neglect as the season progresses. Even if time is no problem, if this is your first garden don't let your enthusiasm carry you into planning more than you can handle. After successfully managing a small garden for one season, you can add on as your gardening experience grows.

WHAT IS THE PURPOSE OF YOUR GARDEN?

The garden size and amount of vegetables you plant will also depend on how you expect your garden to meet your family's food needs. A salad garden is a small patch, usually situated right outside the kitchen door, where the cook can step out and gather an assortment of fresh greens, radishes, scallions, baby carrots or beets, and a few tomatoes. A 3-by-3-foot patch with closely spaced rows and a succession of plantings can produce an adequate supply of salad fixings.

A soup or summer garden is meant to meet the family's fresh vegetable needs throughout the growing season, with no surplus intended for winter storage or processing. Staggered small plantings which mature in sequence over a period of time will provide just the right amount at a single harvest to be eaten fresh, without spoilage and waste.

A surplus garden will meet the family's needs during the growing season, plus produce enough vegetables for storage and processing to feed the family throughout the winter. Such a garden decreases your dependence on outside sources of food and gives you year-round control over how the food you eat is grown and processed. Vegetables especially suited for storage such as onions, potatoes, pumpkins, winter radishes, winter squash, and late cabbages would be found in this garden. Also, when two plantings of crops like beets, carrots, peas, and turnips are made, the later planting would be intended for storage and the earlier planting used fresh. To make processing easier, planting should be made in large blocks so that a sizable quantity of each vegetable matures at one time.

DECIDING WHICH ——— VARIETIES TO GROW ———

Before you purchase seed, whether you do it by mail after leafing through a catalog from a seed company, or whether you buy it off the rack at the local hardware store, you should give careful thought to the vegetable varieties you will grow. Flipping through any seed catalog will reveal the range of varieties available. Choose those which are best suited to your growing conditions and the way you intend to use the harvested crop. To help you with your selection, consider the following points.

SIZE AND GROWTH HABIT

The size of your plot has an effect on which vegetable varieties you can grow. A large garden can accommodate rambunctious, sprawling vine crops like pumpkins and squashes, while a smaller garden planted with the same vegetables would become a choked, snarled mess. However, successful attempts at breeding smaller, more compact bush forms of vine crops which bear standard or near-standard-sized vegetables have made growing these plants in a small area more feasible than it used to be. Dwarf forms of nonvining crops, which are perfect for small gardens, are available, too. If you are working with a small garden area, pay attention to those varieties labeled "dwarf" and "compact" as you read catalog descriptions or seed packets.

DISEASE RESISTANCE OR TOLERANCE

Many varieties are being bred with resistance or tolerance to certain diseases, an important safeguard for the organic gardener. Each term, "resistance" and "tolerance," implies a different response to disease. A disease will not attack a variety which has been specially bred to be resistant to that disease. On the other hand, a tolerant variety will be attacked by the disease, but is able to withstand the damage and continue to grow and bear. There are many resistant or tolerant varieties available now, and you should choose from among them the varieties that are best suited to your gardening area. To be sure which varieties are adapted to your growing conditions, contact your local Extension agent (in the United States, also listed in the phone book under the titles County Agent, Agricultural Agent, or Farm Advisor; in Canada, listed in the phone book under Provincial Government, Department of Agriculture).

TIME TO MATURITY

The time it takes to grow a seed or a transplant to the point where the crop is ready for harvesting is important to consider, especially if you are faced with a short growing season, or if you want to use techniques like succession planting and interplanting. Certain vegetables are quick to mature, and will be

QUICK-MATURING VEGETABLES

Among the vegetables listed here, the longest wait you'll have from garden to table is 60 days, and the shortest a mere 25 days. The numbers in this chart indicate the average number of days to maturity from the time seeds are sown.

Beans, bush snap varieties: 50
Beets: 60
Kale: 60
Kohlrabi: 60
Lettuce, leaf: 45
Okra: 55
Peas, early varieties: 55

Radishes: 25
Scallions (green or bunching onions): 40
Spinach: 50
Squash, summer: 48
Swiss chard: 60
Turnips: 60

in and out of your garden in a relatively short period of time. Of the vegetables which require a longer time to mature, there are often early, mid-, or late-season varieties available. Based on the length of your growing season, you can choose the ones best suited to your garden.

INTENDED USE OR STORAGE

The description of each vegetable variety in a seed catalog or on the seed packet often mentions whether that variety is recommended for canning or freezing, or whether it is best used fresh. Varieties bred for canning or freezing (particularly in beans, cucumbers, squash, and tomatoes) are not always as succulent, sweet, or tender for fresh consumption as other varieties. Instead, they have been developed for their firm textures and lasting flavors when preserved.

VITAMIN CONTENT

Selecting vegetable varieties with the highest nutritive value assures you that your family is harvesting the best possible health benefits from the garden. While all vegetables provide essential minerals and vitamins in varying amounts, the following vegetables can be dubbed the "Top Ten" since they provide substantial amounts of important nutrients like vitamins A and C, calcium, niacin (B_3), riboflavin (B_2), thiamine (B_1), iron, and potassium. Ranked in descending order (based on the combined amount of the

ALL-AMERICA SELECTIONS

All-America Selections (established in 1932) makes awards on a yearly basis for the new vegetable and flower varieties that it feels exhibit qualities that are superior to contemporary varieties. The awards are based on the votes of a council of professional judges who have studied the new varieties at more than 50 trial sites scattered across the United States and Canada. Awards are given out in the form of bronze, silver, and gold medals. A gold medal is the highest possible accolade, designating a significantly superior variety, and is rarely awarded.

Seed entries pour in from around the world, representing years of breeding research done by seed companies, university breeders, government breeders, and even individuals. Each new variety is entered with the name of a comparison variety against which its performance can be judged. When judged against the best-to-date variety of its type, the value of the new variety is readily apparent.

In each of the trial grounds scattered throughout North America, the new varieties are planted side by side with their comparisons, then grown and observed under the same conditions. The criteria for judging include taste, texture, yield, disease resistance, fruit size, climatic adaptability, and novelty or uniqueness. The designated judge at each trial ground rates the new variety on a scale from 0 to 10, based on how the variety is perceived to benefit the home gardener. In order to win, a variety must receive points from at least three-quarters of the trial grounds. This rule ensures that the winning varieties are highly adaptable to different soil and climatic conditions.

Throughout this book, the abbreviation AAS will be used to designate a variety which has won an All-America Selection award. Although the All-America Selection varieties are not perfectly adapted to all gardens, your chances of success are decidedly greater when you select an award-winning variety.

above nutrients each vegetable contains) these nutritional powerhouses are broccoli, spinach, Brussels sprouts, lima beans, peas, asparagus, artichokes, cauliflower, sweet potatoes, and carrots.

OTHER CONSIDERATIONS

There are several ways you can find out which vegetable varieties do well in your particular area. First, talk to neighboring gardeners. You may find veteran vegetable growers who have done variety tests in their gardens, or who save their own seed from year to year.

When you are purchasing seed, check to see if the seed has been treated. Very often bean, corn, and pea seed is treated with fungicide, which is intended to keep the seed from rotting while germinating in cold soil in early spring. You can tell chemically treated seed by its appearance; it is usually brightly colored and coated with a chalky substance. Seed catalogs will usually mention if the seed has been treated, and some seed companies offer untreated seed especially for organic gardeners. Untreated seed sown too early in the spring when the soil is cold will not germinate well. To ensure that a good percentage of the seed germinates, sow bean seed when the soil temperature reaches 65°F, corn seed when the soil temperature is over 60°F, and pea seed when the soil temperature ranges between 55° and 60°F.

SELECTING THE SITE

No gardener, or at best only a select few, will be blessed with the ideal garden site—a loamy, fertile, well-drained plot of land which slopes gently toward the south, where it soaks up eight to ten hours of sunlight, and which is sheltered from the wind but not hemmed in by encroaching tree roots or buildings. If your potential lot doesn't measure up to this fantasy site, select the best location within the context of your own geographical limitations.

LOCATION

Before digging up part of an established lawn or other grassy area for your garden, scout around first and use your eyes before you start using your shovel. Also, you will ultimately save time and energy if you site the garden in close proximity to the compost pile, toolshed, kitchen door, and water source.

If you're strapped for space and are considering using a strip of ground along the walls of your home, garage, or other buildings, be sure to allow a margin of 2 feet between vegetable plants and the wall. Any concrete, stucco, or plaster used in construction may have introduced a large amount of lime, which could be detrimental to your plants, into the soil. Your best insurance is to leave the 2-foot margin and to replace the top 3 or 4 feet of the bed with fresh soil.

LIGHT

In order for most vegetables to grow properly, the garden should receive at least six hours of direct sun daily (eight to ten hours are ideal).

It's helpful to remember as you are deciding where individual vegetables will be planted that the southern and western sides of the garden will receive the most light and heat. Vegetables that will benefit from the extra sun, such as beans and tomatoes, should be planted there, while the crops preferring coolness and shade, like lettuce, should be grown on the northern and eastern sides.

If you are stuck with a spot that is shaded by buildings, trees, shrubbery, or any other tall objects, you'll have to adapt to the situation by concentrating on shade-tolerant vegetables in your garden. You may not be able to grow the sun worshippers like corn, squash, and tomatoes, but you'll make up for their absence by harvesting a bumper crop of crisp and succulent salad greens.

SLOPE

A garden located on a piece of land that gently slopes to the south or southwest will receive more direct sun than a nonsloping plot. The benefit of this arrangement is apparent in the spring when the soil warms up more quickly and in the fall when it stays warmer a bit longer. A slight slope where the air circulates freely will also reduce the chances of frost damage in early spring and late fall. Cold air is dense air, which will fall to the lowest area and settle. A garden located on a slope will not be caught in such a pocket of cold air and can thus escape the ravages of late spring and early fall frosts. Another plus is that the soil on a slope drains well.

While a little slope with the right exposure is beneficial, too much of a slope (when your land drops more than 1 foot in 50 feet) can pose problems. If you have no choice but to contend with a hilly area, terraces and contour rows which run across the slope can help you catch rainfall and prevent erosion from stealing away your valuable garden soil.

DRAINAGE

The drainage of your prospective garden site is another important aspect to consider. Poorly draining soil will hamper the plants' growth and cause them to yellow, since the water which collects interferes with the necessary interaction of air with plant roots and soil microorganisms. Steer clear of low areas where water can accumulate, or areas which receive the runoff from adjacent pieces of property. If you have no alternative but to plant in a low-lying area, try using raised beds. A slight drainage problem can be alleviated by increasing the amount of organic matter in the soil. But if you have a serious drainage problem caused by a hardened, compacted layer beneath the soil, a more involved system involving drainage tiles and gravel may be necessary. Your local Extension Service is the best source of information on how to improve drainage in your garden.

TREES OR SHRUBS ADJACENT TO THE GARDEN

Trees are a particular nemesis of vegetable plants. The outstretched leafy branches that provide a shady haven for sweaty gardeners also, unfortunately, block out the sun needed for vegetable growth. In addition, trees cause undergound interference with their roots, which take nutrients and water from the soil within their dripline, a circular area extending out from the trunk as far as the branches reach.

It's a good idea to give black walnut trees a wide berth, since their roots secrete a substance known as juglone which is harmful to certain vegetables, especially tomatoes. If space allows, provide a margin of 80 feet between the garden and any black walnut trees. When that's not possible, at least plant your vegetables outside the dripline.

WIND EXPOSURE

If your region is often buffeted by winds, they may knock your plants over, uproot them, and otherwise retard their growth. Constant winds also have a drying effect on soil, robbing it of moisture. An effective means of prevention is a windbreak located on the windward side of the garden. Windbreaks can be fences, hedges, trees, or even a sheet of light-admitting fiberglass. Trees and hedges planted as a windbreak should, of course, be located far enough away so they don't interfere with vegetable growth.

MAKING A WORKING DIAGRAM OF THE GARDEN

In order to set the garden plan on paper, you must first pull together some basic information. Once you've pinpointed the best location for your

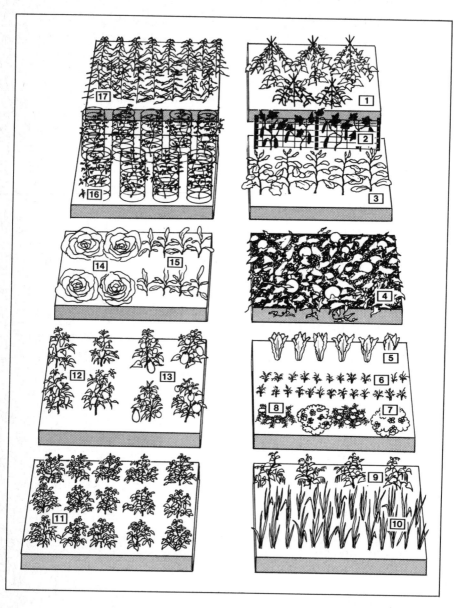

Raised bed garden. Raised beds improve drainage, warm up faster in spring, and keep soil from becoming compacted. Be sure to leave enough room for the paths—they should be wide enough to maneuver a garden cart. (1) Pole beans on teepee trellises; (2) Cucumbers on trellis; (3) Young Brussels sprouts; (4) Bush squash; (5) Swiss chard; (6) Carrots; (7) Nasturtiums; (8) Marigolds; (9) Bush green beans; (10) Onions; (11) Potatoes; (12) Peppers; (13) Eggplant; (14) Cabbages; (15) Broccoli transplants; (16) Tomatoes in cages; (17) Corn.

garden, you will have an idea of what its largest dimensions can be, as dictated by the space available. Your answer to the question of how much time you can devote to the garden should be factored in with the kinds of vegetables you have decided to plant. Add to this the approximate amount of each vegetable you want to harvest to meet your needs, and you'll arrive at the final garden size.

Once you've assembled all this information, you are ready to draw up a scale model of your garden. Measure off the dimensions of your garden using a scale of $\frac{1}{2}$ inch per foot or the premarked grid on graph paper (having each square correspond to a round number of feet or inches of garden space makes the planning easier). Within the perimeter you can now plan where each crop will be grown. Based on the growing system you will use (conventional rows, raised beds, wide-row plantings), note the spacing requirements for each vegetable. These may be found in the individual vegetable entries in An Encyclopedia of Vegetables or on seed packets. Mark off the spaces to be occupied by each crop, and jot down the date each is to be planted. Include any succession crops in parentheses along with their projected planting dates.

This garden diagram serves many purposes. By showing how many plants of each vegetable you have allotted space for, it helps you to determine how much seed to purchase. When you take it along to your garden site, you have a handy planting guide, indicating when and where each crop will go into the garden, and it acts as your seasonal reminder for succession plantings. The diagram will also be a point of reference for future planning. If the 50 feet of carrots you planted this year just weren't enough, next season you'll know by refreshing your memory with the diagram that you need to plant more than 50 feet. And keeping a permanent record of which vegetables grew where will help you plan crop rotations.

PLANNING THE LAYOUT

As you work on your garden diagram, there are certain points you should consider when deciding where to plant each vegetable. No matter which growing system you use, be it conventional rows, raised beds, or wide rows, the following items deserve special attention in the layout.

GROWTH HABIT

Take note of the growing characteristics of the vegetables to be planted. Vining crops such as cucumbers and squash that ramble over a wide area should occupy spots along the border, so they have room to roam outside the garden.

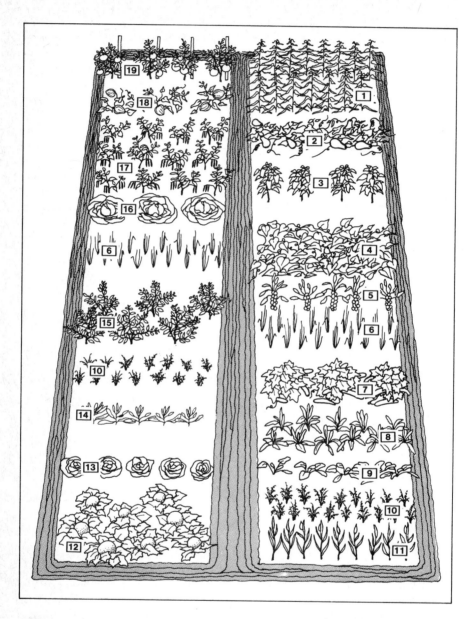

A large row garden. Plants grown in neat rows are easy to see and tend, especially if the gardener weeds the plot by tilling between rows. (1) Corn; (2) Bush summer squash; (3) Peppers; (4) Wide-row sweet potatoes; (5) Brussels sprouts; (6) Onions; (7) Bush cucumbers; (8) Beets; (9) Fall spinach seedlings; (10) Carrots; (11) Garlic; (12) Bush cantaloupe; (13) Lettuce; (14) Fall broccoli transplants; (15) Wide-row block of potatoes; (16) Cabbages; (17) Bush beans; (18) Bush winter squash; (19) Staked tomatoes.

Tall-growing crops like corn, or those that are trellised and staked, such as pole beans and tomatoes, should be planted along the northern side of the garden so that as the sun passes overhead they will not shade any adjacent low-growing crops which need full sun.

ORIENTING GARDEN ROWS AND BEDS

The way you run garden rows depends on the lay of the land and how much sun your particular crops need. If your garden plot slopes, plan your rows so that they will run across the slope to thwart any erosion problems. If your land is flat and you are growing mainly tall to medium-height, sun-loving vegetables, run the rows east to west to maximize the sun's benefits. A north-south orientation works for shade-loving crops when they are grown adjacent to a row of tall plants, which will throw their shadows on their lower-growing neighbors as the sun passes overhead.

SEASON LENGTH

Grouping plants according to their season length can be a big help when the time comes to make succession plantings. When crops that mature early are grown together in a group, harvesting opens up a block of space ready to accommodate the next crop. Grouping long-season crops together means that they will be out of the way as you harvest the early maturers and are busy replanting.

Setting aside a bed for perennials makes sense when it comes time to prepare the soil each season for annual vegetables. By concentrating the perennials in one area, you won't have to worry about dislodging them as you proceed with your plowing or spading of the garden.

GARDENING SYSTEMS

The nature of your layout will depend on whether you are using conventional rows, raised beds, or wide rows. A further discussion of all of these growing systems appears in Chapter 3, Planting. If you're using conventional rows (where seeds or transplants are set in a single row, with specific spacing between plants in the row and between the rows themselves), consider whether you will be cultivating by hand or by machine. If you use machinery like a rotary tiller, you will need to allow extra space between rows and a space for turning at the ends of the rows. When it comes to spacing your vegetables, refer to the distance requirements listed on seed packets or given under individual vegetables in An Encyclopedia of Vegetables, and plan accordingly, row by row. You'll find the spacing described in terms of "inches between plants within the row" and "distance between rows," which makes planning the layout of a garden of this type relatively straightforward.

If you're planning to plant your garden in wide rows (a band of closely spaced plants, about 18 inches wide, as opposed to a conventional narrow row) or raised beds (specially prepared growing areas in which plants are spaced closely together without conventional row spacings between them), remember to leave sufficient pathways so you have easy access to the planting areas. Make sure they're wide enough to allow room for maneuvering wheelbarrows and setting down large tools.

PLANT ROTATION

Alternating the types of vegetables you plant in the same spot in your garden from one year to the next is a simple thing to incorporate into your garden planning. And no garden is too small for you to practice rotation—in fact, small gardens demand it. Because of the concentration of plants within a small area, allowing the same vegetable to occupy the same spot season after season puts an undue strain on the already limited soil resources.

Crops vary as to the type and amount of nutrients they draw from the soil. By growing the same vegetable in the same spot, year after year, you risk depleting the soil of the particular nutrients the plant uses. Rotating vegetables with differing nutrient needs equalizes the drain on the soil's available nutrients. Vegetables can be divided into three groups based on what they take from and give back to the soil: heavy feeders, light feeders, and soil builders. The rotations you should use involve following heavy feeders by light feeders by soil builders, or following heavy feeders by soil builders by light feeders. Never follow light feeders by heavy feeders without some form of soil replenishment.

Rotations also keep a check on soilborne diseases. A vegetable can be host plant to a certain soilborne disease which will continue unabated if the host is continuously grown in the same spot. However, when you remove the host plant and set an unrelated or nonsusceptible plant in its place, you have taken an effective step toward controlling the disease (especially if three or four years pass before the host plant is planted there again). Some fungi, bacteria, and viruses which can be countered by plant rotation include: bean blight, black rot, cabbage black leg, clubroot, cucumber anthracnose, fusarium wilts, and scab.

In addition to countering diseases, rotation may also reduce your pest problems. Each type of insect tends to feed on a very narrow range of plants. So, for instance, one type of insect will zero in on your broccoli, feast away

VEGETABLES WITH SIMILAR NUTRIENT NEEDS

Heavy Feeders		Light Feeders	Soil Builders
Asparagus	Kohlrabi	Carrots	Beans, dry
Beets	Lettuce	Garlic	Beans, lima
Broccoli	Okra	Leeks	Beans, snap
Brussels sprouts	Pumpkins	Onions	Peanuts
Cabbage	Radishes	Parsnips	Peas
Cauliflower	Rhubarb	Peppers	Soybeans
Celery	Spinach	Potatoes	
Corn	Squash, summer	Rutabagas	
Cucumbers	Squash, winter	Sweet potatoes	
Eggplant	Tomatoes	Swiss chard	
Endive and Escarole		Turnips	
Kale			

throughout the season, lay its eggs, and die. If you plant broccoli in the same spot the following season, when the eggs then hatch, the succeeding insect generation will find a ready-made food supply and you'll have to fight the bugs for your broccoli. But the simple act of alternating what you grow from season to season in the same area can help minimize damage by pests. When you alternate crops, keep in mind that insects and diseases tend to attack plants in the same family. Since broccoli belongs to the mustard family, don't plant another family member like cabbage or kale in its place. Instead, choose an unrelated alternate, such as lima beans from the pea family, or eggplant from the nightshade family.

There are several ways you can accommodate rotation in your garden plan. First of all, dividing your garden into sections will help you get a rotation system going. A garden sectioned into beds allows you to work with already clearly defined units of soil, among which you can move the appropriate crop groupings. If you're working with rows, it may help to divide your entire plot into thirds. In the rows of the first third you can plant the heavy feeders; in the second, the light feeders; and in the third, the soil-building crops.

SPACE/YIELD RATIO

These vegetables produce the most in the least amount of space.

Beans (bush and pole)	Onions	Tomatoes
Beets	Peppers	Turnips
Carrots	Radishes	
Lettuce	Summer squash (bush varieties)	

———— TIPS FOR SMALL GARDENS ————

When your gardening expectations exceed the available space, you must try in every possible way to get maximum use out of a minimum of space. The vegetables you want for maximum production are those which keep producing over a period of time so you get a high yield from only a few plants (peppers and tomatoes), and those which yield a bumper crop from a small space (beets, bush squash, radishes). You'll also reap a mighty harvest from a minuscule space by planting "cut-and-come-again" crops, such as cabbage or lettuce.

Whatever you may be lacking in horizontal gardening area you may be able to gain in vertical space. Gardens don't always have to stretch out toward the horizon—they can reach for the sky as well. By erecting a fence or trellis that measures 5 feet tall and 30 feet long, you've gained 150 feet of gardening space. Within the plot itself, you can save space by training vine crops to grow upward instead of sprawling along the ground—thereby making room for more vegetables. Cucumbers, pole beans, melons, peas, vining varieties of summer and winter squash, and tomatoes can be trained to grow vertically.

Raised beds, in conjunction with intensive techniques, make the most efficient use of space. Interplanting or intercropping is an intensive technique by which you can fit more plants into the garden at the same time and increase the yield per square foot. The basic idea is to match up two compatible plants to grow in the same space. These pairings include fast- and slow-growing vegetables, small plants nestled under taller ones, and shade lovers growing in the shadow of taller sun seekers.

Succession planting is another technique that can net you a continuous supply of vegetables by making sure that your garden is working nonstop,

CUT-AND-COME-AGAIN CROPS

More than one harvest is possible if you cut the outer leaves of certain leafy green plants before they fully mature, when they are about 3 to 4 inches long. You can safely pick down to about the six centermost leaves. Take care not to harm the growing point of the plant so that leaf production can continue. With cabbage and broccoli, cutting the main head will stimulate a second crop of sprouts.

Broccoli	Endive and	Lettuce, leaf
Cabbage (early varieties)	Escarole	Swiss chard
Chinese mustard cabbage	Kale	

without any unproductive gaps in the season. This involves planting the same vegetable at two- to three-week intervals to stagger the harvest, or planting early-, mid-, and late-season varieties of the same vegetable at the same time, or replacing a crop with another as soon as it is harvested.

A cold frame or hotbed is a good investment to use in conjunction with a small garden. In addition to growing early and late crops of salad greens, you can also raise transplants which will be ready to pop in as soon as garden space opens up.

TIPS FOR LARGE GARDENS

Wasted space and poor management are just as critical in a large garden as they are in a small one. Even with more space at your disposal, you should strive to make efficient use of the whole area. Remember, more area means that more mulch, water, and compost will be needed. And it's important to keep in mind that a large, unkempt garden can be outproduced by a smaller but better-managed one. Don't take on more garden than you can handle—even if the space is available.

A large garden allows you to grow vegetables well suited for winter storage, such as potatoes, pumpkins, and winter squash, which demand a lot of growing space for a long period of time. More garden area also means you can grow plenty of food for canning and freezing. You can also accommodate a block of corn rows, something which isn't always feasible in a smaller garden.

CHAPTER 2

PREPARING THE SOIL

In the vegetable garden, where most crops have just a few months to develop from seed to edible harvest, soil composition and quality are particularly important. The soil must provide a steady supply of nutrients in order to promote rapid, uninterrupted plant growth. As the growing medium for roots, soil must also provide structural support for all shapes and sizes of vegetable plants, from tomatoes to lettuce to Brussels sprouts. At the same time, it must be loose enough for air and water to penetrate, for germinating seeds to break through, and for root and tuber crops such as carrots.

IMPROVING YOUR SOIL'S STRUCTURE AND FERTILITY

Although an experienced botanist or soil expert can often judge a soil's chemical nature simply by studying the natural vegetation it supports, most gardeners rely on periodic tests. The Agricultural Extension Service of your state or province will test soil samples for a minimal charge, or you can use a do-it-yourself kit. Home nitrogen, phosphorus, and potassium tests aren't

100 percent reliable, and their results should be considered rough estimates of the actual levels of available nutrients in the soil. Results from the Extension Service are much more accurate, but even these should be interpreted broadly.

Since soil changes as new materials are added, and plants, insects, earthworms, and rodents remove and release nutrients, samples should be tested every few years. Structural changes will be obvious as you work the soil, but chemical alterations may be less noticeable. Results from the tests will serve as guidelines for replenishing the supply of organic matter. Any soil, no matter how rich and fertile it is initially, will soon be depleted of its nutrients if it is not continually built up.

YOUR SOIL'S pH

Soil pH is the term used to express the degree of soil acidity or alkalinity, and it is based on a scale of 0 (acid) to 14 (alkaline) with the midpoint of 7 indicating a neutral soil condition. Most vegetable crops prefer a slightly acidic soil with a pH roughly between 6.0 and 6.8. Beans, broccoli, cabbage, corn, cucumbers, peppers, radishes, squash, sweet potatoes, tomatoes, and turnips can tolerate a pH as low as 5.5, but not much lower.

In very acid soils (below pH 5.0), phosphorus becomes locked up in a form that is unavailable to plants. Nutrients such as calcium, potassium, and magnesium have an increased tendency to leach out of overly acid soils. In addition, beneficial soil bacteria begin to slow down their work of turning organic matter into humus, adversely affecting soil structure. An acid condition can even prompt earthworms to move out of your garden to more hospitable ground. The incidence of the disease clubroot, which often strikes brassicas, increases in acid soils.

An overly alkaline soil (above pH 7.5) is no better. A high degree of alkalinity causes most of the trace elements, which are necessary for good plant growth, to be locked up and made unavailable to plants. An alkaline condition also breaks apart humus and in some cases causes a concentration of salts to build up to such levels that they become toxic to plants.

If your soil is too acidic, work in natural ground limestone (especially crushed dolomite), bonemeal, pulverized eggshells, clamshells, oyster shells, or wood ashes to raise the pH. If your soil is too alkaline, add pine needles, cottonseed meal, acid peat moss, leaf mold, sawdust, or wood chips.

NATURAL FERTILIZERS

The secret to successful fertilization in the organic vegetable garden is timing. Natural fertilizers rely on microorganisms to break them down into forms plants can use, and this process takes time. If you apply certain materials

(continued on page 22)

GETTING TO KNOW YOUR SOIL

Soil Type	Texture	Characteristics	How to Improve or Maintain
Clay	Feels rock hard when dry, and sticky, greasy or rubbery when moist. When you squeeze it in your hand, it forms a sticky, compact mass that doesn't break apart easily.	The very small clay particles pack together, discouraging good drainage and aeration. Clay soil is slow to absorb water, but once it does, it is very slow to dry out. It stays cold and wet well into the planting season, but does retain the sun's warmth well into the fall. If worked when too wet, the soil will form rock-like lumps and clods which are very difficult to break apart. Because nutrients don't leach out readily, this soil tends to be rich in nutrients. While a high proportion of clay particles is undesirable, they are necessary to some degree, to give strength and water-holding capacity to the soil. Clay soil is hard to work.	Massive infusions of organic matter are needed to loosen up the soil and to form a crumbly, friable structure that will promote good drainage and root zone aeration. Good materials to add are compost, manure, leaf mold, rice hulls, peat moss, coarse sand, sawdust, and wood chips. Lime helps upgrade the texture and makes the soil nutrients that are present available to growing plants. Green manure crops are very effective in improving clay soils, especially legume crops. Work organic matter into the soil in fall and leave the soil surface in a rough condition over the winter to allow frost action to break up large clods. Don't always dig to the same depth, for this will encourage a hardpan layer to form. As this layer of soil that is never penetrated becomes harder, drainage is hindered and salt concentrations may build up to harmful levels.
Loam	Soil appears to be made of various sizes of crumbs. When you squeeze it in your hand, it molds readily into a ball, which falls apart easily when squeezed.	Generally speaking, a loam consists of 50% sand, 40% silt (gritty particles halfway between clay and sand), and 10% clay with supplemental organic matter. Soils with a higher proportion of clay are termed clay loams, and those with a higher proportion of sand are called sand loams. Loam retains water well,	Keep this "ideal" soil in top shape by continually adding organic matter to maintain fertility and good structure.

GETTING TO KNOW YOUR SOIL
—*Continued*

Soil Type	Texture	Characteristics	How to Improve or Maintain
		with the excess free to drain away. Nutrients are not quickly leached out of this soil. Easy to work and very productive.	
Muck and Peat	Appears very dark brown in color. When you squeeze it in your hand, it may feel like peat moss.	This soil is rich in organic matter like mosses, grasses, and ferns in various stages of decay. The term "peat soil" is used to describe a soil in which the organic matter is not fully decomposed; a muck soil is this same soil at an advanced stage of decay. Muck soils tend to be waterlogged and somewhat deficient in lime. They are rich in nutrients (especially nitrogen), although the proper balance of minerals may not be present for good plant growth. Suited mainly for vegetable crops like celery, lettuce, and onions.	Encourage adequate drainage by adding layers of gravel or drainage tiles. Add lime as needed.
Sandy	Feels grainy and gritty. When you try to squeeze it into a ball, it may be so loose and crumbly that it holds no shape, or if it does, it will crumble apart easily.	Large, irregular particles create open spaces through which water and soluble nutrients quickly flow. Dries out and warms up rapidly, so it is especially suited for early spring crops. Easy to work and well aerated. Because nutrients leach out so quickly, sandy soils commonly have deficiencies of calcium, nitrogen, potassium, and phosphorus. The poor water-retaining capacity of this soil means there is little moisture reserve for plants to draw upon in times of drought.	Continually work in organic matter to hold water and nutrients in the soil where plants can draw upon them. Work manure in deeply in the fall or winter, and add plenty of peat moss, compost, leaf mold, or sawdust to the top layer to help build a fertile, well-structured topsoil. A green manure program will also improve the soil structure.

after you spot deficiency symptoms, the plants may not receive the nutrients in time. If you apply others too early, the nutrient value of the fertilizer may be reduced by leaching. Luckily, a soil rich in organic matter tends to minimize these fertility problems.

Most nitrogenous substances are highly soluble and lose their nutrient value through leaching. Therefore, dried blood, bat guano, and animal tankage, which release nitrogen relatively quickly, should not be applied until just before planting time.

Potassium fertilizers have different rates of release, and you must keep this in mind when deciding at what point to apply a given fertilizer. Mineral fertilizers like granite dust and greensand (found in undersea deposits) take a long time to break down and become available to plants. Apply these in the fall to benefit spring crops, or in the spring for crops to be grown later in the season.

Commonly used phosphorus fertilizers, such as rock phosphate and bonemeal, require time to become soluble, so they are less subject to leaching. They must be applied in the fall in order to supply phosphorus to spring plants, and in early spring to benefit summer plants. Because these materials require a pH above 5.0 in order to break down efficiently, it may be necessary to add some lime at the same time you add the phosphorus-rich material.

The best way for you to get these fertilizers into the garden soil is to broadcast them before the crops are planted. Pulverize mineral substances like greensand and rock phosphate and chop plant matter or wastes like compost, grass clippings, and leaves, so that they may be spread evenly over the soil surface. With mineral substances, the finer the texture, the more quickly the nutrients will be released. With a rotary tiller, plow, or garden rake, work the fertilizers into the top few inches of soil.

COMPOST

As you embark on a soil-building program, you'll find no better source of organic matter than compost. In its finished form it contains roughly two parts nitrogen, one part phosphorus, and one part potassium, with a pH of 7. It releases its nutrients slowly, and they aren't easily leached away by water seeping through the root zone. In addition to its fertility value, compost is a first-class soil amendment that can help turn hopelessly clayey or sandy soils into rich, crumbly, productive loam.

There are several ways you can start out: build an unconfined pile on the ground, start a pile in a 2- to 3-foot-deep pit, or build your pile in a bin. To get your compost pile going, lay down a layer of brush to form the base. Add a 6-inch layer of green or dry vegetable matter, then a 2-inch layer of manure (or other nitrogen-rich substance such as bloodmeal or cottonseed meal)

PERCENTAGE COMPOSITION OF COMMON ORGANIC MATERIALS AND THEIR RELATIVE AVAILABILITY

Organic Material	Nitrogen	Phosphorus	Potassium	Relative Availability
Activated sludge	5.0	3.0	0	Medium
Alfalfa hay	2.5	0.5	2.1	
Animal tankage	8.0	20.0	0	Medium
Basic slag	0	0.8	0	Rapid
Bloodmeal	15.0	1.3	0.7	
Bonemeal (steamed)	4.0	21.0	0.2	Slow
Brewer's grains (wet)	0.9	0.5	0.1	
Castor pomace	5.5	1.5	1.3	Slow
Cattle manure (dried)	2.0	1.8	2.2	Medium
Cattle manure (fresh)	3.0	0.2	0.4	Medium
Cocoa shell dust	1.0	1.5	2.7	Slow
Coffee grounds (dried)	2.0	0.4	0.7	
Colloidal phosphate	0	18–24	0	Slow
Cornstalks	0.8	0.4	0.9	
Cottonseed	3.2	1.3	1.2	
Cottonseed meal	7.0	2.5	1.5	Slow to medium
Dried blood	12–15	3.0	0	Medium to rapid
Fish emulsion	5.0	2.0	2.0	Medium to rapid
Fish meal	10.0	4.0	0	Slow
Fish scrap	7.8	13.0	3.8	Slow
Granite dust	0	0	5.0	Slow
Greensand	0	1.5	5.0	Very slow
Guano	12.0	8.0	3.0	Medium
Hoof and horn meal	12.5	1.8	0	Slow
Horse manure (composted)	0.7	0.3	0.6	Medium
Horse manure (fresh)	0.4	0.2	0.4	Medium
Leaf mold (composted)	0.6	0.2	0.4	Medium
Mushroom compost	0.4–0.7	57–62	0.5–1.5	Slow
Oak leaves	0.8	0.4	0.2	Rapid
Pig manure (fresh)	0.6	0.4	0.1	Medium
Pine needles	0.5	0.1	0	
Poultry manure (fresh)	2.0	1.9	1.9	Medium to rapid
Rabbit manure (fresh)	2.4	0.6	0.1	Medium
Rock phosphate	0	30–32	0	Very slow
Sawdust	4.0	2.0	4.0	Very slow
Seaweed	1.7	0.8	5.0	Slow to medium
Sheep manure (fresh)	0.6	0.3	0.2	Medium
Soybean meal	6.7	1.6	2.3	Slow to medium
Tankage	6.0	8.0	0	
Tobacco stems	2.0	0	7.0	Slow
Wood ashes	0	1.5	7.0	Rapid

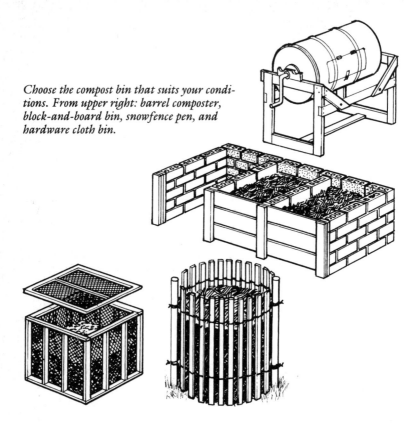

Choose the compost bin that suits your conditions. From upper right: barrel composter, block-and-board bin, snowfence pen, and hardware cloth bin.

followed by a 1/8-inch layer of topsoil. Repeat these layers until the pile stands 3 to 5 feet tall. As you are layering, dampen the materials slightly, but only enough so that they are as moist as a damp sponge. To aid the aeration of the completed pile, insert some poles or pipes down into the pile.

If you've provided the right mix of organic matter, nitrogen, bacteria, moisture, and air, the pile should begin to heat up and shrink in size within a couple of days. You'll need to turn the pile twice to help the decomposition process along. Two to three weeks after the pile has been built, turn it with a spading fork or pitchfork. Turn once again about three weeks later. As you turn the pile, move the outer portions to the inside (where the heat is the greatest) so the organic matter will be uniformly decomposed. Within three months, the material should be reduced to a crumbly, black substance ready to be added to your garden.

If you'd like quicker results and have access to a shredder, you can try the 14-day California Method. For this method, you will need a bin of some sort

COMPOST INGREDIENTS

What to Use	What to Avoid	Sources of Nitrogen (to increase bacterial activity)

Coffee grounds
Eggshells
Ground corncobs
Hedge trimmings
Kitchen wastes
  (vegetable and fruit peels)
Lawn clippings
Pine needles
Sawdust
Shredded leaves
Shredded twigs
Straw
Tea leaves
Weeds and disease-free
  plant debris
Wood shavings
	Material thicker than ¼ inch (shred or chop large pieces to speed up decomposition)
	
	Diseased or pest-laden materials
	
	Plant debris carrying pesticides or herbicides
	
	Meat, bones, grease, other fatty substances (these are slow to decompose and attract undesirable creatures)
	
	Seeds and fruit pits (attractive to rodents)
	
	Cat or dog manure, bird droppings (handling fresh manure and droppings and subsequent use of compost may transmit parasites harmful to humans)
		Bloodmeal
		Bonemeal
		Cottonseed meal
		Manure
		Tankage

to contain the material, which should be a mix of green garden debris or garbage, and dry garden debris. Begin by layering 2 to 4 inches of green materials, then 2 to 4 inches of dry materials. This organic matter should be shredded into pieces no larger than 6 to 8 inches long. Moisten each layer so that the particles glisten, but don't overwater so you end up with a sodden mess. A good size for a bin is 3 feet square, and the pile should range in height from 3 to 4 feet.

Frequent turning is the key to success with this method, for it provides the aeration necessary for the aerobic bacteria to do their breakdown work. You can turn it as frequently as your muscles can stand (not more than once per day), but don't allow more than two or three days to go by without turning. Effective turning involves removing the material from the bin in such a way that the material from the outside (top and sides) ends up on the inside of the new pile. Fluff up the material as you fork it back in the bin. If the pile seems dry, add a little water as your turn it. A well-built, frequently turned

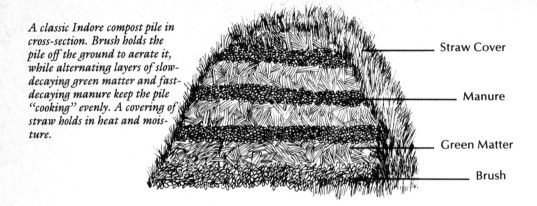

A classic Indore compost pile in cross-section. Brush holds the pile off the ground to aerate it, while alternating layers of slow-decaying green matter and fast-decaying manure keep the pile "cooking" evenly. A covering of straw holds in heat and moisture.

Straw Cover

Manure

Green Matter

Brush

pile can be ready in as few as 14 days, or with less frequent turnings, in a month. The compost is ready to use when the pile has stopped generating heat and the material looks dark and crumbly.

ANIMAL MANURE

In its fresh state, manure is potent stuff; it should never be applied directly to plants or laid down soon before planting to avoid burning seeds, seedlings, and delicate plants. Spread it on the soil the fall before spring planting and plow it under immediately to make sure the nutrients are incorporated into the soil instead of released into the air. The latest fresh manure can safely be applied and turned under is two to three months before planting.

The general rate of application in the garden is a 2- or 3-inch layer spread over the soil, which works out to 10 to 15 pounds per square yard. Dress the soil with approximately 10 pounds rock phosphate per 25 pounds manure to make up for the manure's relatively low phosphorus content. You need apply only half as much chicken manure, which is extremely high in available nutrients, as other animal manures.

Composted or "well-rotted" manure is manure that has been set aside in a pile and allowed to decompose into a moist and relatively odor-free product. Some stables sell this material, or you can oversee the process yourself if you have a quantity of fresh manure available. The easiest way to do this is to layer manure into a standard compost pile, along with green plant matter and dirt. The heat of the decomposition process destroys many harmful bacteria and weed seeds, and diminishes its potency, so you can work rotted manure into the soil up to two weeks before sowing seeds. Decomposition also condenses the pile of manure, due to the breakdown of fibrous material. Although some nutrients are lost through this process, because of the weight loss, composted manure is higher in nutrients pound for pound than fresh manure.

Dried manure is the pulverized, odor-free, bagged product sold through garden centers and nurseries at a steep price. To reach this state, the fresh manure has been dried in an oven to reduce the percentage of water, thereby increasing the percentage of nutrients and humus per unit of weight. As an example, one ton of fresh hen manure that contains 20 pounds of nitrogen, 16 pounds of phosphorus, and 10 pounds of potassium will contain 40 pounds of nitrogen, 30 pounds of phosphorus, and 19 pounds of potassium when dried. To keep the cost of gardening down, use dried manure only if you are gardening in a very small area or in containers.

GREEN MANURE

Animal wastes are not the only or even the best source of nutrient-rich organic matter. Composting is one source, green manure crops are another. In this process, legume or nonlegume (grass or grain) crops are sown and cultivated right on the garden plot, then plowed under while still green. When growing, these crops protect the soil from wind and water erosion. When plowed under, all the nutrients that were used to produce the crop are returned to the soil, along with added organic matter and, in some cases, added nutrients.

The best green manure crops for most areas are legumes, especially alfalfa and the various clovers. These plants produce strong, deep roots that can bring up nutrients from as far as 30 feet below the surface. Legumes harbor bacteria that can harness nitrogen from the air and convert it into forms available to plant roots. When the legume is plowed under, this nitrogen is left for successive crops. To guarantee that legumes have enough *Rhizobia* bacteria to fix adequate quantities of nitrogen, inoculate the seeds with the bacteria before planting.

If your soil is too acid, wet, or infertile to support a healthy vegetable crop, or if you simply want to build organic matter content, then a nonlegume is the best choice. Nonlegume green manures produce considerably more succulent top growth than most legumes, and in a shorter time. Some are quite hardy and can be grown through the winter in northern areas.

Planting and tilling schedules for green manure crops depend upon the crop rotation plan in the garden (incorporating both vegetable and green manure crops), the green manure crop's needs and, of course, local climate and soil factors. Seed may be sown in spring for summer tillage, in summer for fall tillage, or in fall for winter or spring tillage. Broadcast seeds evenly on the smoothed soil surface and cover with a fine sifting of soil.

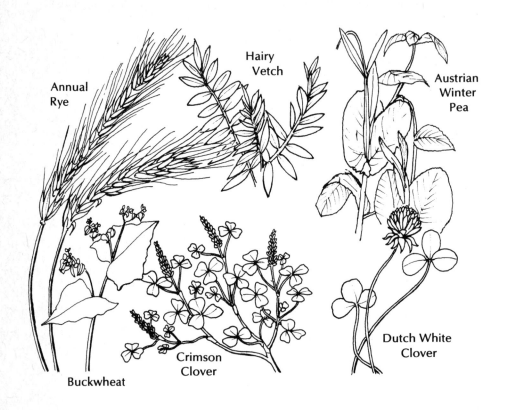

Green manures add nitrogen and humus to the soil while preventing erosion. Regular sowings of green manures also disrupt pest and disease cycles.

You can turn the crop under at any time between its greening and blossoming. As a general rule, till it under just before the first buds emerge. If the green manure crop is to be followed by early vegetables, the best time to turn it under is fall or winter. This allows plenty of time for decomposition during wet, cold months. Summer green manure crops decompose more rapidly and do not need to be tilled under until two or three weeks before planting midsummer or fall vegetables.

You may find that a very dense crop might need scything or mowing before it can be tilled, and even then could require several tillings to break it up. Hand digging, even in a fairly small plot, doesn't really do a complete job.

WORKING THE SOIL

The purpose of working the soil every year—of spading, hoeing, turning, and raking—is threefold: to promote good fertility, drainage, absorption, and soil atmosphere; to remove woody plant residues or diseased debris; and to create a firm seedbed. By beginning cultivation in the fall, you further improve soil in two ways: first, by exposing overwintering insect pests to birds, cold temperatures, and wind; and second, by leaving the ground open to frost action. The work to be done in the spring is minimal, and since less time is needed to get the seedbed in shape, you can start planting much earlier, a real advantage in boosting the yield of your garden.

CLEANING UP

The first step of cultivation, whether the ground is to be worked by machine or by hand, in the fall or in the spring, is to remove the diseased and woody plant materials left over from the previous vegetable garden. (In the interest of disease control, remove all diseased plant debris in the fall, to give harmful organisms less time to become established.) Pull up cabbage, cauliflower, and broccoli stalks, tomato vines, and bean plants. When this work is done in the fall, some clean plant matter should be left in place since it will add bulk and will probably decompose during the winter. If you're doing this preliminary work in the spring, clear the plot of all plant matter, since there is not sufficient time for it to break down before planting. Add wastes to the compost heap, and bury them deeply in the pile to eliminate any pests.

SOLARIZING YOUR SOIL

Soak the bare soil with water, then cover it with sheets of clear plastic (not the black plastic used to control weed growth). After several weeks in the sun, the soil will be "solarized"—almost 100 percent free of harmful organisms in the top 12 to 18 inches. But be ready to begin weeding, for that clear plastic acts as a greenhouse, providing a near-perfect environment for some pesky plants.

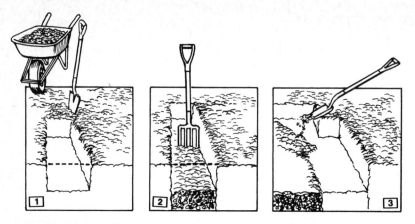

Double-Digging. (1) Open a trench the width and depth of a spade across the end of the proposed bed. Put soil from trench in wheelbarrow. (2) Loosen second foot of soil in trench with spading fork. (3) Open second trench alongside the first, spading its soil into the first trench. Continue steps 1 and 2 down the length of the bed, filling the final trench from the soil in the wheelbarrow.

DIGGING

After rough plant material and undecayed matter have been cleared away, turn the soil and add pH-adjusting materials and fertilizers. If you are working your soil in the fall, you can safely add natural fertilizers that require a long period of time to break down and release their nutrients. If you are working your soil in the spring, you should concentrate on fast-acting fertilizers, those that make their nutrients available relatively quickly.

Depending on how large your garden is, you can turn the soil by hand or by rotary tiller. If you are using a rotary tiller, simply pass over the garden after the lime and fertilizer have been spread on the soil, following either a row-by-row or a circular pattern, spiraling in toward the center of the plot. Although the process consumes a lot more time and energy when done by hand, in some instances it is the only way to get the soil into the best shape possible for planting. The best time to cultivate is when the soil is crumbly in texture and damp but not soggy. If too wet, it will compact and eventually form hard clods; if too dry, it will be reduced to a fine powder.

Probably the most common way of preparing fairly good, ordinary garden soil by hand involves digging a series of trenches. Begin by digging a trench about 1 foot wide and just 8 inches deep along one end of the garden. Using a wheelbarrow, move this top layer of soil you have just removed from the trench to the far end of the garden patch, where it will be used to fill in the last trench. Next, dig a trench parallel to the first one, turning the dirt you lift from this second into the first trench. Continue this process, filling each trench with the soil from the succeeding one. Be sure to chop up any plant matter you uproot as you go, and bury it at various depths in the soil, particularly if your are spading sod. Fertilizers and lime may be added trench by trench, or you can broadcast them, raking the materials lightly into the soil after the entire plot has been turned.

SHAPING YOUR GARDEN: ROWS AND RAISED BEDS

The conventional row garden isn't necessarily the best plan for the home gardener. First of all, with the soil nearly level to the surrounding yard, drainage is poor and the soil takes longer to warm in spring. Also, you must devote a large portion of the cultivated ground to paths that run between the planted rows. And when you walk on them during the season, they become compacted and all the more unsuitable for cultivation the following year.

Raised beds are the solution to these problems. These beds are raised some 6 to 12 inches above ground level, and are 3 to 5 feet wide, an easy reach for an outstretched arm during weeding and planting. Because you don't need to step into the beds to work, the soil remains loose and friable. Drainage and aeration are much improved, allowing the growing season to begin quite early in spring.

ROWS

You can easily plan the conventional row garden on paper in early spring. When the time comes to prepare the soil, you do your work in one large rectangular or square area, turning the soil, incorporating the appropriate organic matter, and adding the necessary fertilizers. The large, single area allows easy access for rotary tillers, plows, and other mechanical equipment. Not only is this a help in preparing the soil for a large garden area, but also for weeding and cultivating where mulching is not desired or practical. When you are ready to plant, define the rows by following the recommendations for in-row spacing and between-row spacing given in the individual vegetable entries in An Encyclopedia of Vegetables or on the seed packets themselves.

GROWING BEDS

In this system, the garden area is divided into rectangular beds, intersected by narrow paths. These beds are slightly raised, narrow areas that are never walked on once they have been prepared. For this reason, they

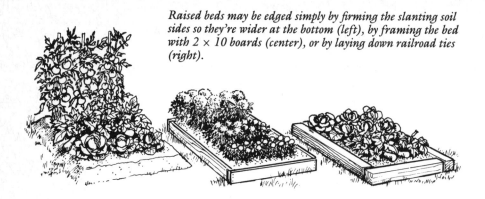

Raised beds may be edged simply by firming the slanting soil sides so they're wider at the bottom (left), by framing the bed with 2 × 10 boards (center), or by laying down railroad ties (right).

should be no wider than 3 to 5 feet—3 feet where there is access from only one side, up to 5 feet where the bed can be reached from both sides. Length depends on your own tastes and the available space. Allow for paths 1 foot or wider between beds, and consider running a wider central path of 2 to 3 feet the length of the garden area, to make room for wheelbarrows and garden tools.

Growing beds are double-dug. As you work the soil, you are loosening it to a depth of 20 to 24 inches, which improves drainage and aeration considerably. Unless your soil is in excellent condition, as you dig you should add rotted manure and other organic materials. With these infusions of organic material, the level of the beds should be some 4 to 5 inches above ground level. This further improves drainage and tends to create a warmer soil for growing plants. The high organic matter content (at least 20 percent for best results) helps the garden support heavy, intensive crop production. Yields are generally as much as four times that of the same square footage planted in conventional rows.

STRUCTURED-SIDE BEDS

One variation of the raised bed often brings even higher yields, particularly where native soil is quite heavy or otherwise of poor quality. By adding structured sides to the beds, you can raise soil as much as 2 or 3 feet above ground level. This enables you to improve you soil by piling compost, loamy soil, rotted manure, and other organic matter on top of a bed. Railroad ties, masonry "walls," cement blocks, stones, bricks, or wooden frames may be used for the sides.

CHINESE MOUNDS

Gardeners who wish to avoid the hard work of double-digging will find the Chinese mound system a practical alternative to growing beds. Like growing beds, these are narrow, slightly raised areas with a series of permanent paths connecting them. However, unlike growing beds, these are only single-dug, saving both time and labor. Studies at the University of Maine indicate that where soil is not excessively compacted, double-digging will not make a significant difference over single-digging or rotary tilling. If your soil is basically in good shape, you can simply turn it, and incorporate plenty of compost, manure, and other materials into the first 12 inches. This procedure will raise the bed and sufficiently loosen most soils. If you're planning on building a series of mounds, you should have an ample supply of organic matter on hand.

The exact dimensions of your Chinese mounds will vary according to your gardening space. You can make them any length you desire, but they should be about 4 feet wide at the base and 3 feet wide at the surface, with gently sloping sides. After adding the organic matter, the soil in the mound should extend about 6 inches above the surrounding ground level. As with growing beds, you must allow room for dirt paths alongside the beds.

CHAPTER 3

PLANTING

Before planting the garden, learn when to expect the last frost in your area and how to manage the idiosyncracies of your garden climate. Decide which crops will be direct-seeded in the garden and when they should be planted, as well as which crops will be raised from transplants.

DETERMINING THE FROST-FREE DATE

A fairly sound prediction of the last frost date, and hence the frost-free date, is necessary in planning just when to start certain seeds indoors, transplant other crops, and direct-seed in the garden. One way to make more accurate predictions is to keep your own records. Each year, note the date of the last spring frost as it occurs in your garden area. If you are new to the area, find out about its general climatic history from the local weather service office. Then speak with neighboring gardeners to find out when they start to plant, harvest fall crops, and the like. Make a note of the approximate date of the last frost, add two or three weeks, and you will know the frost-free date for your area.

Another point of reference you should use in conjunction with plant hardiness and the frost-free date is soil temperature. Each vegetable has an

PLANT HARDINESS AND OUTDOOR SEED-SOWING DATES

Cool-Season Crops		Warm-Season Crops	
Hardy: withstand subfreezing temperatures. Plant 4 to 6 weeks before frost-free date.	*Half-Hardy:* withstand some light freezing (short-term exposure to subfreezing temperatures). Plant 2 to 4 weeks before frost-free date.	*Tender:* fruit and leaves injured by light frosts. Plant on frost-free date.	*Very Tender:* need warm temperatures (above 70°F) for growth. Any exposure to temperatures just above freezing will damage fruit or leaves. Plant 1 week or more after frost-free date.
Broccoli	Beets	Beans, dry	Beans, lima
Brussels sprouts	Carrots*	Beans, snap	Corn (depending on
Cabbage	Cauliflower	Corn (depending on	variety planted)
Chinese cabbage	Celery	variety planted)	Cucumbers
Chives	Endive and Escarole	Cowpeas	Eggplant
Garlic	Lettuce*	Okra	Melons
Kale	Parsnips	Soybeans	Peanuts
Kohlrabi	Potatoes	Tomatoes	Peppers
Leeks	Radishes*		Pumpkins
Onions	Swiss chard		Squash, summer
Peas			Squash, winter
Rhubarb			Sweet potatoes
Rutabagas			Watermelon
Scallions			
Spinach			
Turnips			

*These plants are classed as half-hardy because they withstand only light freezing; however, they can be planted at the same time as hardy crops and protected from extreme cold.

optimum temperature range at which its seed will germinate, and for best results, you should plant only when the soil temperature is within that range. For example, crops like beans and corn will rot if the soil isn't warm enough. Germination temperatures are given in individual entries in An Encyclopedia of Vegetables. A soil thermometer is a relatively inexpensive garden tool available in many garden centers or through mail-order catalogs. For judging when to start seeds indoors and when to set young plants outdoors, use the frost-free date, the number of weeks it takes to grow a seedling to transplant size, and air temperature as your guidelines.

THE DAYLENGTH FACTOR

One other factor that can influence planting time and crop development is daylength. For certain crops, flowering and fruiting are induced by daylength (or photoperiod) as well as by temperature. There are even a few crops that are entirely governed by daylength. Fortunately, most crops are day-neutral, which means their flowering and fruiting are brought on more by temperature and moisture conditions than by daylength, so they are easily adapted to a variety of latitudes and planting dates.

However, when you are planting spinach, potatoes, and onions, you must keep their daylength requirements in mind. Both spinach and potatoes are long-day plants that require short nights to flower or form tubers, and these processes are inhibited if nights are longer than a certain critical length (which differs among plants). Since flowering signals the end of spinach's usefulness as an edible crop, you want to plant it in early spring when the days are short and nights are long to inhibit the natural cycle of flowering and seed production. Conversely, you want to plant potatoes, which you are growing specifically for their tubers, with respect to their need for long days (longer than 10 hours) and short nights (less than 14 hours). Certain varieties of onion form bulbs under short-day conditions, while others require long days to form bulbs.

——— STARTING SEEDS INDOORS ———

Starting seeds inside in flats not only speeds up the harvest date, but ultimately saves money on transplant costs and increases the variety and range of the crops grown in the outdoor garden. Determine when to start your seeds indoors by taking the setting-out date (when seedlings can be safely moved to the garden) and counting back the number of weeks it takes to grow the vegetables to transplant size. Timing is important: If you start your seeds too soon, the plants will outgrow their pots and become tall and gangly. It's better to err on the side of lateness when starting seeds, for young plants transplant more successfully than old ones.

Use the chart, Guide to Figuring Indoor Planting and Setting-Out Dates, and a calendar to help you with your calculations. The spring setting-out dates for the various vegetables are given in terms of weeks before

GUIDE TO FIGURING INDOOR PLANTING AND SETTING-OUT DATES

Vegetable	Column I Weeks to Transplant Size (from time of sowing)	Column II Spring Setting-Out Dates (in relation to frost-free date) Weeks Before	Weeks After
Asparagus	12–14	—	4
Beans, lima	3–4	—	1–2
Beans, snap	3–4	—	1–2
Beets	4	4	—
Broccoli	6–8	4	2–3
Brussels sprouts	6–8	4	2–3
Cabbage	6–8	5	2–3
Carrots	5–6	4	—
Cauliflower	6–8	4	2
Celery	6–8	3	3–4
Corn	4	—	2–3
Cucumbers	2–3	1	—
Eggplant	8–10	—	2–3
Endive and Escarole	4–5	4	2
Garlic	4–6	2–4	1
Kale	6–8	5	2
Kohlrabi	6–8	5	2
Leeks	4–6	5	2
Lettuce	4–6	2	3
Okra	6–8	—	3–4
Onions, bulb-type	4–6	6	2
Parsnips	4–6	4	3–4
Peanuts	4–6	Plant on frost-free date	
Peas	4	4	2–3
Peppers	6–8	—	2–3
Spinach	4–6	3–6	—
Squash, summer	4	—	4
Squash, winter	4	—	3–4
Sweet potatoes	6–8	—	2–3
Swiss chard	4	3–4	—
Tomatoes	6–10	—	4
Turnips	3–4	4	—

and after the frost-free date. To pinpoint these dates for your own area, start by determining the frost-free date (two to three weeks after the local last frost date). Make a note of the frost-free date in the appropriate spaces on your calendar. Depending on the hardiness of your crops, you will then either subtract or add the weeks given in Column II to this date, to arrive at the precise setting-out date for each vegetable. Mark the setting-out date on the calendar also.

Now use this setting-out date as your starting point and count back the number of weeks it takes to grow your particular vegetable seed to transplant size (given in Column I). This date is when you can start your seed indoors.

GERMINATING MEDIA

Germinating seeds, young seedlings, and maturing plants all have slightly different needs, and the same mix should not be used for all three stages of growth. From the sowing to the thinning stage, the growing medium should be quite loose, fine, and able to hold moisture without becoming soggy. It must also be firm enough to hold a tiny seedling upright, particularly after watering.

Soil used for seed starting must be sterile, or at least pasteurized, so it is free from disease-carrying organisms, harmful insects, and viable weed seeds. Sterile soil or planting mix can be bought at most garden stores; pasteurized soil can be made by placing your own garden soil in an oven set at 180°F for 30 to 45 minutes. This will not produce absolutely weed-free, organism-free material, but it will virtually eliminate the chances of damping-off or other soilborne problems.

SEED-STARTING MIXES

2 qt. peat moss	1 qt. loamy soil,	1 qt. peat moss	1 qt. peat moss
1 qt. vermiculite	pasteurized	1 qt. vermiculite	1 qt. loamy soil,
1 qt. perlite	1 qt. peat moss	1 qt. perlite	pasteurized
1 tbsp. dolomite	1 qt. sharp sand		1 qt. perlite

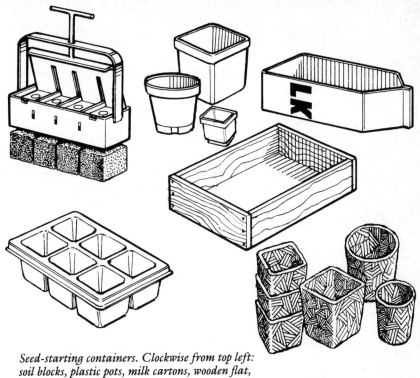

Seed-starting containers. Clockwise from top left: soil blocks, plastic pots, milk cartons, wooden flat, peat pots, and plastic six-pack.

CONTAINERS

The most common planting containers are plastic or wooden flats sold in garden shops. These shallow, rectangular boxes are used for starting large numbers of plants, and are especially good for easily transplanted crops such as cabbage, lettuce, and tomatoes. A foil roasting or loaf pan will serve the same purpose, provided you have cut drainage slits in the bottom. You can also construct your own flat from scrap lumber.

Some gardeners prefer to sow seeds in individual pots so that seedling roots do not have to be untangled during transplanting. This is especially critical when starting any temperamental crops that don't tolerate disturbance of their roots. To avoid serious setbacks when these plants are transferred to the garden, grow them in individual containers which can be gently peeled away from the root mass, or which will decompose in the ground, thus eliminating the need for separating container and plant. Any biodegradable containers like milk cartons, sections of rolled newspapers, or peat pots will do. Since no potting up will be done as the seedlings are maturing, start these crops in a rich growing medium which will nourish their growth until they are set out in the garden.

Peat pots are often recommended for seed starting, but they are expensive and tend to dry out, draining water away from plant roots. If you do use them, moisten the pots at least half an hour before filling them with soil (six to eight hours before is even better). Place them in flats, filling spaces between the pots with moist peat moss or soil. Keep the whole setup well watered.

Probably the simplest, most reliable individual containers are round or square plastic pots. Yet another option is lightweight plastic trays with attached individual growing compartments, which allow you to easily push the seedlings from the compartments without damage to the roots.

SOWING THE SEEDS

Prepare flats and pots by placing a layer of perlite, fine gravel, coarse sand, sphagnum moss, or other light material on the bottom. If container holes are large, cover the bottom with a layer of peat or damp paper towels before you add drainage material. Fill with moistened soil or germinating mix to within $\frac{1}{2}$ inch of the container's rim. If peat moss or vermiculite is being used, thoroughly moisten the material before trying to fill planting containers. Otherwise, you'll end up with a dusty, scattered mess. Press gently so that the medium is firm, yet not packed solid. With a spoon handle, stick, or planting dibble, mark off shallow furrows, about 1 inch apart, in flats.

As a general rule, seeds are buried at a depth two to three times their diameter. In individual pots, sow at least three seeds so you can be sure of getting one good plant. In the flats, place large seeds about 1 inch apart in the furrows, and medium seeds just $\frac{1}{2}$ inch apart. Plant fine seeds as thinly as possible, shaking them from the corner of the packet, or dropping them in pinches from between your thumb and forefinger. Very fine seeds may be mixed with sand or light soil for more even sowing. Press the seeds lightly into the soil surface, then cover with soil or mix.

Once you have sown the seeds in pots and along the marked furrows in flats, water very gently with a mister. Next, label, date, and cover the containers with burlap, cheesecloth, or plastic in order to maintain a moist soil surface. Do not allow the covering to rest on the soil, and be sure to leave a small opening for air to enter and escape. Place the container in a warm spot, preferably where air temperatures will not fall below 65°F. To keep soil temperatures sufficiently high during germination, you can set containers on top of the refrigerator or television, above a fluorescent light ballast, or on a plate warmer.

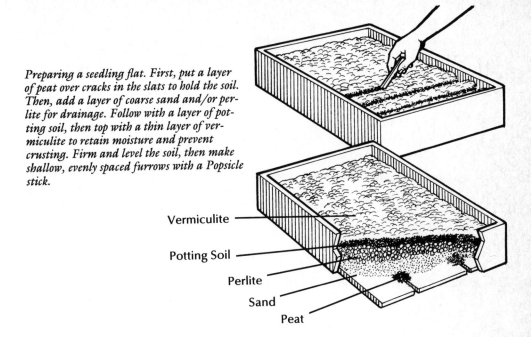

Preparing a seedling flat. First, put a layer of peat over cracks in the slats to hold the soil. Then, add a layer of coarse sand and/or perlite for drainage. Follow with a layer of potting soil, then top with a thin layer of vermiculite to retain moisture and prevent crusting. Firm and level the soil, then make shallow, evenly spaced furrows with a Popsicle stick.

Vermiculite

Potting Soil

Perlite

Sand

Peat

Most seeds will germinate in total darkness, so there is no need to worry about light levels until germination has occurred and seedlings have broken the soil surface. The one common exception to this rule is lettuce, which does need some light for germination. You can make sure lettuce receives enough light by not covering the seeds with growing medium.

CARING FOR SEEDLINGS

As soon as you see green shoots appearing on the soil surface, remove all coverings. Mist daily with lukewarm water, and allow the moisture to soak in gradually.

When plants are 2 or more inches tall and have developed their first two sets of leaves, they should be watered less frequently, allowing the soil surface to dry between soakings. Since they are strong enough to withstand heavier streams, use a watering can.

Seedlings need a minimum of 6 hours of full sunlight, with most young plants benefiting from 12 to 15 hours a day. Although it is possible to supply the necessary light through a sunny, southern window, a more reliable light source is fluorescent lighting. Regular, industrial-type hanging fixtures suspended by chains can easily be raised or lowered as plants grow.

A light garden lets you start seed-lings indoors under an even source of light. For sturdy, regular growth, seedlings grow best with 12 to 15 hours of light a day.

A two-tube, 4-foot-long fixture will provide adequate light for a 1-by-4-foot area. Three fixtures, hung 8 inches apart, create a 3-by-4-foot "mini garden." Special fluorescent tubes emitting light from the red end of the spectrum have been developed for indoor plant growth. These "grow-light" tubes are certainly very good for raising transplants, but the ordinary "cool white" or "warm white" tubes will also do nicely. The best combination is often said to be one of the special plant tubes alongside a cool white tube. These lamps remain cool, so you can start with flats just 3 inches beneath the tubes, and gradually raise the lights or lower the flats as seedlings grow.

Plants are ready to be thinned after they emerge. Check over the seedlings just as the first true leaves are appearing. Prime candidates for thinning are seedlings with distorted leaves, mechanical injuries, or those that are overcrowding their neighbors. Simply cut off their stems with a small pair of scissors, clipping just at the soil surface, leaving roots in the soil.

TRANSPLANTING SEEDLINGS

Unless seeds are sown in deep, individual containers or spacious flats of rich soil, transplanting is necessary even before the plants are moved to the

RICH MIXES FOR SEEDLINGS

1 qt. compost	1 qt. leaf mold	4 qt. loamy soil	1 qt. sand
1 qt. loamy soil	2 qt. loamy soil	2 qt. peat moss	1 qt. vermiculite
1 qt. sand, perlite, or	1 qt. compost or	2 qt. leaf mold	1 qt. loamy soil
vermiculite	well-rotted	2 qt. vermiculite	1 qt. peat moss
	manure	6 tsp. dolomite	1 qt. perlite

garden. Seedlings need richer soil for growth than they do for germination. By transplanting them just after their first true leaves appear, seedlings will recover rapidly from the shock of the move.

Select flats or pots at least 3 inches deep so that roots will have adequate room for growth. Line all containers with a thin layer of drainage material. Fill the containers with the soil mix to within 1/2 inch of the rim.

Remove seedlings from flats by using a dibble or pointed stick. Lift the plant, holding it by the leaves, not by the stem or the fragile growing point, both of which are easily bruised. As each seedling is lifted from the flat, gently place it in a hole deep enough so that it can be buried up to its first set of true leaves. Make sure that the seedling roots are in firm contact with the surrounding soil. Water slowly, allowing moisture to gradually seep downward to the roots.

After transplanting, don't water again for several days. The plants are in shock and should be allowed to rest out of direct sunlight or strong artificial light. Wilting may occur, but this will usually pass in a day or two as the plants become established. When they are well rooted and standing upright again, resume normal care by watering whenever the soil dries out, and fertilizing with a weak solution of manure tea or fish emulsion every week or two.

HARDENING-OFF

Before being moved outdoors, seedlings must be "hardened-off," or adjusted to the harsher environment of the garden. About two weeks before seedlings are to be transplanted to the garden, allow slightly more time between waterings. Do not let the plants wilt, but do force their roots to reach down for water. At the same time, discontinue all fertilizing.

A few days after this drying out has begun, start placing flats outside on a shaded porch or in a well-ventilated cold frame during the warmest part of each day. Begin by leaving them out for an hour or two, and gradually increase

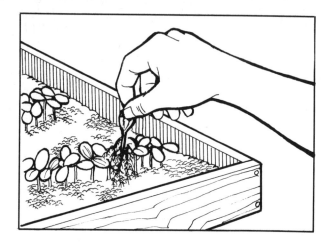

When transplanting, lift seedlings by their leaf tips so you don't crush the delicate stems or growing points.

the period until, within ten days, they are able to stay outside all day. Bring them in at night to prevent frost damage.

Seedlings planted in flats can be further hardened-off by a process known as "blocking." About ten days before planting out, cut between plants so that each seedling has a block of soil at least 3 inches by 3 inches. Use a sharp knife, and make clean, straight cuts. This severs the large lateral roots and forces new branch roots to form.

DIRECT-SEEDING IN THE GARDEN

Direct-seeding requires less work and planning on your part and avoids the initial shock of transplanting for the plants.

PREPARING THE SEEDBED

Before seeds can be sown or plants set out in the garden bed, soil must be raked smooth and leveled. This is best done on a dry day, just before planting. If final preparations are made too far in advance, a hard crust may form on the soil surface, making further cultivation necessary before seeds can be planted.

Clear away any undecayed green manure or woody plant debris still remaining in the garden. By allowing such materials to remain in the soil, you are simply inviting disease and insect damage. Rocks brought to the surface through winter frost-heaving should also be removed, and large clods broken apart with your fingers, hoe, or rake. Don't pound the soil, for this will compact it. If a clod doesn't break apart with a light tap of the hoe or rake, then just rake it aside. The goal is to have a perfectly smooth, light, fine soil to a depth of 8 to 12 inches, or even slightly deeper for root crops such as long carrots or parsnips. To keep the soil as loose as possible, avoid walking on it. If you have opted for a gardening system like the growing bed or Chinese mound, then this will be no problem. However, if you are working in a standard one-plot vegetable patch with rows, then you will be unable to avoid walking in it and compacting some of the soil. The best solution is to lay down boards to walk on, or at least to walk only in the places where paths will be laid out at planting time.

Next, rake the garden area smooth so that the tops of any raised beds are level, with only a gradual slope on the sides. If the slope is too great, wind or rain will cause the beds to collapse. Furrows, pits, and small irregularities in the soil surface will result in puddling or drying out and will cut down on the germination of your seeds. The smoother the seedbed, the better the germination and initial growth will be. When the bed is completely raked and clean, water it lightly with a fine mist, not a heavy stream, and allow it to rest for a few hours before planting. This brief waiting period gives the water a chance to percolate into air pockets in the soil and lets the ground firm up.

When the seedbed has been properly prepared and the soil has reached the appropriate temperature for the crop you are planting, choose a calm, sunny day to begin planting. Rows and raised beds should be carefully marked off according to the garden plan you have drawn up. Follow the plan closely, measuring out the planting areas, so that all the vegetables you intend to grow will fit into the garden. Don't feel you must fill every inch of the available garden space with seeds. Remember that when thinning time comes, you may want to transplant some seedlings.

SEED-PLANTING TECHNIQUES

There are two basic ways to plant seeds by hand. Where entire beds or blocks of space within a bed are to be planted in the same crop, the seeds may be broadcast—scattered randomly over the soil surface. For conventional rows, hill planting, and intensive plant spacing patterns in raised beds and wide rows, seeds are sown individually, which gives you more control over spacing and placement.

Broadcasting: Scatter seeds over the prepared seedbed by flinging them outward in even motions. The idea is to scatter the seeds in midair so that they fall evenly on the soil. Fine seeds may be broadcast more easily if mixed with sand or dry peat moss before spreading. When the entire area has been seeded, broadcast a covering of fine soil or peat moss, so that the seeds are covered to a depth appropriate to the type of seed planted. Water with a gentle spray from a sprinkler or watering can.

Conventional Rows: For row seeding, mark off furrows by using the corner of a regular hoe blade for large ones, and a stick or garden tool handle for shallow ones. Remember that seeds are sown about two or three times as deep as they are wide. Small seeds can be sown directly from the packet, or by dropping them in pinches from between your forefinger and thumb. Or you can mix them with fine sand and spread the sand/seed mixture. You can also rig up a seed spreader from household cast-offs like spice shakers. At the completion of a row, cover seeds with compost or rich, fine soil to prevent loss of moisture from the ground, and press seeds into the soil. Larger seeds, from spinach- to pumpkin-sized, are easy to handle, so uniform spacing in rows is no problem.

Hill Planting: Certain crops, including beans, corn, cucumbers, melons, pumpkins, and squash, are often planted in hills or mounds to provide seeds with a warmer germinating area. To prepare a hill in a garden with loamy, fertile soil, form a 2- or 3-inch-high mound, about 12 inches square. If the soil is poor, or if the crop being grown is a heavy feeder, dig a hole 12 inches deep and 12 inches square before you form the mound. Add 8 inches of well-rotted

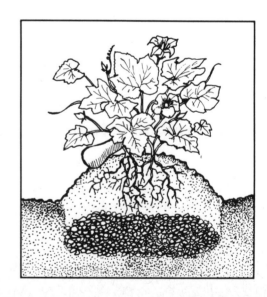

Heat-loving heavy feeders like squash and pumpkins thrive when planted in hills. Fill the bottom of a 12-inch hole with 8 inches of well-rotted manure or compost, then mound 8 inches of soil on top. The hill will warm fast for quick germination, and hungry crops will feast on the extra nutrients.

VEGETABLE SPACING FOR INTENSIVE CULTURE

Crop	Inches	Crop	Inches
Asparagus	18	Okra	18
Beans, lima	9	Onions, bulb-type	6
Beans, snap	6	Onions, bunching	
Beets	6	(scallions)	3
Broccoli	18	Parsnips	6
Brussels sprouts	18	Peanuts	18
Cabbage	18	Peas	6
Carrots	3	Peppers	15
Cauliflower	18	Potatoes	12
Celery	9	Pumpkins	36
Chinese cabbage	12	Radishes	3
Corn	18	Rhubarb	36
Cucumbers	18	Rutabagas	9
Eggplant	24	Spinach	6
Endive and Escarole	18	Squash, summer	24
Garlic	6	Squash, winter	36
Kale	18	Sweet potatoes	12
Kohlrabi	9	Swiss chard	9
Leeks	6	Tomatoes	24
Lettuce, head	12	Turnips	6
Lettuce, leaf	9		

compost, manure, or other organic material, then cover this with 8 inches of soil. Depending on the crop being grown, plant three to six seeds in the mound, evenly spaced along the top and sides, and buried at the correct depth.

Raised-Bed Systems: There are a number of seeding patterns you can use when planting raised beds that will space plants closer together than is normally recommended in gardening guides. These closer spacings allow you to grow more plants within the concentrated area of the bed.

The bed-row system is easy to set up. In a row-planted bed, crops are placed in closely spaced rows, with a different crop in each row. This allows for a diversified crop mix, and takes advantage of interplanting and companion-planting techniques. The trick to planning bed rows is to determine distances between individual rows of different crops. To calculate this distance, average the recommended planting distances for the two neighboring crops.

More plants can be grown in the same space using equidistant spacing (right), which uses staggered rows, than with the more traditional square-center spacing (left), where there is the same spacing between rows and between plants in a row.

Square-center spacing is a grid-type pattern that is useful in beds planted with a single crop. With this spacing, the plants are treated as if they were individual squares which together form a gridlike pattern across the surface of the bed. With the center of each plant acting as the center of a square, the distance from the center to each of the square's sides is the distance given in the spacing chart. This means that when you are planting, you allow the same distance between the plants in a row as between the rows themselves.

Equidistant plant spacing is an even more efficient spacing pattern for single-crop beds. In this pattern, the plants are treated as circles, with the result that the rows will fit more closely together. Here, it is the distance between plant centers that corresponds to the spacing on the chart, while the actual distance between rows shrinks. This is done by planting staggered rows so that the plant centers are not perpendicular.

Wide-Row Planting: This is a useful management for small and large seeds alike. Also called band planting, it involves sowing seeds in several very close rows that together form a single 18-inch-wide band of one crop. A similar effect can be obtained by simply broadcasting or scattering seeds evenly across the 18-inch-wide strip. Individual bands are spaced about 24 to 30 inches apart.

The most striking advantage of these wide bands is their high yield, sometimes as much as four times the yield produced by the same area planted in single rows. Individual plants produce less, but the overall yield of the area goes up. Beans, beets, lettuce, onions, radishes, and most other compact plants do well in wide rows.

THINNING AND TRANSPLANTING OUTDOORS

Weak or overcrowded seedlings need to be thinned in the outdoor garden, just as they do when grown indoors in flats or pots. Whether or not the seedlings are saved, they must be removed with a certain amount of care in order to spare remaining plants. Choose a cloudy, calm day for thinning and transplanting. Late afternoon is usually a good time, for it allows plants to become established while the sun is low in the sky. If you are planning on transplanting some of the thinnings, prepare a weak manure or compost tea and bring along a putty knife or hand fork, a trowel, some compost or rich soil, and a sharp stick or pencil.

Begin by watering the row so that the soil is loose and easy to handle. Use the hand fork or putty knife to separate a section of soil and plants. How many plants you remove depends on the desired spacing for that particular crop. Wilting will probably occur the next day, and perhaps for several days afterward. This is to be expected since the plants have been traumatized by the move. As long as you have planted them at the right depth and firmed the soil around them, daily waterings should help them recover without any significant setbacks.

BUYING TRANSPLANTS

Limited time and space make it necessary for many gardeners to rely on professional growers for at least some of their spring and fall transplants. Do not be lured into buying the largest plants in the hope that they will produce bushels of early fruit. Very large plants will be sharply set back by transplanting, and although they may already show a few fruits or blossoms, they could turn out to be far behind others in producing the main crop. Instead, choose short, sturdy seedlings with healthy green leaves that show no signs of insects or diseases. Scrape away the soil surface around cabbage and other cole crops to check for clubroot.

Seedlings growing in individual containers, or widely spaced and blocked off in flats, are superior to those crowded into flats. This is especially true with hard-to-transplant crops such as beans and cucumbers. Check to be sure that seedlings have been given adequate rooting depth, and that roots have not grown out several inches from the bottom of the pot or flat. Chances are that seedlings you pick up in a greenhouse have not yet been thoroughly hardened-off and will require very gradual hardening.

PLANTING OUT

Purchased seedlings, as well as those raised in the home or cold frame, may be planted in the garden as soon as they have been hardened-off and outside conditions permit. Specific soil and air temperature requirements differ from crop to crop. It is best to set out plants on a cloudy, damp day. If you must work on a sunny day, hold off until late afternoon or early evening when the sun is low in the sky.

Following the garden plan, dig a hole for each transplant. A transplanting trowel, narrower than the ordinary garden trowel, is excellent for this, for it allows you to make deep, straight-sided holes without disturbing other nearby seedlings already in place. Most seedlings should be planted at least at their potted depth, and up to 1 inch deeper. Members of the cabbage family must be planted deeply to prevent the center stalk from growing crookedly. Make sure the holes are deep enough so these plants can be covered with soil up to their first set of true leaves. Pour warm water or starter solution around the transplant to settle the roots and firm the soil further.

In all but the wettest seasons, you should mulch the plants as soon as they are set out in the garden. (Note, however, that if you are planting warm-season crops like peppers and tomatoes a little early, you shouldn't mulch right away, to give the soil a chance to warm up some more.) Mulch heavily, but keep the material well away from stalks until the plants have been established. If an inorganic mulch like black plastic is being used, it should be set down before the seedlings are planted.

TECHNIQUES FOR HIGHEST CONTINUAL YIELD

In order to guarantee top yields all year long, you may wish to use two intensive gardening methods—succession planting and interplanting. Succession planting is the raising of new crops in spaces just vacated by others. Interplanting is the planting of different crops within the same garden area.

SUCCESSION PLANTING

One way to succession plant is to sow long- and short-season crops together in a row or bed. You can space plants more closely together than usual since the short-term crop will be removed by the time the long-term crop needs its full complement of growing space. Typical plantings of this sort are radishes and cabbage; early cabbage and tomatoes; Chinese cabbage and eggplant; lettuce and turnips; and radishes and beans. In all cases, the first vegetable of the pair is harvested before the second achieves full growth. As long as the short-season crop is given its minimum required intensive gardening space, it can be grown between or beside the long-term crop.

A variation of succession planting is relay planting. Relays are the successive plantings of the same vegetable over a period of time. This guarantees a dispersed harvest over the course of several weeks or months. It is especially useful for crops which are desired continuously but in small quantities such as beans, lettuce, scallions, and radishes, or for popular crops that are needed in full supply all summer long, such as corn and potatoes. The only requirement for a relayed crop is that it be one with a broad tolerance of daylength and temperature; otherwise, ripening problems may occur. Plant relays every seven to ten days, in the same rows or bed.

A similar relay effect may be achieved by simply planting early-, middle-, and late-maturing varieties of the same crop at the same time. Although differences are usually slight with most crops, certain vegetables (such as cabbage, corn, squash, and tomatoes) do have a wide range of maturity rates among their varieties.

The most commonly practiced sort of succession planting is probably the planting of one crop in the space recently vacated by another. This technique is a must with short-season crops such as cabbage, peas, and spinach, which are soon harvested and must be replaced with another crop.

INTERPLANTING

Interplanting, or intercropping, takes advantage of certain plant needs and growth characteristics to increase the yield per square foot of garden space. With this system, several different vegetables are grown close together in the same planting area, such as tall crops near short ones, or deep-rooted with shallow-rooted. You can carry the idea one step further by interplanting within each row or bed. This not only makes your garden space more productive, but it may also improve the health of your crops.

Small, compact crops such as beets, onions, parsley, and radishes can be planted among almost any larger upright plants. Taller plants may help shade, and therefore cool, the smaller ones, aiding in moisture conservation. Match

CHARACTERISTIC ROOTING DEPTH

Shallow Rooting (18 to 36 inches)	Medium Rooting (36 to 48 inches)	Deep Rooting (more than 48 inches)
Broccoli	Beans, snap	Artichokes
Brussels sprouts	Beets	Asparagus
Cabbage	Carrots	Beans, lima
Cauliflower	Cucumbers	Parsnips
Celery	Eggplant	Pumpkins
Chinese cabbage	Peas	Squash, winter
Corn	Peppers	Sweet potatoes
Endive	Rutabagas	Tomatoes
Garlic	Squash, summer	
Leeks	Swiss chard	
Lettuce	Turnips	
Onions		
Potatoes		
Radishes		
Spinach		

shallow-rooting crops with medium- or deep-rooting ones, and medium-rooting with deep-rooting crops. Shallow roots absorb water and nutrients from upper soil zones, while larger, longer roots draw moisture and food from lower levels. Try pairings of onions with tomatoes, radishes with snap beans, leeks with carrots, or Swiss chard with parsnips.

CHAPTER 4

CARE THROUGH THE GROWING SEASON

While good gardening does take time, it need not be an all-consuming hobby. The best approach is a sensible, "preventive" attitude toward garden care in which plants are given all the materials they need to grow and produce without constant attention from you. Crop rotation, interplanting, companion planting, thorough soil preparation, mulching, and other good gardening techniques actually produce crops that can withstand unfavorable conditions to some degree.

Of course, some special care is needed during the course of the growing season. Even where a heavy mulch has been laid down, some watering may be necessary in order to get plants through dry spells. Extra feeding may be necessary for a few crops, or for transplants set out later in the season, and weeds and insect pests need to be kept in check. There may be some crops that require pruning, staking, blanching, or other special care. Finally, there are crops to be harvested and new ones to be planted from week to week.

WATERING

Water is the most misunderstood of all plant needs. Essential for growth and development, it carries minerals from the soil to the leaves, and acts as the raw material from which plants manufacture food. In order to benefit crops, it must be supplied to the main roots—not just to the leaves and the top inch of soil.

Light daily waterings can do more harm than good by encouraging roots to grow along the wet soil surface, rather than reaching down where moisture and nutrients remain in fairly stable supply. For best results, you should water less frequently, and when you do, make sure it is for a long enough period so that moisture soaks deeply into the soil, reaching the main root masses of the plants. With mulch covering the soil surface, little moisture is lost by evaporation when the water has been allowed to soak deeply into the ground.

WHEN TO WATER

There are two simple ways you can determine whether the garden should be watered: by the feel of the soil, and by the look of the plants themselves. When the soil is holding as much water as it possibly can without any puddling or runoff, its particles stick together, forming a durable, pliable ball that will stick to your hands as you shape it. At this point, the soil is said to be at "field capacity." The more crumbly the soil, the less water it contains, and the further it is from field capacity. Generally, when the soil around a plant's roots is below 50 percent field capacity (when it is holding half the water it is capable of holding), it is time to water. To test this, don't judge by the surface soil. Just because it appears to be dry doesn't mean the root zone is dry. In a vacant spot in the garden, dig down to the approximate depth of the crop's root mass. Press some of the soil from that depth between your fingers. If the soil barely holds together, then it's time to water.

A simpler check can be made with a hollow metal rod or a specially designed probe. Insert the probe deeply into the soil, once again in an unoccupied space. If it penetrates easily to root zone, chances are there is plenty of water available. If the probe does not penetrate easily, or if it comes out perfectly clean, then the soil is probably below field capacity and should be watered.

Plant behavior is also an indication of the soil's moisture content. The most obvious plant response to low moisture is wilting, although this can be misleading. Some plants wilt in response to excessive heat, whether or not adequate moisture is available in the soil. Cucurbits, eggplant, lettuce, peppers, tomatoes, and others will wilt almost every day in the heat of the summer sun, but they quickly recover as the sun sets and temperatures drop. This temporary wilting does not necessarily indicate a need for additional water. If, however, a plant does not recover by evening or begins wilting early in the morning, then water immediately, for soil moisture reserves are certainly depleted.

Under normal soil conditions, plants' moisture needs change dramatically according to their level of development. Generally, large amounts of water are needed during early growth, flowering, and fruit set. If they don't get the moisture when they require it, crops will be of poor quality. Blossom-end rot in tomatoes, splitting in cabbages, and blossom drop in peppers are just a few examples of water-related problems.

In all but emergency cases, watering should be carried out in late afternoon or early evening. Earlier waterings are mostly lost to evaporation. Therefore, water several hours before sunset, giving leaves a chance to dry before dark. If you water too late in the day and the garden is left wet during the night, fungi and related diseases set in.

In deciding how much water to give plants, follow the guidelines for determining when to water. When the soil around the plants' root zone is near field capacity and sticks to a probe, enough water has been applied. This may require 1/4 inch of water, or 1 inch, depending on the amount already present and on the soil type. Use the chart, Characteristic Rooting Depth, which appears in Chapter 3 to assure that moisture is being supplied to the right level, and water evenly beneath each plant's canopy of leaves so that the entire root mass is moistened.

WATERING SYSTEMS

The drip or trickle method is one of the most efficient ways to water. For this system, a special hose is required—either a rubber or canvas soaker, with tiny pores through which the water passes, or a perforated plastic hose with a row of tiny holes along its entire length. Since moisture is released all along these hoses, there is no need to move them once they have been set in place. Either hose may be buried under a mulch, or set atop the soil surface. The plastic and rubber types can be left buried under a mulch throughout the summer, provided you have enough hose length to cover the entire bed or patch. Since the canvas soaker type might weaken or clog, it should not be buried for long periods of time.

All three hoses are well worth the investment and make the job of watering very simple and efficient. The water that trickles out soaks in slowly in a concentrated area. Their only real disadvantage seems to be a loss of water where the hose crosses unplanted areas. Since they emit water wherever they are, water is wasted on paths, lawn, or other areas crossed to get to the vegetable garden. You can avoid this problem by purchasing one that attaches to an ordinary garden hose.

If you have a fairly reliable source of water, and one that is relatively close to the garden area, you may want to consider installing a formal, permanent system of drip irrigation. Such a system has the advantages of the portable soakers and perforated hoses, but may be left in place all year long. Usually, it

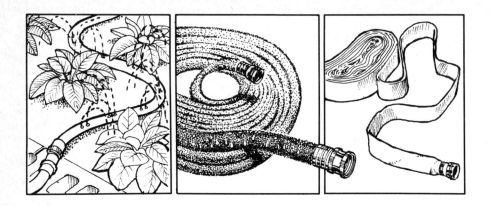

Drip irrigation provides a slow, steady supply of water, with little loss to evaporation.
Left to right: soaker hose, rubber ooze hose, canvas hose.

consists of two soft, flexible plastic perforated pipes for each 5-foot-wide raised bed, or one pipe every 2 to 3 feet in the conventional row garden. A main pipe along one side of the beds or patch connects to these smaller feeder pipes. The feeder pipes may be installed on the soil surface or underground, although aboveground pipes have fewer problems with clogging. As water is pumped through the system, it drips through the tiny holes, evenly supplying the growing area. Again, as with the plastic and canvas hoses, water goes only where it is needed. No runoff occurs and no water is wasted outside the crop root zones. By reducing and increasing the pressure, you can regulate moisture flow to suit any soil type, gradient, or crop requirement. However, unlike the hoses, which can be easily maneuvered and removed for cultivation, this system is to a large degree permanent. The main supply lines, often placed below ground, usually remain in place, with feeder lines possibly being more mobile. For this reason, wait to install a permanent system until the ground has been gardened for several years and is in near-optimum condition. Also, if you use a rotary tiller to work the soil, be careful not to disrupt the pipe system when you till.

SUPPLEMENTAL FERTILIZING

As long as the soil has been properly prepared, very little supplemental feeding is necessary in the organic vegetable garden. However, in order to keep levels of certain nutrients in reserve for succeeding crops, you should continue to work organic substances into the soil whenever the opportunity arises. This is especially important for potassium-rich substances which, because of leaching losses, are best applied in small doses throughout the season. Crops requiring medium to heavy amounts of potassium should be generously fertilized with wood ashes at least once during their growth. After an early crop is harvested, work in additional compost, well-rotted manure, or other materials.

APPLYING THE FERTILIZER

Midseason fertilizers may be applied in liquid form to the soil or sprayed on the leaves, or they can be side-dressed in dry form alongside established crops.

With one type of solution feeding, you pour enriched water onto the soil, where it can soak down to the plants' roots. You may use either manure or compost tea or a dilute solution of fish emulsion or seaweed extract. The latter two are available commercially in concentrated form, and directions are given on the package for diluting them. The usual solution is 1 tablespoon concentrate per gallon of water.

When you water with these enriched solutions, you want to apply them as close to the plants as possible, so the nutrients will seep directly down to the root zone. Because these are dilute solutions, there is no concern about burning the plants.

Instead of applying nutrients to the roots, in the case of foliar feeding you are spraying them on the leaves in weak solutions. Since the leaves absorb the nutrients almost immediately, this method of fertilizing gives the most rapid results. Foliar feeding is especially helpful during very wet or very dry spells when nutrient uptake through the soil is hindered. The fertilizers to use are seaweed or fish emulsion concentrates, diluted as directed on the package. Because the nutrient benefits are not long-lasting, you must spray plants with these enriched solutions every two to three weeks throughout the season.

Side-dressing calls for applying the dry fertilizing material in a shallow furrow alongside the crop. It has been shown to increase the rate at which some materials become available to plants, especially bonemeal and rock phosphate. Side-dressing is a good method to use with potent materials such as fresh chicken manure, which could burn plants if applied too close to the roots.

To side-dress plants, dig a 2- to 3-inch-deep furrow about 4 inches away from each plant, between rows, or around a block of bedded plants. Apply the material, then push back the soil with a hoe to cover the furrow. If you are side-dressing newly sown seeds, the material may be placed slightly closer, but no nearer than 2 inches.

Timing of fertilization can be critical, particularly in dealing with nitrogen fertilizers. Plants just preparing to flower or fruit are winding down

NUTRIENT DEFICIENCIES—
THEIR SYMPTOMS AND REMEDIES

Nutrient	Function	Deficiency Symptoms	Common Organic Sources	Deficiency Occurrence
Nitrogen (N)	Required for all phases of growth and development (roots, stems, leaves); excesses increase leaf and shoot growth, causing delay in maturity of certain crops.	Leaves are light green or yellowish (lower leaves first to show discoloration); plant is stunted; some nitrogen deficiency symptoms are normal during fruiting.	Bloodmeal, cottonseed meal, sewage sludge, animal tankage, farm manure, poultry manure, compost.	Mostly on very light soils where leaching occurs; may result wherever planting has been heavy and fertilization inadequate.
Phosphorus (P)	Constituent of plant's genetic material; found mostly in the growing points of plants (shoot tips and roots); increases rate of crop maturity; strengthens stems; helps in resistance to pests and diseases; necessary for proper fruiting, flowering, seed formation, and root branching.	Lower leaves and stem have reddish coloring; upper leaves are dull, pale; plant is stunted; failure to flower or produce fruit.	Bonemeal, animal tankage, rock phosphate, fish meal.	On acid soils; temporary deficiency occurs on cold, wet soil.
Potassium (K)	Required for formation of sugars, starches, and proteins, and for action of certain enzymes; contributes to cold-hardiness; enhances	Lower leaves are spotted, mottled, or curled; leaves may appear scorched along edges or tips; corn leaves	Nonwoody plant residues (particularly hulls, peelings, and rinds),	Leaches from very light soils; most likely to be deficient in upper layers of soil since

NUTRIENT DEFICIENCIES—
THEIR SYMPTOMS AND REMEDIES
—*Continued*

Nutrient	Function	Deficiency Symptoms	Common Organic Sources	Deficiency Occurrence
	flavor and color of some crops; needed for development of root crops; also aids in development of fruit and seeds.	appear streaked; root system is underdeveloped; yields are low; fruit is misshapen, small; grain is chaffy; stem tissue may appear weak.	manure, seaweed, wood ashes, greensand, granite dust.	plants remove it from these levels.

their development of leaves and shoots. If you boost the available nitrogen supply at this point, crops will revert back to an earlier stage of development and the harvest will be delayed. Similarly, since nitrogen tends to make crops succulent and tender, late plantings of salad crops and greens, or any perennials, should not be given nitrogen fertilizers in the fall. This would only promote top growth, making the plants an easy target for frost damage.

———— MULCHING ————

In addition to the obvious advantages of water conservation and weed control, mulch provides physical protection for growing crops. Soil compaction is reduced, so there is less opportunity for root damage. During the winter, mulch protects perennials from freezing and heaving. In the spring and summer, it forms an insulating blanket, reducing sharp temperature shifts which could shock exposed plants. A mulch also keeps cool-weather plants cooler in the spring and summer. And in the fall, a good mulch may extend the garden season several months beyond the first frost.

Whether you are applying an organic or inorganic mulch, it is necessary to wait until the ground is prepared, and is neither soggy nor dry. A mulched wet soil stays wet; a dry one will remain dry. The same principle also applies to cold and warm soil.

ORGANIC MULCHES

For an organic mulch to be effective, it must be thick enough to provide a good soil covering. When loose material such as straw or leaves is used, make the mulch 8 to 10 inches thick. Once the material has been on for a while, it will compact down to about 4 inches. There's no need to apply finer materials as thickly. For example, just 2 or 3 inches of sawdust form a satisfactory weed barrier.

Where tiny seedlings are just getting established, or where plants have not yet emerged, pile mulching material in windrows alongside the rows or around the raised bed. This will protect the plants from excessive exposure to sun and wind until they become established. When they have reached thinning size, gently pull the mulch around each plant, allowing some room around plant stems. With heat-loving crops, mulching too soon before the soil has a chance to warm up can retard their development.

Transplanted stock should be mulched as soon as it is set out, but be wary of allowing organic matter to touch the plant stalks at this early stage. Leave an unmulched circle around the base of each plant, until plants are over their shock and have built up their resistance to diseases and insects. Contact with damp or rotting mulch as soon as they are set out in the garden could cause tender transplants to fall victim to damping-off.

You must replenish organic mulches throughout the summer in order to replace material that has decomposed. If your mulch supply is limited, try placing a heavy layer of newspapers beneath the main mulching material.

With the arrival of fall, organic mulches may be left in place, raked to the side, or incorporated into the soil. Most soils respond well to a good mulch that has been tilled under at the end of the season and allowed to break down over the course of the winter. As long as the soil's nitrogen level is sufficiently high to break down that amount of woody material, the soil will not only be structurally improved, but nutritionally enriched as well. On the other hand, soils with barely enough nitrogen to supply the needs of the current season's plants may be in poor shape for spring planting if a woody, high-carbon mulch is tilled under in fall. Combining the mulch with a green manure crop or a nitrogen-rich material such as bloodmeal or cottonseed meal would correct the problem and make decomposition more complete.

INORGANIC MULCHES

Plastic, foil, or "carpet" mulches are strictly for use during the growing season, and should not be left in the garden after harvest. Far from replacements for organic mulches, these should be viewed as supplements. They may

Cut x-shaped slits at desired spacings in a sheet of black plastic mulch and you can transplant directly into it. The mulch warms soil fast to get heat-loving seedlings off to an early start.

be placed on top of layers of compost, straw, leaves, or manure, or used alone in specific sections of the vegetable beds.

Black and clear polyethylene are sold in rolls of several hundred feet, or in some hardware stores by the yard. Three or 4 feet is the most widely available width, and the easiest to handle in the garden. In a row garden, lengths of plastic may be laid between rows, with narrow spaces left open for planting, or the sheeting may be placed over rows with slits cut for planting. Since 3 feet is a bit wide for most between-row spacing, the latter method is usually preferred. By covering the entire area with plastic, you eliminate places for weeds to emerge. However, it does become necessary to cut holes in the material, and this may make it harder to use the following year.

Raised beds and band plantings are easily mulched with plastic since the entire area can usually be covered with one length of sheeting. If you plan on using plastic mulch, consider shaping your growing beds to fit the widths available. This will save lots of time and trouble.

WEEDING AND CULTIVATING

Nothing helps eradicate weeds better than a clean, thick layer of organic material or a single sheet of black polyethylene. Those weeds which do

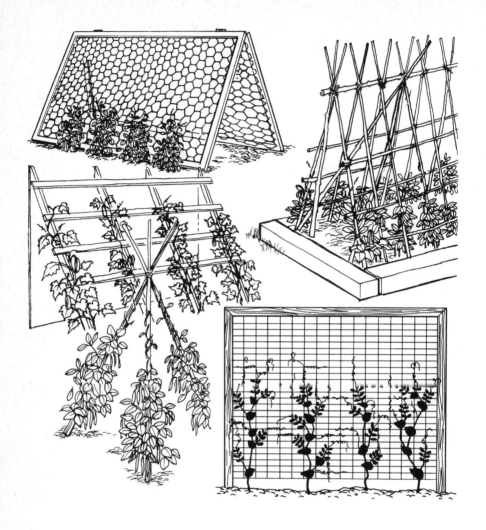

Teepees and trellises make the best use of vertical space. Clockwise from top: wire-and-wood A-frame trellis, oriental-style bamboo trellis, wire fence trellis, wooden tripod, and slanted wooden wall trellis.

manage to force their way through a mulch can be quickly spotted and easily uprooted. Occasionally, gardeners find that their mulch actually increases the weed problems in the vegetable garden. This occurs when unfinished compost, hay, uncomposted manure, or other material containing viable seeds is used. To avoid the problem, compost manures before using them as mulches. Use straw, which contains no weed seeds, instead of hay, or rely on grass clippings, salt hay, or wood chips.

Unmulched gardens usually require cultivation by hoe or rotary tiller in order to keep weeds under control and to loosen soil. Begin cultivation for weed control some three days after the first seeds have been sown. It is necessary to begin this early so that weeds do not get a head start on the crops you are trying to raise. This preemergent cultivation is a job requiring painstaking care, for while you need to destroy the weeds, you must not disturb the yet-unsprouted vegetable seeds. When tiny weeds appear on the soil surface, use a steel rake to gently uproot them in the between-row areas. If you planted seeds fairly deep, go ahead and rake the entire area. In the raised bed, rake cultivation is possible, but a hand cultivator may be easier to manage. Where seeds have been broadcast or equidistantly spaced, the old-fashioned method of hand-pulling is best.

When seedlings have emerged and begun to make good growth, you do not need to be quite so cautious in your cultivation. The steel rake is still a fine tool for the job in a row garden since it does not disturb the seedling roots and allows you to weed quite close to the plants without harming them. You can also employ a pointed Warren hoe or a flat-bladed draw hoe, but do not hoe deeper than 1 inch. A hoe is meant to push or pull the soil, not to chop it. A special scuffle hoe (or Dutch hoe), with a sort of stirrup-shaped blade, will even get rid of weeds without moving the soil at all. When you push it across the ground, it chops off the weeds at ground level, diminishing their chances for survival.

The best time for weeding is midafternoon. Weeds come up most easily from damp soil, but you can't work in soggy ground, and shouldn't weed among crops when their leaves are damp for fear of spreading disease.

A wheel cultivator or rotary tiller is helpful in managing large areas, or in eliminating pernicious weeds that cannot be handled by manual hoeing. Do not use such tools as routine methods for cultivation, however, for they may damage soil structure.

FROSTPROOFING YOUR GARDEN

An important part of early spring and late fall gardening is simply knowing how to protect plants from frost. It is the occasional, sporadic frosts characteristic of these times of year that keep you from planting out as early as you might, or from extending the season beyond that fateful first fall frost. Plenty of warm Indian summer weather remains after that first night freeze, so take advantage of those days. Use the tips presented below to help vegetable crops survive frosty nights.

Hotcaps, Cloches, and Row Covers: These frost guards are not only valuable in the spring garden as protectors for seedlings and tender transplants, but in the fall garden as well. Cover late-planted salad greens or root crops with paper hats, bottomless glass jugs, or plastic hotcaps. Ripening of

Plastic or cloth covers can protect rows or beds from frost and/or insects. Slitted polyethylene sheeting (top) provides automatic ventilation; clear unslitted sheeting (center) can be opened at the ends for air flow during the day, then closed at night. Plastic should rest on wires or stakes, but Reemay (bottom) can rest directly on the plants and allows free passage of air and water. Bury all ends in soil for stability and insect protection.

late melons can be speeded under such a covering. For larger plants such as beans, eggplant, or peppers, invert a cardboard box or bushel basket over the plant and cover it with a sheet, burlap, or plastic. Use old feed bags or dog food bags to cover groups of corn plants or single tomato plants. Entire rows

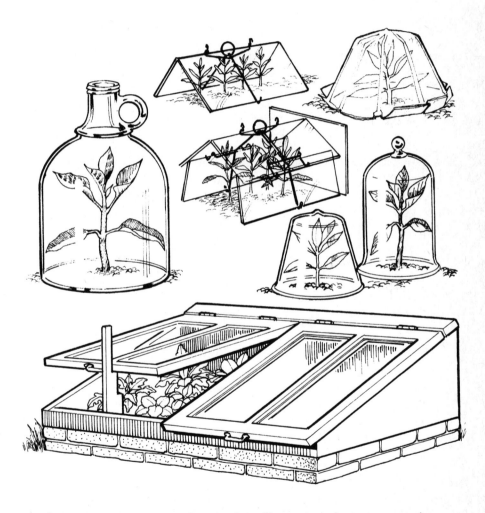

Plant protectors let you put tender transplants like peppers and tomatoes out early. Cover them at night if frost threatens. Clockwise from top: glass tent and barn cloches, commercial hotcap, bell jars, cold frame, and bottomless gallon jug. A permanent cold frame can extend the season in both spring and fall.

or raised beds may be protected with wooden or wire frames covered with polyethylene or cloth. Early the next morning, be sure to remove any cover you have laid down so that humidity does not build up; this is particularly important if plastic or glass is used.

Mulches: Draw hay, straw, chopped leaves, or other dry material closely around the plant base and, if possible, lightly cover its crown to form an insulating blanket to ward off frost. The thicker such a mulch is, the more effective it will be, so don't skimp on materials. Celery, root crops, salad greens, and almost any other crop will respond well to this sort of frost protection. Black plastic mulches will also help insulate crops by protecting the roots from freezing. In fact, any dark-colored material will absorb more heat than lighter-colored mulches will.

Cold Frame: Move celery, lettuce, spinach, Swiss chard, and other cool-season crops from the garden after the first frost and transplant them into the cold frame. They will continue to grow there for at least another month's worth of harvest. Consider cold frames an important extension of the garden, not just a separate structure for starting new plants in spring. During autumn, leave the frame open during the day, and close and cover it only when frost threatens.

DEALING WITH INSECTS
——— AND DISEASES ———

Building a rich, well-structured soil should be first priority not only for high yields, but for insect and disease control as well. Equally important is the maintenance of a clean growing area; remove and dispose of garden debris, or periodically rake it under the soil surface where it will decompose. Where soil is wet and cold, avoid placing a heavy mulch around plants, for this would only encourage fungal diseases, molds, and other problems. Since many diseases are spread by contact, you should wash your hands after working around diseased plants, and sterilize any tools that you used by dipping them into a 10 percent bleach solution. (Rinse and dry these tools promptly to keep rust from forming.) In fact, it is a good idea to wash your hands whenever you go out to work in the garden, for powerful chemicals and cigarette tars that they may carry can transmit some diseases. Furthermore, try to avoid ever touching a bean plant that is wet, for this spreads rust, anthracnose, and several other diseases. Most other vegetables can be handled safely when wet.

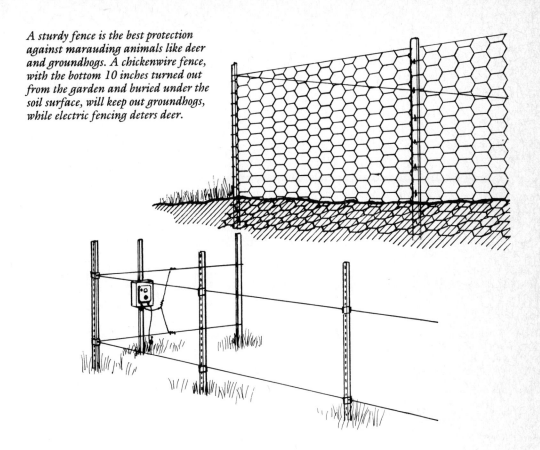

A sturdy fence is the best protection against marauding animals like deer and groundhogs. A chickenwire fence, with the bottom 10 inches turned out from the garden and buried under the soil surface, will keep out groundhogs, while electric fencing deters deer.

Rotation, interplanting, and companion planting are particularly effective ways of preventing serious pest problems. They not only limit insect and disease problems once they begin, but they also keep most from ever taking hold. Where plantings are diversified, pest populations will be relatively small, so that natural predators like the chalcid wasps, ladybugs, and praying mantids can control them.

Next in your line of defense should be the selection of resistant varieties and certified seed. Read catalog selections carefully and, where possible, select varieties that can withstand the diseases or pests you know are present in your locale. Choose disease-free seed and stock, and do not plant seeds or transplants that look suspiciously abnormal.

INSECTS

As an organic gardener, you have various alternatives to consider when combating insect pests, without having to unleash a flood of chemical poisons that taint your harvest and cause long-lasting damage to the garden environment. These alternatives are effective as long as you are a good observer and become familiar with the visual clues that tell you what's ailing your plants.

Potentially harmful insect populations can often be managed if their life cycles and living habits are known to the gardener. Altering planting times so that crops are not available when insects feed is probably one of the best, and least practiced, organic controls. Because the timing of planting depends on when the insects begin feeding and laying eggs in your locale, it is also the most difficult to explain. Begin by keeping garden records of insect "attacks." Write down when they occur, how long they seem to last, and any likely reasons for them, such as too heavy a mulch, weakened plants, or overwatering. This, along with some information about life cycles from a reliable insect guide (see the Bibliography), should provide you with enough information to alter future planting times of the host plant. Thus, squash plants that are normally devastated by borers in early July might be planted a few weeks later so that they will miss the onslaught.

When the time comes to set out transplants, physical barriers will serve as protectors against many insects. Paper collars are the most common example. These are used around young broccoli, Brussels sprout, cabbage, cauliflower, and tomato seedlings to keep cutworms and cabbage maggots from attacking the stems. Use stiff roofing paper or triple-thick newspaper to make an upright collar that penetrates at least 2 inches below the soil surface and stands 1 or 2 inches above. There should be a ½-inch margin between the collar and seedling stem. Some gardeners place slitted asphalt shingles on the ground around the plant, or a thick layer of gritty sand or diatomaceous earth as a mulch. These materials work by abrading the insect's waxy outer coat, allowing its internal fluids to dry up. All such devices should be set in place as soon as seedlings are planted out, or if direct-seeded, when seedlings emerge.

Physical barriers also work in controlling certain beetles. Try covering cucumbers and other cucurbits with Reemay or cheesecloth early in the season to prevent cucumber beetles from setting up house on the leaves. This technique is effective only when the entire plant is covered, for if cucumber beetles get a chance to chew on any portion of it, bacterial wilt infection most likely will result.

Most common insect problems can be managed with daily handpicking. Always try this method of control first—it costs nothing but your time and may stop the problem before it gets really serious. Remove not only feeding adults, but the larvae and eggs. Check around the bases of plants, under leaves, and in surrounding mulch to be sure you find them all. Drop captured pests

(continued on page 75)

COMMON INSECT PESTS

Insect	Description	Feeding Habits	Vegetable Hosts	Natural Controls
Aphids	Come in a variety of colors; soft-bodied; pear-shaped; winged or wingless; less than $\frac{1}{10}$ in.	Suck leaves, vegetables, and stems, causing foliage to curl, pucker, and yellow; transmit viral disease	Most vegetables	Foil mulch; soap-and-water spray with clear rinse; rotenone; predators will take care of most aphid infestations before serious damage occurs.
Beetles	Hard wing covers meet in straight line in middle of back.	Chew on leaves, fruit, roots.		
Asparagus beetle	Blue-black with 4 white square patches and reddish margins; oblong shape; $\frac{1}{4}$ in. long.	Chews spears and leaves.	Asparagus	Rotenone dust for serious infestations; otherwise, handpick.
Blister beetle	Yellowish with black stripes or black with gray wing margins.	Chews foliage, fruit.	Most vegetables (although seldom a problem)	Handpick, wearing gloves for protection from insect's secretion.
Colorado potato beetle	Yellow with black stripes and orange head covering; convex shape; $\frac{1}{3}$ in. long; eggs bright yellow; larvae red, plump.	Chews foliage.	Eggplant, peppers, potatoes, tomatoes	Clean cultivation; heavy mulching; handpick and remove eggs; use rotenone as last resort.
Cucumber beetle	Yellow with black stripes or spots; oblong shape; $\frac{1}{4}$ in. long; eggs orange; lar	Chews leaves, flowers; transmits mosaic and bac-	Beans, corn, cucumbers, eggplant, melons, peas,	Handpick; cover plants with cheese-

(continued)

COMMON INSECT PESTS—*Continued*

Insect	Description	Feeding Habits	Vegetable Hosts	Natural Controls
Cucumber beetle (*continued*)	vae found near plant base.	terial wilt.	potatoes, pumpkins, spinach, squash, tomatoes	cloth; use rotenone or pyrethrum as last resort.
Flea beetle	Shiny, black; may have yellow or white markings; very active; $\frac{1}{10}$ in. long; jumps like a flea when disturbed.	Chews tiny holes in foliage; transmits viral and bacterial disease.	Most vegetables, especially cole crops, eggplant, radishes, Swiss chard, turnips	Lime; diatomaceous earth; or rotenone dusts.
Mexican bean beetle	Yellow to gold with 16 black spots; round; $\frac{1}{4}$ in. long; yellow eggs; orange larvae.	Chews holes in leaves.	Beans	Handpick; rotenone; pyrethrum dusts.
Bugs	Small triangular patch on back; overlapping heavy wings have thin membranous tips.	Suck fluids from plant tissue; carry diseases.		
Harlequin bug	Patterned in shiny black and red; shield-shaped with large triangle on back; $\frac{1}{4}$ in. long.	Sucks leaves, causing them to wilt and die; white blotches may appear.	Brussels sprouts, cabbage, cauliflower, kohlrabi, radishes, rutabaga, turnips	Handpick; control weeds; plant trap crops of turnips near main crop; pyrethrum for serious infestations.
Squash bug	Brown to black with light-colored outline on abdomen; $\frac{1}{2}$ in. long; brown shiny eggs; greenish gray nymphs.	Sucks leaves; plant wilts as vines are damaged.	Cucumbers, pumpkins, squash	Handpick; practice clean cultivation and rotation; select resistant varieties.
Tarnished plant bug	Yellow to brown with darker markings; $\frac{1}{4}$ in. long.	Sucks stem tips, buds, fruit, causing black spots and pitting.	Most vegetables	Practice clean cultivation.

COMMON INSECT PESTS—*Continued*

Insect	Description	Feeding Habits	Vegetable Hosts	Natural Controls
Carrot weevil	Brownish with hard shell; ⅛ in. long; pale, brown-headed larvae with no legs.	Larvae chew celery hearts and tunnel into the tops and roots of carrot, destroying most of the plant's tissue.	Carrots, celery	Practice crop rotation and clean cultivation.
Caterpillars	Larval stage of butterflies and moths.	Chew leaves, stems, fruit, or roots.		
Cabbage looper	Light green with yellowish stripes; loops as it walks; round white eggs; adult brown moth.	Chew leaves.	Beans, broccoli, cabbage, cauliflower, celery, kale, lettuce, peas, potatoes, radishes, spinach, squash, tomatoes	Handpick; diatomaceous earth; *Bacillus thuringiensis* for serious infestations.
Corn earworm	White to greenish red with 4 prolegs; spined; 1½ in. long; adult brown moth.	Chews buds, leaves; plant may be stunted; ears are destroyed from tip down; tomato is destroyed from stem end.	Beans, corn, peas, peppers, potatoes, squash, tomatoes	Apply half a medicine dropper of mineral oil to silk; remove pests after silk has browned; *Bacillus thuringiensis* for serious infestations of garden vegetables.
Cutworm	Grayish, possibly with markings; curls up when disturbed; hides during the day; 1 to 2 in. long; adult is mottled night-flying moth.	Chews stems at or below ground level.	Most vegetables, particularly when young	Protect seedlings and transplants with a collar.

(continued)

COMMON INSECT PESTS—*Continued*

Insect	Description	Feeding Habits	Vegetable Hosts	Natural Controls
European corn borer	Grayish to pink with darker head and spots on each segment; white eggs in groups on foliage; adult yellowish moth.	Chews leaves and tassels of corn; bores into stalks and ears later in season; may chew stems or leaves of other crops.	Beans, corn, peppers, potatoes, spinach, Swiss chard, tomatoes	Make relay plantings; handpick.
Imported cabbageworm	Light green with 1 yellow stripe; leaves soft green excrement; 1¼ in. long; bullet-shaped white to yellow eggs; adult white moth.	Chews leaves.	Brussels sprouts, cabbage, cauliflower, kohlrabi, radishes, turnips	Cover plants with cheese-cloth; handpick; garlic spray; diatomaceous earth; *Bacillus thuringiensis* or rotenone for serious infestations.
Potato tuberworm	Pinkish to white with dark head; ½ in. long; adult grayish moth with mottled wings.	Tunnels into leaves, stems, and tubers.	Eggplant, potatoes, tomatoes	Remove infested vines or tubers; practice clean cultivation.
Squash vine borer	White with dark head; 1 in. long; adult orange and black clear-winged moth with black stripes around the abdomen.	Chews base of stems in early summer, then moves into other plant parts, causing plant to suddenly wilt.	Cucumbers, pumpkins, squash	Alter planting dates; practice clean cultivation; when signs of infestation occur, slit stem and remove borer, then cover damaged stalk with soil; during the season,

COMMON INSECT PESTS—*Continued*

Insect	Description	Feeding Habits	Vegetable Hosts	Natural Controls
				bury every fifth leaf node on trailing squash (this causes them to take root and keep the vine going).
Tomato hornworm	Green with white stripes and a horn projecting from rear; 4 in. long; adult grayish brown moth.	Chews leaves and fruit.	Eggplant, peppers, potatoes, tomatoes	Handpick; if larva has papery cocoons on its back, natural parasite has already doomed it, so do not kill.
Flies (maggots)	One pair of clear wings; maggots are small, white, legless worms.	Maggots feed within host plant; flies lay eggs in plant tissue.		
Cabbage maggot	Adult resembles housefly; maggot white, ¼ in. long.	Maggots tunnel into plant roots and stems; wilting, bacterial diseases may result.	Broccoli, Brussels sprouts, cabbage, cauliflower, turnips	Dust base of plant with wood ashes, rock phosphate, or diatomaceous earth.
Carrot rust fly	Black fly with long yellow hairs and yellow head and legs; maggots yellow to white, ⅓ in. long.	Maggots chew roots, causing plants to be dwarfed; soft rot bacteria may become a problem; entire plant quickly decomposes.	Carrots, celery, parsnips	Alter planting dates; practice clean cultivation; prevent egg laying by sprinkling rock phosphate around plant base.

(continued)

COMMON INSECT PESTS—*Continued*

Insect	Description	Feeding Habits	Vegetable Hosts	Natural Controls
Leafminer	Small black fly usually with yellow stripes; tiny yellowish larvae.	Maggots feed between the upper and lower surfaces of leaves; white tunnels or blotches appear.	Beans, beets, cabbage, lettuce, peppers, potatoes, rutabagas, spinach, Swiss chard, turnips	Remove and destroy infested leaves before maggot matures; cover with wire screening.
Onion maggot	Humped-back fly; white maggots found near bulb or neck.	Maggots chew into neck and bulbs in spring and early summer.	Onions, radishes	Scatter onion plants throughout the garden, rather than planting them all together; dust with diatomaceous earth.
Pepper maggot	Yellow to orange fly with brown marks on the wings; maggots white, pointed, quite small.	Maggots enter fruit from any end and feed within; infested fruit is decayed and falls prematurely.	Eggplant, peppers, tomatoes	Remove and destroy infested plants; sprinkle talc, diatomaceous earth, or rock phosphate on fruit in midsummer during egg-laying season.
Leafhoppers	Green, wedge-shaped with wings held in a rooflike position above their bodies; very active; 1/4 to 1/3 in. long; move sideways.	Adults and nymphs of various species suck juices from leaves and transmit various diseases.	Beans, beets, celery, eggplant, potatoes, rhubarb, spinach, tomatoes, and other vegetables	Dust susceptible plants with diatomaceous earth; cover potato plants with netting in early summer.

COMMON INSECT PESTS—*Continued*

Insect	Description	Feeding Habits	Vegetable Hosts	Natural Controls
White-flies	Small, mothlike, dusty white-winged adults; yellowish nymphs are legless, resembling scales at certain stages.	Nymphs and adults suck juices from plant leaves, buds, and stems; plants weaken.	Most vegetables, particularly greenhouse-grown transplants	Spray with soapy water; predators will control when in the garden.
Wire-worms	Dark brown to yellowish; hardshelled; cylindrical; ⅓ to 1½ in. long; adult black beetles.	Wireworms chew seed, roots, and tubers.	Most vegetables	Rotate crops, practice clean cultivation; trap wireworms in pieces of potato buried 1 inch below the ground for 1 or 2 days.

into a can of turpentine, gasoline, or paint thinner, or simply drown them in soapy water.

Insects too small for handpicking should be sprayed off with clear water. A harsh spray of water early in the day will often be sufficient to control aphids, mites, and whiteflies. If this does not work, try adding an insecticidal soap to the water. This type of mild insecticide not only does away with aphids and mites, but discourages leafhoppers, leafminers, and some caterpillars as well. Some gardeners suggest rinsing plants after such a dousing, while others claim that the soap residues should be left on the plant for a few days to discourage a return infestation. If you do decide to leave the residue on, watch your plants carefully. If they show signs of flagging, rinse the residue off immediately; certain plants are damaged by the presence of this film on their leaf surfaces.

As a last resort for very serious infestations, organically derived insecticides and pathogens may be necessary. Although these are not as harmful as the so-called chemical insecticides, they are by no means "safe." Use them only as a last resort, and handle them as carefully as you would any harsh cleanser or other poisonous material.

Bacillus thuringiensis: Also called Bt, this material is sold under the names Dipel, Thuricide, Biotrol, and others. A naturally occurring bacteria, it is dusted or sprayed on plant leaves, flowers, or fruits. When feeding insects ingest it, they become ill from the spores and toxin, stop feeding, and die soon after. Bt is only effective against caterpillars, such as cabbage loopers, cankerworms, corn earworms, European corn borers, gypsy moths, and imported cabbageworms.

Diatomaceous Earth: This material is sold as Perma-Guard. It consists of the ground, dried skeletons of microscopic algae. The fine, sharp particles of this material abrade away the outer, waxy layer of soft-bodied insects that come in contact with it and they simply die by loss of body fluids. Dust it on infested plants just after a fine rain or light watering so that the material will not be blown away. Cover the entire plant thoroughly, particularly the undersides of leaves. It is effective in controlling beetle grubs, caterpillars, aphids, fly maggots, and other soft-bodied creatures. Earthworms will not, however, be affected.

Pyrethrum: This material is derived from the flower heads of several chrysanthemum species. It, too, is effective against soft-bodied insects, but also kills certain beetles, bugs, and leafhoppers in their adult stages. Because of its extreme potency, use pyrethrum only when absolutely necessary.

Rotenone: Also called derris, this is another of the plant-derived insecticides. It is very potent, but its effects last for only a short time. Apply it periodically to clear up any insects that have not been controlled by other, less drastic means. A spray of 1 percent solution is usually strong enough to do away with insects.

DISEASES

Controlling diseases in the home garden is not as easy as coping with insect pests. For that reason, prevention is absolutely essential, and resistant varieties should be used wherever possible. Do not plant so closely that lower leaves never receive sunlight. Constantly wet conditions, particularly where summers are humid, favor diseases.

Some diseases are carried through seeds, so certified seed is essential to good gardening. Do not plant blackened, shriveled, or soft seeds. Other diseases are carried through plant matter or soil. When you find a diseased plant in the garden, remove it—roots, surrounding soil, top growth, and all—and burn it. If it is a disease such as clubroot, which remains in the soil for several years, you will have to forgo growing host crops in that area until the disease disappears. Avoid infesting your soil with such diseases by carefully checking any transplants and seeds for signs of clubroot, stem rot, black rot, or similar fungal diseases.

VEGETABLE CROPS AND THEIR COMMON DISEASES

Crop	Symptoms	Disease	Natural Controls
Asparagus	Reddish yellow spots on stem, branches; gradually entire plant yellows, weakens, and eventually dies.	Asparagus rust	Use rust-resistant varieties; do not plant in a damp or low-lying area; dust with sulfur.
	Wilted, stunted spears with brownish surface color.	Fusarium wilt	Select healthy stock; do not plant in infected soil.
Beans, snap	Dark red, sunken spots on leaves and stems; pinkish red spots on pods; seeds are often black.	Anthracnose	Use disease-free, western-grown seed; do not work near plants when they are wet; rotate crops.
	Large brown blotches on leaves, possibly bordered with yellow or red; water-soaked spots on pods; seeds may be discolored.	Bacterial blight	Use resistant varieties.
	Plants stunted; leaves crinkled with mottled areas; pods may be rough, misshapen.	Mosaics	Control aphids; use resistant varieties.
	Many small, reddish orange to brown spore masses on leaves and possibly stem; leaves rapidly yellow, dry up, and drop.	Rust	Use resistant varieties; remove diseased plant matter at the end of the season; use new stakes each year; dust leaves with lime if case is serious; avoid handling wet plants.

(continued)

VEGETABLE CROPS AND THEIR COMMON DISEASES—*Continued*

Crop	Symptoms	Disease	Natural Controls
Cabbage (also broccoli, Brussels sprouts, cauliflower, turnips)	Leaves yellow, veins become black; plant becomes stunted and heads of cabbage, cauliflower, or Brussels sprouts are one-sided or nonexistent; stem cross section shows a brown, woody ring.	Black rot	Use hot-water-treated seed; practice clean cultivation; avoid wetting plant foliage; rotate crops.
	Yellowed leaves that wilt during the day; plants may be stunted; roots misshapen and enlarged with club-shaped knots that eventually rot.	Clubroot	Check seedlings before purchasing and transplanting; maintain pH above 7; sprinkle a mixture of wood ashes and whitewash lime around the plant base in spring; rotate crops.
	Seedlings develop purplish lesions on leaves and stems; white downy substance covers these areas; plants die very rapidly after contracting the disease.	Downy mildew	Dust with lime, flour, or sulfur.
	Lower leaves yellow, turn brown, and finally drop; heads may appear stunted and taste bitter; symptoms similar to black rot.	Yellows	Use resistant varieties.
Carrots	Yellow to whitish spots on leaves; girdling of roots; water-soaked spots or lesions on roots.	Alternaria leaf blight	Use hot-water-treated seed; cultivate soil thoroughly; use 4-year rotation where infection has occurred.
	Small galls on lateral rootlets; pimple-sized swellings on main root; plants may be yellow and stunted.	Root knot nematode	Rotate carrots with grain, velvet bean, or cowpea crops, which are resistant to nematodes.
Celery	Greenish or water-soaked spots on leaves; sunken lesions possible on stalks;	Blights (early and late)	Transplant seedlings before they become overcrowded; use seed more

VEGETABLE CROPS AND THEIR COMMON DISEASES—*Continued*

Crop	Symptoms	Disease	Natural Controls
	growth may be stunted; spore threads may be visible in wet weather.		than 2 years old; select resistant varieties.
	Reddish tissue on stalks and leaves; yellowing of foliage.	Fusarium yellows	Select resistant varieties; practice clean cultivation.
	Water-soaked spots on stalks; bitter-tasting, rotted stems; damping-off may occur in an infected seedbed.	Pink rot	Use resistant varieties; avoid planting cabbage, celery, or lettuce in the same soil; destroy sick plants.
Corn	Pale, streaked leaves; yellow, sticky substance exudes from a cut stem.	Bacterial wilt	Control flea beetles which carry the disease; use late-maturing varieties; plow under stubble in fall.
	Large galls develop on stalk, ears, and roots; later, grayish galls blacken and release spores; ripened spores appear oily or powdery.	Corn smut	Gather and destroy smutted plants before spores are released; use disease-resistant seed; practice clean cultivation.
Cucumbers (also squash)	Small, dark spots on leaves; eventually spots grow together and entire leaf is destroyed; fruit may blacken and drop; problem develops in warm, moist conditions.	Anthracnose	Three- to 4-year crop rotation with nonvining plants; use disease-free plants and seed.
	Leaves wilt quickly, possibly while still green; white sticky material might be seen when a stem is cut.	Bacterial wilt	Remove affected plants and destroy; control spotted cucumber beetle; use resistant varieties.
	Yellow to purplish spots start on leaves, gradually cover entire plant.	Downy mildew	Use resistant varieties; remove infected plants.
	Leaves of cucumber and squash develop rough, mottled surface; cucumber fruit may be entirely white; plant may be stunted and yellow.	Mosaic	Use resistant varieties; keep area weed-free; do not grow host plants near catnip or milkweed.

(continued)

VEGETABLE CROPS AND THEIR COMMON DISEASES—*Continued*

Crop	Symptoms	Disease	Natural Controls
Cucumbers (also squash) *(continued)*	Round, white spots on undersides of leaves; eventually entire leaf is covered with powder; fruits ripen prematurely and have poor flavor and texture.	Powdery mildew	Use resistant varieties of squash and cucumber; dust squash with sulfur if infection is severe (cucumber will be harmed by sulfur).
	Dark spots on fruit of cucumber and pumpkin; leaves may have water spots and stems shallow lesions; sap oozes from fruit, then greenish mold develops.	Scab	Do not grow cucumbers in the same soil more than once every 3 years, particularly in the northern states; select resistant varieties.
Eggplant	Brownish spots on leaves; damage is particularly bad during wet weather when fruit may develop small tannish cankers which later rot.	Fruit rot	Use resistant varieties; practice rotation on a 4-year basis.
	Yellowing of foliage and gradual defoliation; plants may become stunted.	Verticillium wilt	Do not grow eggplant where potatoes or tomatoes have just been raised; use clean seed.
Onions (also garlic, leeks)	Early symptoms are sunken spots on leaves; later, a purplish mold develops over spots.	Downy mildew	Rotate crops; use resistant varieties; be sure that soil is well drained; do not overwater plants.
	Mature bulbs and sets develop sunken, dried areas around the neck, usually during storage; only attacks injured bulbs or sets.	Neck rot	Pungent varieties are less susceptible than mild-tasting ones; store sets and bulbs at correct temperatures (near 32°F) with good air circulation; do not plant diseased sets.
	Roots turn pinkish or red, eventually rot; plant is stunted, with wilted tops.	Pink root	Once soil is infested, do not grow any bulb crops; select tolerant and resistant varieties; grow on well-drained soil.

VEGETABLE CROPS AND THEIR COMMON DISEASES—*Continued*

Crop	Symptoms	Disease	Natural Controls
	Black spots on leaves and between the sections of the bulbs; young plants may have twisted leaves; common in North.	Smut	Use healthy sets and resistant varieties.
Peas	Leaves shrivel and die; roots and lower stems may blacken and rot; disease overwinters on plant debris.	Ascochyta blight	Use western-grown seed; rotate crops on a 3-year basis; practice clean cultivation.
	Brownish or yellow blotches form on leaves and pods; stems may turn purplish; leaves eventually yellow.	Bacterial blight	Protect plants from physical injury that could allow bacteria to enter.
	Stems and leaves discolor, turning yellow, then brown. Plants wilt and eventually die.	Fusarium wilt	Pull and destroy infected plants; use resistant varieties; solarize soil with clear plastic.
	Stems, leaves, and pods dusted with white powdery mold; black specks appear later in the season; plants are stunted and vines shriveled.	Powdery mildew	Do not wet foliage during the afternoon; dust infected plants with sulfur; practice clean cultivation.
	Yellowed, gangly plants with rotting roots and lower stems; plant may die before pods form.	Root rot	Plant early on well-drained soils; practice long rotation with nonlegumes.
Peppers	Dark, round spots on fruit; entire pepper may rot or dry up; serious problem particularly in southern and central regions.	Anthracnose	Use clean seed; do not touch wet plants; separate bean and pepper plantings.
	In dry areas, leaves develop yellowish spots with darker margins; older leaves eventually drop.	Bacterial spot	Practice clean cultivation; rotate crops; select resistant varieties.
	Blossom end of fruit becomes soft and spotted, eventually shrivels.	Blossom-end rot	Water continuously after flowering; avoid overfertilization with nitrogen-rich materials.

(continued)

VEGETABLE CROPS AND THEIR COMMON DISEASES—*Continued*

Crop	Symptoms	Disease	Natural Controls
Peppers *(continued)*	Leaves yellow, curl, and become mottled; early fruits are stunted; later flowers fail to set fruit.	Mosaic	Keep garden area free of weeds, particularly nightshade and wild cucumber; control aphids; wash hands after handling infected plants; use resistant varieties.
Potatoes	In warm, moist climates plants become stunted and leaves yellow and roll; stem base develops brown rotted areas on the inside; inside of tubers show darkened blotches and a soft rot that worsens during storage.	Black leg	Plant certified seed potatoes where disease is prevalent; plant only whole tubers; use well-drained soil.
	Spots develop in rings on leaves; eventually leaves may die; tubers develop puckered skin and shallow rough lesions; mold may result.	Early blight	Select clean, certified seed potatoes; use well-composted humus to prevent infection.
	Tissue just beneath the skin on tubers breaks down, eventually turning black; condition does not appear until after harvest and storage.	Internal black spot	Carefully handle tubers during harvest; do not overfertilize with nitrogen materials.
	Mottled, crinkled foliage; brown specks appear on tubers and plants may droop and die prematurely.	Mosaic	Plant certified tubers; select resistant varieties.
	Dark brown cankers appear on young sprouts; mature stalks may become brown; tubers are covered with hard black "scurfs"; tubers may also be roughened in a cross-patched pattern.	Rhizoctonia	Plant certified seed; rotate potatoes with cereal or corn crops; in wet, cold ground, plant either shallow or very deep with thick mulch covering to encourage rapid growth.

VEGETABLE CROPS AND THEIR COMMON DISEASES—*Continued*

Crop	Symptoms	Disease	Natural Controls
	Late in growing season plants begin to decay below ground; just under skin of tuber, ring of rotting tissue appears; eventually, entire inside rots, leaving a shell of firm tissue.	Ring rot	Use disease-free stock; disinfect tools that have come in contact with infected plants.
	Potato tubers are spotted or covered with brown corky pits or scabs.	Scab	Rotate crops on a 4-year basis; do not use manure, wood ashes, or lime on potatoes; lower pH to 5.0–5.5; use resistant varieties; buy certified seed pieces.
	Late in season, older leaves yellow; affected vines die prematurely; stem tissue discolors from base; tubers may be pinkish.	Verticillium wilt	Rotate crops on a 4-year basis; use resistant varieties.
Spinach (also Swiss chard)	Yellowish, curled leaves; stunted leaves and plants.	Blight	Control aphids; maintain weed-free growing areas; select resistant varieties.
	Plants are stunted and yellowed, producing numerous spindly stems.	Yellows	Maintain weed-free growing areas; control leafhoppers or grow spinach under pest-proof cover such as Reemay; remove and destroy infected plants.
Tomatoes	Fruit develops small, round, water-soaked spots; later, fruit darkens and rots.	Anthracnose	Rotate crops; use hot-water-treated seed; practice clean cultivation; do not let ripe tomatoes remain on the vines.
	Seedlings wilt, become stunted; older plants may show dried leaves; cankers develop on stems; small, raised white spots show on fruit; these spots darken eventually.	Bacterial canker	Use clean seed; rotate on a 3-year basis; sterilize infected tools; practice clean cultivation.

(continued)

VEGETABLE CROPS AND THEIR COMMON DISEASES—*Continued*

Crop	Symptoms	Disease	Natural Controls
Tomatoes *(continued)*	Irregular, water-soaked spots may develop on leaves; plant becomes partly defoliated; seedlings may girdle; stem end of fruit becomes grayish green; blossoms or young fruit may drop.	Blights (early and late)	Rotate all solanaceous crops on a 3- or 4-year basis; practice clean cultivation; select resistant varieties.
	Blossom end of fruit darkens, eventually becomes sunken, black, and leathery.	Blossom-end rot	See Peppers.
	Leaves yellow and droop; cross-section of stem shows brownish liquid within; fruit usually decays and drops.	Fusarium wilt	Do not grow in contaminated soils; practice crop rotation; select resistant varieties.
	Mottled leaves; young leaves are bunched or puckered; plants are stunted; yield is reduced; in some types of mosaic, fruit is also mottled.	Mosaics	Eradicate perennial weeds; keep tobacco oils away from plants; spray infected seedlings with milk once a week; control aphids.
	Older leaves thicken and roll upward; young leaves curl; plant is spindly; fruit is soft.	Psyllid yellows	Control psyllids with a garlic spray; keep area free of ground cherry and other weeds.
	In midsummer, old leaves develop small, dense spots with grayish centers; later spores appear in the centers of the spots; fruit is seldom affected.	Septoria leaf spot	Practice crop rotation; keep area weed-free; maintain fertile soil.
	Lower (older) leaves turn yellow, then dry up and fall off; terminal leaflets curve upward at the margins; cross-section of stem shows tan layer beneath the skin.	Verticillium wilt	Plant resistant varieties; solarize soil with clear plastic to kill fungus; destroy infected plants.

CHAPTER 5

GROWING VEGETABLES IN CONTAINERS

Apartment and condominium dwellers, inner-city residents, mobile-home owners, and other would-be gardeners whose ground space is limited or nonexistent don't have the luxury of thinking in terms of conventional garden plots. They must improvise and adapt their gardening endeavors to their situation. Container growing is a multifaceted solution—it encompasses everything from window boxes to pots and planters scattered on doorsteps, patios, and balconies, from elaborate high-rise rooftop layouts to hanging baskets. As long as you can provide the basics—light, water, a container full of growing medium, and fertilizer—you can grow fresh vegetables for your table.

The trend in vegetable breeding toward compact, bush varieties expands the realm of vegetables suitable for container gardening. The availability of dwarf and midget varieties of garden favorites like cabbage, carrots, eggplant, lettuce, peppers, and tomatoes means that the container gardener's selection isn't limited, even if his space is.

Container gardening can be decorative as well as productive. You can raise your crops in a wide variety of containers, including half-barrels, window boxes, planters, hanging baskets, and clay or plastic pots.

There are other advantages to gardening in containers. Container growing offers a flexibility that ordinary gardens just can't match. Pots can be moved from place to place, to expand the garden and extend the growing season. In midsummer, a lettuce crop can be set in the shade where it won't bolt. On frosty fall nights, a tomato plant can be brought indoors, then put out again the next morning to continue ripening fruit in the warm sun. Containers have the further advantage of needing less care than in-ground gardens. There is no hoeing and little weeding. It is easy to tailor soil and water conditions to specific plant needs. An acid-loving plant may grow right beside one needing a higher pH. Crops that require lots of fertilizer, special insect controls, or other treatments can be cared for individually, with less effect on surrounding plants.

Containers also have decorative value. With a little imagination and experimentation, potted vegetable plants can be used to break up a monotonous stretch of bare wall, cover an unsightly drain hole, or soften a sharp change

THE HAZARDS OF HEAT, LIGHT, AND WIND

These factors often cause special problems in high-rise container gardens where conditions change drastically almost by the hour. Wind velocities on a twentieth-story balcony may frequently exceed 25 mph; temperatures may peak at 105°F in the afternoon, then drop to the 40s at night; and sunlight may beat down with desertlike intensity one moment, then disappear completely soon after. Heat can wreak havoc in your garden by killing the pollen of such plants as melons, thereby robbing you of the harvest. While you can't eliminate these quirks of the weather, you can soften their effects. Here are some tips:

Heat and Light

- Buffer plants from intense heat by choosing light-colored pots. White, beige, yellow, and metallic containers will reflect sunlight, making the soil a bit cooler.
- If your patio or deck is a dark color, set plants on a bed of white gravel, a light-colored sheet, a piece of white plastic, or some other reflective surface.
- Keep thin plastic pots and plastic pillowpack containers up off the ground to avoid root burn.
- Store hoses and reservoirs in the shade. Intense sunlight can weaken certain plastics and make the water hot enough to kill plants.
- If containers are portable, move plants to a cool, shady spot.
- Tack burlap, cheesecloth, netting, or other lightweight fabric to sturdy frames to make sunscreens, or use rollup bamboo porch screens.

Wind

- Use large, wide-bottomed containers.
- In very windy locations, don't use hanging baskets or Styrofoam, pulp, and flimsy plastic containers.
- Bolt window boxes firmly in place.
- Group freestanding plant pots close together.
- Use heavy drainage material like gravel in the base of each pot.
- Anchor trellising and supports firmly in the containers.
- Take advantage of built-in supports such as railings, pipes, and walls.

in the yard's elevation. They can define space, accenting the boundary between the patio or terrace and lawn or swimming pool. And you can use them like annual flowers to add color and life to the midsummer landscape.

CARE FOR
———— CONTAINER GARDENS ————

You can start your container garden either by seeding directly in the containers or by transplanting seedlings you've bought or started indoors. See Chapter 3, Planting, for information on growing transplants, and refer to individual vegetable entries in the chart, Vegetables for Container Gardening, for specifics.

Container-grown vegetables need the same amount of light as those grown in the backyard plot. All vegetables need at least six hours of light daily to grow well. As a rule, leafy greens and some root crops can get by with less light and still produce, but fruiting plants need nearly full sun for a successful harvest. Containers equipped with wheels or set on a dolly can be moved around to take advantage of the available light. If your containers are too heavy to move or for some other reason must remain stationary, you can increase their light ration by making use of reflected light. Place the containers against light-colored walls or aluminum-foil reflectors.

Soil in containers dries out more quickly than soil in the garden. In fact, your containers may need one watering a day, and even two in very warm weather. Check them daily, and if the top inch of soil feels dry, water thoroughly—until you see the water draining out the bottom. City gardeners should let the chlorine and fluoride in their tapwater dissipate by drawing the water the night before they plan to use it. Mulching will help conserve moisture and cut down on watering. Use compost, leaf mold, or a half-inch of vermiculite or perlite. (Don't use peat moss as a mulch. It draws water out of the soil and is nearly impossible to remoisten once it has dried.)

Frequent waterings rapidly leach nutrients out of the containers. This means you must fertilize often throughout the season to replace what is lost. Feed your vegetables at every third watering or a least once a week. Use dilute solutions of manure or compost tea (made by steeping a burlap bag full of manure or compost in a bucket of lukewarm water for a few weeks), liquid

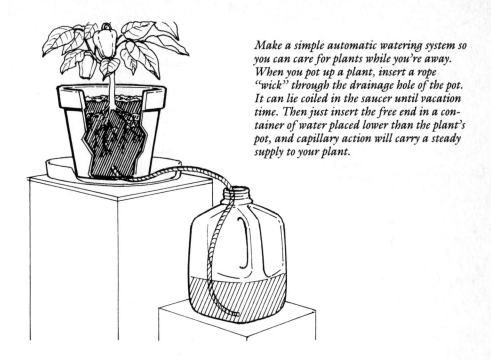

Make a simple automatic watering system so you can care for plants while you're away. When you pot up a plant, insert a rope "wick" through the drainage hole of the pot. It can lie coiled in the saucer until vacation time. Then just insert the free end in a container of water placed lower than the plant's pot, and capillary action will carry a steady supply to your plant.

seaweed, or fish emulsion. Or feed every third week with a nutrient-rich solution of equal parts bonemeal, granite dust, flaked seaweed, bloodmeal, and either fish emulsion or manure tea.

POTTING SOIL

Good potting soils are not necessarily soils at all. In fact, the best garden loam usually makes a rather poor growing medium when used alone in a container. Although its nutritional quality may be excellent, its texture is usually less than ideal. Even the most well-drained loam tends to bring about waterlogging in small containers. Garden soil has other disadvantages as well.

POTTING MIXES
FOR CONTAINER GARDENING

These mixes are used successfully at the Rodale Research Center.

Soilless Medium
   1 part peat moss
   1 part perlite
   1 part vermiculite
      dehydrated chicken manure (follow package recommendations)

Potting Soil
   1 part screened compost
   1 part peat moss
   1 part perlite
   1 part vermiculite
      dehydrated chicken manure (follow package recommendations)

It is heavy, and it can harbor disease organisms which cause some seeds to rot and seedlings to damp-off.

Soilless mixes are available commercially under a wide variety of trade names. They are all composed of vermiculite, peat moss, fertilizers, and trace elements in varying proportions. You can mix up your own with little trouble and at little expense. Just blend together three parts peat moss and one part coarse sand, perlite, or vermiculite. Add 6 ounces of ground dolomitic limestone per bushel of this mix to neutralize the acidity of the peat moss. A soilless mix will release all the nutrients it has absorbed at once, as compared to releasing them over a long period as mixes with soil do. This means that you must be diligent about replenishing the nutrients which the vegetables require for growth.

The best long-term mixes contain compost, leaf mold, loam, or manure. Where damping-off or other diseases are a concern, pasteurize the material, don't sterilize it. Heating soil in a 150° to 200°F oven for 20 minutes destroys most harmful bacteria while sparing the beneficial ones. It is a smelly process, but the result is safe potting soil that may then be combined with texture enhancers (such as peat moss, perlite, and vermiculite) for use in seedling flats and the like.

TRAINING VEGETABLES

A few vegetables require some sort of training in order to thrive in containers. To save space, vines that ordinarily sprawl over the ground with abandon must be trained to grow upwards, along trellises or stakes. Among container-grown vegetables commonly trained along vertical supports are pole beans, cucumbers, tomatoes, melons, peas, and squash. Trellising and support material may consist of anything from 1-inch bamboo rods to fancy

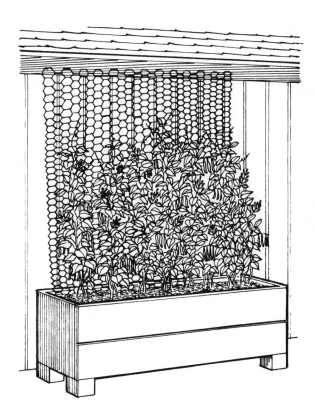

Climbing plants like beans can be grown on a trellis attached directly to the planter, making optimal use of vertical space. Here, the trellis is tacked to the back of the planter box and secured under the roof overhang.

wooden fan trellises. Container shape and size, wind conditions, and the plants themselves determine which materials you select.

As long as they are firmly set in the base of the container, wooden stakes are fine for tomatoes, cucumbers, and squash. They are practical in individual pots, and in closely planted large containers as well. To avoid damaging mature, spreading roots, set stakes in place when you plant.

Nylon netting hung stapled at top and bottom to sturdy wooden dowels or boards and hung against a wall makes a neat trellis that can be easily rolled up, stored, and reused every year. In the container garden, it is most practical when used in conjunction with rectangular planters and window boxes that can be set right against it. Let the netting hang down over the container so that when the plants are about 8 to 10 inches tall, they can begin climbing up the netting without having to bend or reach. Select small, $1\frac{1}{2}$-by-$1\frac{1}{2}$-inch mesh for pea and bean crops, and larger 4- to 6-inch mesh for cucumbers, melons, and tomatoes. These larger openings let you reach through to get to your harvest. (Wire mesh is not recommended—hot metal will sear plants.)

FALL AND WINTER
CLEANUP

Compared to conventional gardens, your container garden requires little in the way of maintenance and autumn cleanup. At the end of the growing season, after you've grown all you can outdoors but before the soil has frozen solid, begin uprooting spent vegetable plants. Chop and compost disease-free plant debris. Throw out diseased material that might contaminate the compost.

Turn soil in large, permanent planters and add a layer of manure, leaf mold, or compost, working it in. Protect filled planters from the erosion caused by heavy rain and snow by covering them with old blankets or burlap bags, or even a thick layer of newspapers weighted down with rocks or other heavy objects. If you hope to plant early in the spring, you may wish to simply cover large planters with black plastic.

Small pots, particularly those made of clay or ceramic, should be cleaned and emptied in the fall. Frost heave is a serious problem in container gardens, and the uninformed gardener who leaves clay or ceramic pots filled with soil outdoors to overwinter may find that they've cracked beyond repair come spring. The destructive force is nothing more than the expanding and

Companion planting makes this barrel a showpiece. Swiss chard is surrounded by marigolds, which are ringed around the barrel's rim with carrots.

contracting of the water in the soil as it freezes and thaws. Empty your containers and you'll have nothing to worry about.

There's another reason not to postpone container cleanup until spring. After soil dries on clay or ceramic containers, it is terribly hard to remove. As you dump out the soil, use a rubber spatula to scrape the sides and bottom clean. Then soak clay and plastic pots in warm sudsy water to remove the rest of the soil. Soak again in a mild bleach solution (one part bleach to ten parts water) to sterilize, and rinse. Let pots dry before stacking and storing upside down.

Very dirty clay pots that are encrusted with debris and the telltale white marks that point to salt buildup must be scrubbed with baking soda and water or even with brick cleaner, trisodium phosphate. After cleaning, soak in warm water and rinse well.

Wooden planters need less cleanup. Scrape out the soil and set the boxes in the sun. After a few days, use a whisk broom or vacuum cleaner to remove the dried soil.

VEGETABLES FOR CONTAINER GARDENING

Vegetable	Growing Medium	Container Size for One Plant	Light	Ideal Temperature (°F)
Beans, bush	Good potting mix rich in nitrogen	8" wide × 8–10" deep	Full sun; tolerates partial shade	65°–85°
Beans, pole	Good potting mix rich in nitrogen	12" wide × 8" deep	Full sun; tolerates partial shade	65°–85°
Beets	Very light, slightly alkaline soil rich in phosphorus and nitrogen	6–12" deep; add 3" width for each beet planted	Full sun or partial shade	40°–50°
Broccoli	Loamy soil rich in nitrogen and potassium	12" wide × 12" deep; 5 gallon capacity	Diffused sunlight preferred	50°–60°
Cabbage	Loamy soil rich in nitrogen and potassium	8–10" wide × 12" deep; 3–5 gallon capacity	Shade part of day to prevent overheating	60°–65°

VEGETABLES FOR CONTAINER GARDENING—*Continued*

Planting	Watering	Fertilizing	Suitable Varieties	Comments
Direct-seed 4" apart outdoors after danger of frost is past; indoors 2–3 weeks earlier.	Keep soil slightly dry until budding, then constantly moist.	Feed dilute solution of compost or manure tea, fish emulsion, or liquid seaweed.	Any variety	Keep leaves as dry as possible; never touch leaves when wet.
Direct-seed 8" apart outdoors after danger of frost is past; indoors 2–3 weeks earlier.	Keep soil slightly dry until budding, then constantly moist.	Feed dilute solution weekly until flowering.	Any variety	Same as for bush beans; Provide 6–8' sturdy stakes, trellis, or net.
Direct-seed 1–3" apart; for continuous yield, sow every few weeks from late spring until late summer.	Keep soil moist, but not soggy.	Apply foliar spray every week, after establishment of plant.	Baby Canning (12, 20), Spinel Baby Beet (11)	Young leaves as well as root are edible.
Start indoors in flat or peat pots for 6–8 weeks. Transplant to containers (18" apart) 4 weeks before last frost.	Needs frequent watering; keep soil moist.	Side-dress or apply foliar spray every week after establishment of plant.	Crusader Hybrid (WA)	Provide good drainage and keep cool and moist.
Start seeds indoors 10–12 weeks prior to last expected frost; 4 weeks before last frost transplant to containers (10" apart).	Don't let soil dry out completely; may require daily watering.	Apply side-dressing or foliar spray every week.	Baby Head (WA), Dwarf Morden (9)	Handpick worms; brush away white eggs on the leaves.

(continued)

VEGETABLES FOR CONTAINER GARDENING—*Continued*

Vegetable	Growing Medium	Container Size for One Plant	Light	Ideal Temperature (°F)
Carrots	Rich, very loose soil high in phosphorus and potassium; extra spoonful of wood ashes and bonemeal added to each pot of soil mix	10–12" deep; add 2" width for each carrot planted	Tolerates some shade; direct sunlight only if soil is kept moist	45°–65°
Cauliflower	Loamy soil rich in nitrogen and potassium	8–10" wide × 12" deep; 3–5 gallon capacity	Shade part of day to prevent overheating	60°–65°
Corn	Well-drained, very fertile medium with good water-holding capacity	21" wide × 8" deep (for 3 plants)	Full sun best	65°–85°
Cucumbers	Slightly heavy, moisture-retentive soil with plenty of organic matter like	8" wide × 12" deep; 1–2 gallon capacity	Full sun best; tolerates diffused light part of day	65°–85°

VEGETABLES FOR CONTAINER GARDENING—*Continued*

Planting	Watering	Fertilizing	Suitable Varieties	Comments
Direct-seed 2" apart, 2 weeks before last frost.	Keep soil moist.	Make mid-season side-dressing of wood ashes.	Baby Finger Nantes (33), Gold Nugget (WA), Oxheart (WA)	Ample rooting depth is important.
Start seeds indoors 10–12 weeks prior to last frost. 4 weeks before last frost, transplant to containers (10" apart).	Keep soil moist.	Apply side-dressing or foliar spray every week.	Early Snowball (WA), Snow King (WA)	Blanching (gathering leaves around head and tying) lets head remain white and sweet as it develops.
Start seeds indoors in peat pots 2 weeks before last frost. Set out after danger of frost is past.	Don't let soil dry out, especially during ear formation and tasseling.	After establishment, apply weekly foliar spray with a balanced fertilizer.	Golden Midget (WA), Polarvee (WA), Golden Miniature (33), Midget Sweet Corn (12)	Growing corn in containers requires much room, since each stalk requires several gallons of soil.
Start seeds indoors in peat pots or portable containers, 4" between plants.	Frequent watering is needed.	Apply foliar sprays; when vines are several inches high, side-	Bush Crop (12), Patio Pick, Pot Luck,	Standard indeterminate types can be trained up

(continued)

VEGETABLES FOR CONTAINER GARDENING—*Continued*

Vegetable	Growing Medium	Container Size for One Plant	Light	Ideal Temperature (°F)
Cucumbers (continued)	compost or leaf mold			
Eggplant	Loose, rich soil that drains quickly; rotted manure and compost added before planting	12" wide × 12" deep; 3–5 gallon capacity	Full sun best	above 70°
Endive and Escarole	A variety of soil conditions	6" wide × 6" deep	See Lettuce	See Lettuce
Garlic	Loose, rich soil with good moisture-holding capacity	2–3" wide × 10–12" deep	Full sun	55°–75°
Kale	Any rich, well-drained soil with ample well-rotted manure added	8" wide × 8" deep	Prefers some shade during the day	60°–65°

VEGETABLES FOR CONTAINER GARDENING—*Continued*

Planting	Watering	Fertilizing	Suitable Varieties	Comments
		dress with a balanced organic fertilizer.	Space-master (all WA)	trellises, etc., to form attractive screens. Small varieties do well in hanging baskets.
10 weeks before last expected frost, start seeds indoors in flats or peat pots. Set out in early summer (12" apart).	Water regularly to keep soil moist.	Apply a weak solution of balanced fertilizer weekly.	Dusky (WA), Morden Midget (24)	
See Lettuce	See Lettuce	See Lettuce	Deep Heart Fringed (8), Batavian (WA)	Requires blanching before harvesting to avoid bitter taste.
In early spring, about 6 weeks before last frost, sow seeds in permanent containers (about 4" apart).	Water frequently to keep soil constantly moist; mulch.	Every 2 to 3 weeks, side-dress with a balanced fertilizer.	Any variety	
When soil warms to 60°, direct-seed 8" apart.	Keep soil constantly moist.	Side-dress (at midgrowth) with nitrogen-rich fertilizer. Apply foliar spray weekly.	Blue Curled Scotch, Dwarf Blue Curled Vates, Dwarf Flowering (all WA)	Frost improves the flavor.

(continued)

VEGETABLES FOR CONTAINER GARDENING—*Continued*

Vegetable	Growing Medium	Container Size for One Plant	Light	Ideal Temperature (°F)
Lettuce	Very rich soil with a lot of well-rotted manure and compost	8" wide × 6–8" deep	Partial shade or diffused light	60°–65°
Melons	Well-drained soil rich in compost, manure, or leaf mold	24" wide × 24" deep; 5 gallons soil	Full sun for 6 hours a day	65°–80°
Onions	Loose, rich soil with good moisture-holding capacity	2–3" wide × 10–12" deep	Partial shade to full sun	55°–75°
Peas	Any good potting mix fairly rich in nitrogen	4" wide × 12" deep	Full sun, but tolerates partial shade	45°

VEGETABLES FOR CONTAINER GARDENING—*Continued*

Planting	Watering	Fertilizing	Suitable Varieties	Comments
Sow seeds in soil about 55°. Can be seeded outdoors about 3 weeks before last frost or started indoors 3–10 weeks before last frost (8" apart).	Keep soil constantly moist.	Apply fertilizers weekly; side-dress at midgrowth if plants are pale.	Bibb (loose-head), Oak-leaf, Tom Thumb (loosehead) (all WA), Midget Lettuce (12)	Any varieties are suitable for containers, but leaf and loose-heading types are more successful.
3 weeks before last frost, start seeds indoors in peat or permanent pots. Set out after danger of frost is past. Plant in groups of 3 (8" apart).	Keep soil constantly moist and increase watering as fruit forms.	Apply foliar sprays once or twice a week. Side-dress with rich compost or balanced fertilizer at midgrowth.	Cantaloupe varieties: Ha-Ogen (36), Minnesota Midget (WA), Short 'N Sweet (24). Watermelon varieties: Sugar Bush (5), Kengarden (24)	May need to train the 24" vines to small trellises or netting. Support fruit with "slings" tied to trellis.
Sow seeds in permanent container in early spring, about 6 weeks before last frost. Thin plants to stand 2" apart.	Keep soil constantly moist; mulch.	Side-dress once every 2–3 weeks with balanced fertilizer.	Beltsville Bunching, Japanese Bunching, White Pearl (all WA)	
Direct-seed (4" apart) outdoors about 8 weeks before last frost.	Slightly dry soil is best until flower buds appear. Then keep soil	Feed with dilute fertilizer every week until flowering.	Any dwarf or standard vining types. Dwarf	Provide tall peas with 6–8' trellis; Dwarf peas with

(continued)

VEGETABLES FOR CONTAINER GARDENING—*Continued*

Vegetable	Growing Medium	Container Size for One Plant	Light	Ideal Temperature (°F)
Peas (con- tinued)				
Peppers	Loose soil that drains easily	24″ wide × 12″ deep; 2 gallon capacity	Full sun needed	70°–90°
Radishes	Any ordinary soil mix	2″ wide × 4–6″ deep	Any light conditions	60°–65°
Spinach	Loose fertile soil with a lot of nitrogen	8″ wide × 4–6″ deep	Some shade pre-ferred	60°–65°

VEGETABLES FOR CONTAINER GARDENING—*Continued*

Planting	Watering	Fertilizing	Suitable Varieties	Comments
	constantly moist until harvest.		counterparts of Sugar Snap are Sugar Bon, Sugar Pie, Sugar Rae (all WA)	twigs or low trellis.
Start seeds indoors in peat pots 8 weeks before last expected frost. After frost danger subsides, set out (1' between dwarf plants; 2' between full-sized).	Don't let soil dry out, especially when blossoms and fruit appear.	Avoid high-nitrogen fertilizers. Side-dress with a high-phosphorus fertilizer as blossoms appear.	Any hot pepper variety. Sweet pepper varieties: Canapa (13, 21, 33), Italian Sweet (12), Pepper Pot (24), Gypsy Hybrid (WA)	Can be grown indoors in fall if adequate light is provided.
Direct-seed in early spring (3 weeks before last frost). Thin plants to stand 2–3" apart. Sow every 10 days to spread out harvest.	Moisture must be constantly and evenly supplied.	No major fertilizing is necessary; can treat with foliar sprays.	Cherry Belle & White Icicle (both WA)	
Direct-seed very early in spring (2–3 weeks before last frost). Thin plants to stand 6" apart.	Constant moisture is important.	Apply nitrogen-rich fertilizer every week or two.	Any variety	

(continued)

VEGETABLES FOR CONTAINER GARDENING—*Continued*

Vegetable	Growing Medium	Container Size for One Plant	Light	Ideal Temperature (°F)
Summer squash	Rich, very fertile, well-drained soil	24" wide × 24" deep; 5 gallon capacity	Full sun is essential	65°–80°
Swiss chard	Loamy soil very rich in nitrogen	12" wide × 8–12" deep	Diffused sun or shade; tolerates full sun	60°–65°
Tomatoes, dwarf and standard	Loose, neutral to slightly acidic soil rich in phosphorus	6" wide × 6" deep; 1 gallon capacity, for dwarfs; 12" wide × 24" deep, 2–3 gallon capacity, for standards	Full sun at least 6 hours per day	70°–80°
Turnips	Light but moisture-retentive soil	6" wide × 10–12" deep	Partial shade	60°–65°

VEGETABLES FOR CONTAINER GARDENING—*Continued*

Planting	Watering	Fertilizing	Suitable Varieties	Comments
Direct-seed in permanent location (indoors or out). Pots may be set out after danger of frost is past (24" between plants).	Continuous waterings are needed to keep soil evenly moist.	Weekly application of balanced fertilizer after seedlings are established.	Early Yellow Summer Crookneck, Gold bar, Straight Neck, Scallopini (all WA), Park's Creamy (24)	Hand pollination may be necessary (use a paint brush to transfer pollen from male to female blossoms).
Direct-seed in permanent containers after danger of heavy frost is past. Thin plants to 8" apart.	Must keep soil moist, especially while plants are becoming established.	Apply balanced fertilizer weekly, after plants are established.	Any variety	
6–8 weeks before last frost, start seeds indoors. Transplant outdoors when all danger of frost is past (6" apart).	Water on a regular basis; mulch lightly.	When seedlings are up, apply a balanced dry fertilizer. After establishment, apply liquid fertilizer weekly.	Patio VF, Pixie, Small Fry, VFN, Sweet 100, Toy Boy, Tumblin' Tom, Yellow Pear (all WA)	Use stakes, trellises, or cages for large varieties.
Direct-seed about 4 weeks before the last expected frost. Thin plants to stand 4" apart.	Keep soil constantly moist.	Fertilizing isn't necessary. Occasional dose of a weak balanced fertilizer for lush greens.	Purple-Top, White Globe, Shogoin, Tokyo Cross (all WA)	

PART TWO
AN
ENCYCLOPEDIA
OF VEGETABLES

ARTICHOKES
Cynara scolymus

If you have 100 frost-free days in your gardening season, you can raise artichokes. Most of the country qualifies. But artichokes are virtually unknown as a garden crop outside of California. Two mistaken notions about how the artichoke plant grows are at the root of the problem. The first is that the artichoke must be grown as a perennial and does not bear the first season.

Researchers grew artichokes from seed at the Rodale Research Center in Maxatawny, Pennsylvania, and harvested the first edible buds the same season—about the time the first tomatoes ripened. Farther north in the Berkshire mountains of western Massachusetts, the season is shorter, but you can pick artichokes from seed-grown plants about the second week of August. There are at least six weeks of harvest time after that.

The second erroneous idea is that artichokes can't tolerate intense heat. True, the plants wilt very severely under intense sunlight, even when the ground is loaded with moisture. They look bad for a while, but so do squash or cucumber leaves on any hot, sunny day. Squash and cucumbers recover later—and so do artichokes. But while heat doesn't affect the health of the plant, it can ruin the eating quality of the buds. They develop quickly during a hot spell and tend to be small and tough. When the weather cools, though, the plant will start producing high-quality artichokes.

Soil Preparation:
Artichokes are most tender when they are encouraged to grow fast. That means rich soil and prompt watering whenever the soil dries. If you apply generous amounts of manure or compost to your garden each year, it should be in good shape to start artichokes. If your soil is heavy, plant the artichokes in a well-drained spot and consider working in some sand and organic matter to improve its moisture-holding characteristics. Artichokes like the soil pH at 6.0, which is slightly acid.

How Much to Plant:
A rough guideline is two to four plants per person.

Planting:
To get bigger plants the first year, buy dormant roots from California nurseries. All of them will bear good buds, but some will probably mature quite late. Where the growing season is long and easy, it's nice to have some plants peaking early and others coming on later. But if you're racing bad weather, you want plants that mature on time.

An artichoke plant demands a lot of space in the garden. Where the growing season is long, each plant can grow at least 3 feet high and 4 feet wide. You'll need a row 25 feet long for half a dozen plants. Where the season is short, an artichoke grows only 2 feet tall and 2 to 3 feet wide. But since production is lower, you'll need twice as many plants. Set each plant into a 12-by-12-inch hole that is filled with compost. If the garden is not manured, work four to five pounds of manure (a little more of compost) into the soil around each plant shortly after planting.

Growing from Seed:
In short-season regions, the best way to start artichokes is from seed. Plan to start artichoke seeds at the same time you plant your first vegetable seeds indoors. To break dormancy, store the seed in the refrigerator in moist peat moss for two

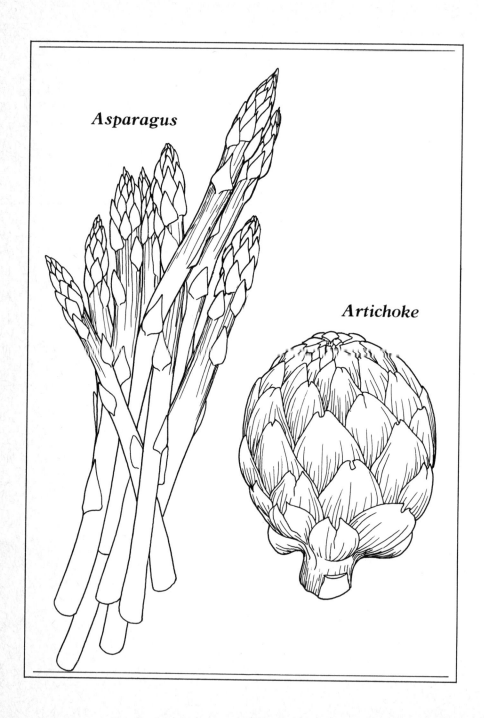

Asparagus

Artichoke

weeks before planting. Use bottom heat for quick germination. Transfer the seedlings to individual containers soon after germination, because the plant quickly begins to grow a long, deep root. Don't set the plants out unprotected until all danger of frost has passed. If you use cloches or other protective devices, you can set them out two weeks earlier.

Growing Guidelines: At monthly intervals throughout the growing season, side-dress each plant with bloodmeal, cottonseed meal, or some other high-nitrogen fertilizer. Or use manure or fish emulsion tea. Fish emulsion is especially good because it is high in calcium, the nutrient that, after nitrogen, will most severely restrict artichoke growth when in short supply.

An artichoke plant must never be short of water when you are pushing it into production, especially when the temperature gets above 75°F. But in the South, where the plant may be ready to flower during unfavorably hot weather, you want to hold it back until about 100 days before the daytime high temperatures dip back into the mid-70s by trimming back flower stalks and big leaves as needed. Be very sparing of water during this period and withhold all supplemental feeding.

Mulch is an invaluable aid to artichoke culture. When the weather turns warm, cover the soil with a thick organic mulch. When the weather has cooled, remove most of the mulch. Some is needed to prevent erosion, but you want to let sunlight reach the ground and warm it.

Where winters are not severe but still bring freezes, gardeners have developed ways of carrying artichokes through the cold weather. The simplest method is appropriate for mild climates. After the first killing frost, cut off the large, damaged leaves, but leave the stems (which can be tied together) to protect the crown and the growing point from the earth that is mounded generously around each plant. Don't allow any dirt to get into the center. Where the weather is colder, first cover the trimmed-back plants with a wooden box, then cover the boxes with a heavy blanket of earth and mulch. Where there are prolonged heavy freezes, some gardeners pile sifted ashes 1 foot deep over each trimmed plant. Any extra protection goes over the ashes, which apparently prevent decay. Layers of manure or compost, however, almost always rot the plants.

Remove the protective coverings promptly when all danger of ground freezing has passed. There is a danger, if the plants are protected too long, that shoots will start up too early. They will be tender and very vulnerable to light spring frosts. But after the ground has thawed and the chance of a penetrating frost is over, take off all the mulch. Then the plants should come out of dormacy very slowly, matched to the weather. Use cloches if heavy frosts threaten young leaves later in the spring.

Where deep ground-freezes are a threat, artichoke roots should be dug and stored indoors, because the crowns are very likely to rot under mulch. The roots can be safely stored all winter if they are kept in a fairly dry place that is maintained between 33 and 40°F. Cut back the leaves to within an inch or so of the crown and carefully dig and brush the roots clean. Keep them loosely packed in fiber bags (don't use plastic) or on a shelf. An even surer way of keeping them is to plant each one in a large pot. Put the pots in a cool, bright place. The crowns will

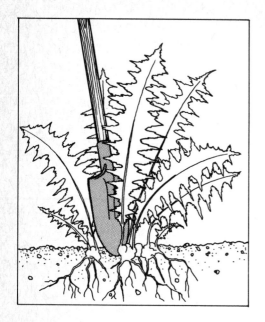

Dividing a globe artichoke plant.

be strongest when the season comes to a close, while suckers taken after the dog days run less risk of succumbing to heat and dehydration.

The best-sized shoot for propagation has a piece of root with it that is $2\frac{1}{2}$ to 3 inches long and at least an inch thick. Carefully dig around the base of a likely-looking side shoot. If it has a good-sized piece of root with it, cut it gently away from the parent, saving as many rootlets as possible. Trim off all the large leaves, keeping only one or two small leaves that will be protected by the stalks of the leaves you have cut away. Plant it right away, water it often, and shade it a bit, if necessary.

immediately begin to regrow, but do not feed them, and water very sparingly until shortly before the time comes to set them out in spring.

Keys to Top Yields:

Artichoke plants become overgrown with the years. Old plants need to be constantly replaced with new ones to maintain steady production. Some growers do this every three years, while others keep the plants producing for six or seven years. To renew a bed every four years, for example, one-fourth of the planting should be replaced each year.

The best way to do this is with suckers, or side shoots, taken from the best plants. Artichokes continuously grow new side shoots, and they can be taken from the plant at any season for propagation. Suckers removed early will

Harvesting and Storing:

Large size has little to do with good eating qualities in artichoke buds. Prime buds can range from 2 to 5 inches across. A perfect artichoke's bud scales are tight and flat. When they begin to point out, the most tender stage has passed. The stem of a bud that's perfect for eating should be soft and pliable for 2 to 3 inches below the bud. Cut each bud with about 2 inches of stem for a handle. Buds can be kept up to one month in the refrigerator. Cooked artichoke hearts can be pickled, frozen, or canned.

Choosing Varieties:

A superior variety, GRANDE BEURRE, appears to produce fast-budding plants in 50 to 80 percent of its seedlings. GREEN GLOBE, the most common American variety, may produce no plants that form edible buds in the first season. GREEN GLOBE is therefore best suited to warm climates.

Pests and Diseases:

Curly dwarf is a virus that stunts and eventually kills

ARTICHOKES

Variety	Description	Sources*
Grande Beurre	150 days; best to start from seed; consistant, fast budding; 3' high, 3' wide	36
Green Globe	180 days; harvest when heads are young; thick, heavy, large, flavorful scales	WA

*Listings correspond to seed companies listed under Sources of Seeds at the back of the book.

artichokes. Botrytis is a fungal disease that is a problem in areas of high humidity and moderate temperature. The principal insect pest is the artichoke plume moth. Aphids, caterpillars, slugs, and snails can also be problems. Generally, however, the homegrown artichoke is free of most diseases and pests.

Nutritional Value: Artichokes are rich in potassium, calcium, and iron.

ASPARAGUS
Asparagus officinalis

Asparagus need no longer be limited to a spring delicacy. For very little more work than mulching it each year, you can depend on it for meals through three seasons for decades to come.

What makes the best asparagus? At the Michigan Agricultural Research Stations, scientists loaded a shear-press, which measures toughness, with asparagus. "Results show that spear toughness increases with decreasing diameter and with increasing distance from the spear tip," they reported. And at Washington State University, scientists also found

that "larger spears are more tender than smaller spears." The more spears per plant and the greater the diameter of the spears, the more tender the asparagus.

The Washington scientists further discovered that emerging spears were tougher following cold spells in the spring than when the weather was warmer. Finally, researchers at Michigan State University reported that "as the amount of rainfall increases during spear growth, the spears contained less fiber."

Soil Preparation: How asparagus beds are prepared and plants are set in has everything to do with the size of the spears those plants will produce. First, choose the site carefully. The bed will be there for a long time. Most references put a bed's life expectancy at about 25 years, but beds much older are still producing. The site should be in a well-drained area, because asparagus will die quickly if its roots stand in water for even a few days.

Since spears grow tougher after a cold snap in the spring, plant the bed along a sunny south wall if possible. If you have no wall, make sure the bed gets full spring sunlight. Some growers hasten soil warming by laying lengths of black plastic along the sides of the bed in the

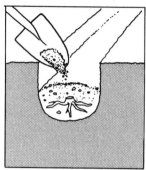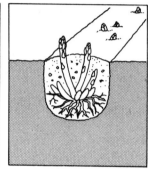

Trench-planting asparagus crowns.

spring. Sandy soil warms up more quickly than heavy soil, and it drains well, too, so sand is an important ingredient in the bed.

For double-row asparagus, dig a trench 1 foot deep and a little more than 2 feet wide. When replacing the soil later, you'll want to mix a quarter sand and a quarter rich humus (such as rotted manure, leaf mold, or compost) with the ordinary soil from the trench. Asparagus likes a soil with a pH of 6.5.

How Much to Plant:
A rough guideline is 40 crowns per person. Planted 2 feet apart each way in double rows, two double rows of 40 feet each will be more than enough for a family of four. If 40 crowns per person seems like a lot, it is. It's double the recommended number found in almost all gardening publications. We're suggesting you plant twice the number because that is the key to all-season production.

Planting:
Five inches is the usual planting depth recommended for asparagus in the Midwest and East, 8 inches or more for the sandy or peat soils of California. But scientists at the University of Illinois planted crowns at 5 and 10 inches deep to see what effect varying depths would have on spear yield and thickness. They found that "the shallower plantings came into production a week earlier each year than the deeper plantings (perhaps an advantage for the deeper setting, since they emerge later into warmer air and that can mean more tender spears). While there were fewer spears from the deeper plantings, the individual spears were much larger and heavier," the researchers stated.

For later emergence of tender, much larger spears, then, make the trench 12 inches deep with plants set at 10 inches. That leaves room for a 2-inch mound of compost or good soil in the bottom (ridging) over which the young plants' roots are spread. Scientists at the Luddington Experimental Horticulture Station in England found that the total number of spears was 40 percent higher from flat rows than from ridged rows. But, they also found that almost 60 percent of the spears from the ridged rows were of the two largest grades, while only 35 percent of those from flat rows were in the premium grades. When they compared weights, the ridged rows produced

2½ times the amount because of the larger, thicker spears.

A California test several years ago involved varying the distances between plants to see the effect on yields. The results showed that crowns 2 feet apart produced twice as many spears, and heavier spears, than crowns spaced more closely. In an experiment reported in *California Agriculture,* "a significantly greater number of larger spears was obtained each season in the double-row plantings than in single rows. Our data also show that the average spear size was reduced in plantings with more than two rows per bed." This is understandable when we realize that in light soils, asparagus roots can grow to fill a 6-foot circle, and that in heavy soils, roots can still reach a diameter of 4 feet. So, for top yields space plants 2 feet apart each way in double rows 7 feet apart.

Growing from Seed: While gardeners have traditionally planted one-year-old roots, there are advantages to starting your own plants from seed. There's little chance of importing fusarium root rot on seed. Roots shipped through the mail or purchased from a store undergo a severe transplant shock, while plants grown from your own seed should have a 100 percent "take" when set into the garden. After a few years, plants started from seed outproduce those from roots, and continue to make slightly larger (and more tender) spears. Also, purchased roots may be either male or female plants. Females have a higher mortality rate and lower yields than males. If you allow your seedlings to bloom, you can mark the males and make your permanent bed entirely from these more vigorous plants. It's assumed that females are not as fruitful in terms of spears because part of their food reserves, stored in the fleshy roots, goes for berry production. (Asparagus flowers are small, bell-shaped, and yellowish green. The male flower is larger and longer than the female, containing six well-developed stamens, while the female has a three-lobed, well-developed pistil. A hand magnifying glass should quickly show you the differences.)

Plant seeds one to a peat pot in late February or early March and make sure they get daily sun. Seeds germinate best at about 77°F. Seedlings grow well at temperatures from 60 to 70°F, which a sunny windowsill or a spot in the greenhouse will provide. Let them grow about 12 weeks, or until they are about 12 inches tall. Plant them 2 to 3 inches deep in a nursery bed if you're going to select the males, or right in the permanent bed if you don't mind the lower (by 25 to 30 percent) production from a mixed-sex planting. Unused seed is good for three years.

Handling Seedlings: The following June, dig a trench and mix sand and rotted manure, leaf mold, or compost into the excavated soil. Make ridges in the bottom and set in the crowns or the seedlings. Cover the young plants only about 2 inches deep with the soil mixture, and water well. Come back in a week or two and move another inch or two of soil into the trench to smother young weeds. Pinch off any low, emerging branches that might be covered as you add soil. Over the summer, repeat this procedure until all the soil has been moved into the trench and the soil is slightly mounded in the bed. It will settle during the coming winter. At this point, mulch the bed with leaves, compost, rotted manure, or grass clippings. Don't let weeds take hold, as asparagus will respond to the competition by diminished yield and spear size.

Growing Guidelines: According to the USDA, "Asparagus must be grown for two full growing seasons before harvest begins. This is necessary to allow the plants to develop an adequate storage root system to produce spears in coming years. Any harvesting or damage to the ferns during the first two growing seasons dwarfs the plants and can reduce yield for the life of the bed." In that first harvest year, pick spears only for two weeks. When the bed is four years old, you can increase the harvest season to four weeks, and at five years, to the full eight weeks (in California, make that a 4-8-12-week succession).

Where feasible, asparagus rows should parallel the direction of the prevailing winds. The ferns support each other in winds, reducing the chance of breakage and consequent setback to the plant. Don't start an asparagus bed in an area recently used for strawberries. A virus that attacks both strawberries and asparagus could wipe out your planting.

After winter arrives and the ferns turn brown, don't remove them. They tend to hold the snow, providing extra groundcover and protection against deep freezing and thawing, which can injure the roots.

If you have an established asparagus bed that's been giving you lots of spindly spears, no matter how much organic fertilizer you give them, the crowns may have grown too close to the soil surface. Crowns grow about an inch upward each year, but heavy mulches also raise the surface. Here's a way to increase spear size. When the harvest season for your bed, whether spring or fall, is about half over, ridge 6 inches of soil carefully over the rows. This has the effect of increasing the depth of the crowns, which has the further effect of increasing spear size and enhancing tenderness.

Keys to Top Yields: The best idea for extending the asparagus harvest comes from Dr. Frank H. Takatori, an asparagus specialist at the Department of Plant Sciences at the University of California, Riverside: "I encourage gardeners to plant double what they'll need. I tell them to harvest half the bed until early summer, then let it grow to fern. At that point, cut down the ferns that have grown on the unused half of the bed. That portion will send up spears that can be cut until cold weather slows production. The spring bed should be harvested in spring only, and the fall bed only in the fall." Beds can be marked off into more sections, also, allowing eight weeks of harvest from each for a whole-season harvest time.

Dr. Takatori explained that in most of the country, asparagus is limited to an eight-week cutting season because it needs the rest of the year to leaf out into ferns that manufacture the plant's food, which is stored in the fleshy roots. Too long a cutting season means less time for food manufacture and storage, and tougher, thinner, and fewer spears next year. A 12-week cutting season is recommended for California's gentle climate. An eight-week season is long enough for the Midwest and East—usually from early April through the first week in June. But in the bed for fall harvesting, food manufacture and storage goes on during the spring and early summer. Cut down the fall bed's ferns in late July and enjoy spears until October's frosts. Meanwhile, the spring bed has leafed out, producing food for next spring's bounty.

Harvesting and Storing:

Crowns can be injured by jabbing a knife into the soil to cut off spears. Unemerged portions of spears will likely be too tough to eat, and that knife could be injuring roots or spears just starting upwards. The proper way to harvest is to snap the spears off at ground level with the fingers. Cooked asparagus can be frozen or canned.

Pests and Diseases:

Asparagus diseases and pests should be checked early, since insects can damage the ferns' ability to make food—and if the damage occurs in the first few years, it can permanently injure the bed.

Asparagus rust can be a problem in areas with wet growing seasons, such as

Asparagus beetle (Crioceris asparagi). This ¼-inch-long, metallic blue to black beetle chews spears in the spring and may defoliate plants in the summer.

in the East. Damage only becomes visible about midsummer, when rusty brown spots break out on the stalk and branches of the plant. A light dusting of the plants with elemental sulfur about three weeks after cutting stops, and another a month after that, will control the rust.

The asparagus beetle is probably the worst pest of this crop. It has a design on its back of white square patches against a dark background. Its dark eggs, laid in rows along the fernlike leaves of the plant, hatch into larvae of light gray or brown with black heads and feet. This and the 12-spotted asparagus beetle may be controlled by allowing several spears on either end of the bed to grow as a trap, then dusting the infestation with rotenone. If you plan to allow a spring bed to grow to fern for fall cutting, look for the beetles and their larvae on that bed's ferns, which will be leafed out through the spring. The asparagus miner makes zig-zag tunnels on the stalks and branches. Tear out any infested ferns in the late fall or in the spring.

Nutritional Value:

Asparagus is a very good source of the B vitamins, calcium, iron, and vitamin C.

Choosing Varieties:

MARY WASHINGTON is the most widely grown and available variety, and it's tolerant of asparagus rust. WALTHAM WASHINGTON and MARTHA WASHINGTON are also rust tolerant, although less widely available. These, along with RUTGERS BEACON, are especially suited for gardens in the East and Midwest. The VIKING strain is recommended for gardeners in the northernmost parts of the country. U.C 157 and 500 have been developed for the special climate of the West Coast. Asparagus, which needs a dormant period caused either by freezing or drought, doesn't grow along the mild, wet Gulf Coast and Florida, but it will do fine in the mid-South.

ASPARAGUS

Variety	Description	Sources*
Martha Washington	tight, uniform buds; tolerant to asparagus rust and fusarium; good freezer	13
Mary Washington	heavy yields; straight, thick spears; tolerant to aspara-gus rust; 60-day cutting season	WA
Rutgers Beacon	suited for East and Midwest	18
Viking	vigorous, heavy yields; large spears, tight buds; suited to northern parts of U.S.	WA
Waltham Washington	consistent; highly resistant to asparagus rust; buds hold tight longer; sweet flavor	12

*Listings correspond to seed companies listed under Sources of Seeds at the back of the book.

BEANS, DRY
Phaseolus vulgaris

If your area gets 120 frost-free days, dry beans are fairly simple to grow, harvest, and store, and each variety has a distinct taste that is especially welcome during the winter. A diversified family, dry beans go by many names and come in many sizes, shapes, and colors. Kidney, navy, and pinto beans are all related and are all widely cultivated in "bush" form across the country. Of another species entirely, runner beans grow as high as 10 feet when trellised. Any mature, edible legume seed that is dried in the garden and used for baking, chili, or other bean dishes qualifies as a dry bean.

Soil Preparation: Dry beans can be grown in a wide range of soils, from sands to clays, although heavier soils don't allow the seeds to mature properly. They generally prefer lighter, slightly acid soil (pH 5.8 to 6.5), and many New England growers get excellent yields on extremely sandy land. Regardless of soil type, make sure it is rich and in good physical condition with plenty of potassium and phosphorus.

How Much to Plant: A rough guideline is 100 feet of row per person, for an average yield of 10 pounds of dry beans.

Planting: "The best advice to remember is that beans need what I like to call a 'good view,'" says Rob Johnston, Jr., of Johnny's Selected Seeds in Albion, Maine. "Well-drained soil is essential, as is proper air circulation around the plants. Give dry beans lots of room. Planting on a slope is fine, provided the plants get as much sunlight as

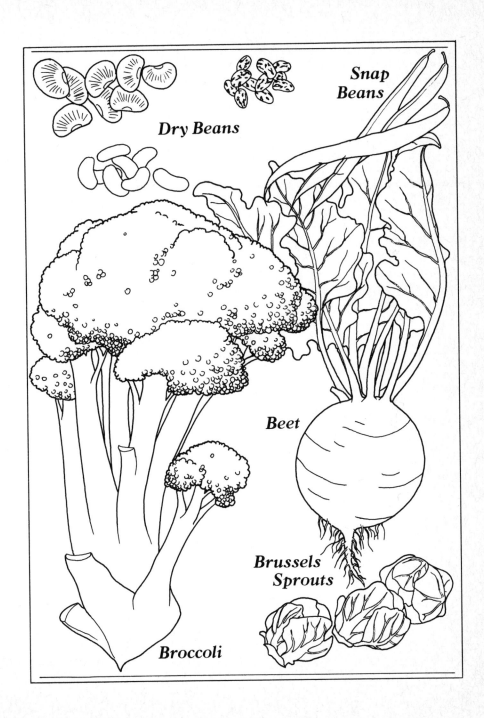

Dry Beans

Snap Beans

Beet

Brussels Sprouts

Broccoli

possible. Shade will stunt plant growth and cause staining. Trying to grow dry beans in a low spot that tends to get sultry during the summer is one of the biggest mistakes a gardener can make."

Plant your dry bean row 20 inches apart with 4 inches between each seed. Sow seeds 1 to 2 inches deep. To assure maturity in short-season areas, sow within a week of the last frost. The soil temperature should be 60°F or higher. If you plant dry beans too early, the germinated seeds will probably die because beans have no frost tolerance. Cover the seeds, pressing the soil over them to insure contact. Keep the soil moist—but not too wet—until the seeds have germi-nated (within a week, usually), and then water only if you are faced with a dry spell. Don't drench your bean plants! Bean experts have found that no vegeta-ble seed rots more quickly under cool, damp conditions than the bean, because of the large quantity of food stored in the seed. Unused seed is good for three years.

Growing Guidelines: Keeping the organic content of your soil high and conscientiously rotating beans with non-legumes like tomatoes, corn, or squash at least every other year are the surest ways to guarantee that your dry bean crop gets enough nitrogen.

DRY (SHELL) BEANS

Variety	Description	Sources*
Black Turtle Soup	85–115 days; bush-type plant; jet-black seeds; popular in the South; good in soups and stews	38
Garbanzo (also Chick-Pea)	100 days; suited to Southern climates; small seeds; distinctive flavor; excellent in salads	12
Great Northern	65–90 days; hardy, 24", prolific plants; fine, white seeds; excellent baked or in soup	WA
Jacob's Cattle (Trout)	90 days; compact, 23" plants; white seeds speckled with maroon; good for short-season areas	38
Maine Yellow Eye	90 days; compact, 18" plants; hardy and prolific; excellent for soup and baking	15, 38
Pinto	85–90 days; strong vines need space; related to Red Kidney; excellent for baking, Mexican dishes	24, 38
Seafarer	90 days; high-yielding Navy bean; small, round, shiny white seed; good texture and flavor	15
Soldier	90 days; compact plants; good choice for cooler climates; excellent flavor for soup or baking	15

*Listings correspond to seed companies listed under Sources of Seeds at the back of the book.

A few inches of organic mulch will not only keep the weeds down and feed the topsoil, it will help retain moisture during the long growing season. In fact, mulch is probably the best defense against unexpected cold or hot spells. Bean plants have their own built-in stress indicators to help you keep tabs on their health. "A gardener can see when his bean crop is suffering," says Dr. A. W. Saettler of Michigan State University. "There are visible indications—beans will wilt when the climate is dry. And if it gets very hot and dry, the blossoms will drop off and no pods will form."

So keep your eyes on your beans all summer long. Try to maintain the best growing climate possible, which can mean watering plants during particularly hot weather and putting away the watering can during less extreme periods.

Harvesting and Storing:

It's easy to tell when dry beans are ready for harvesting. When at least 90 percent of the leaves have fallen off the plant, and the pods are so dry that you can rattle the beans inside, you should pull the plants out by the roots. Finish drying them under cover if the weather is damp. Seed-shattering is not a problem unless your crop has been drenched by rain just before harvest time.

There are as many ways of threshing dry beans as there are excellent varieties of the crop. If you have a lot of patience, you can shell each pod by hand. Otherwise, you might want to try a method Dr. Saettler learned while he was visiting South America a few years ago. "It's very simple, really," he says. "After they have pulled the mature plants, they pile them in the middle of a burlap sheet and beat them with a half-inch-thick stick. A variation of this method is to place the plants inside a burlap sack, tie the top, and hit them until the pods have broken open." Whichever way you choose to thresh your dry beans, make sure you don't beat them on a hard surface like concrete, since that will damage the seeds themselves.

Storing shelled dry beans is simple—just seal them in jars and place the jars in a cool place. Add a sachet of dried milk powder to each jar to absorb moisture.

Pests and Diseases:

With beans, pest and disease problems are interrelated. Quality seeds, resistant varieties, a good rotation program, and sanitary garden practices will help break the insect-disease chain.

Dry beans can be attacked by potato leafhoppers, black bean aphids, bean weevils, and several kinds of beetles. To a great extent, the preventive measures you take to control bean plant diseases will also help control insects. If you do have trouble with bean pests, use rotenone dust—but only when the problem gets out of hand. "Make sure there isn't a lot of old organic debris lying around," recommends Dr. Saettler. "That makes an excellent breeding ground for insects."

Dr. Jack P. Meiners, a bean-plant disease expert, works in the USDA's Applied Plant Pathology Laboratory in Beltsville, Maryland. He explains that most seed-borne diseases like anthracnose and bacterial blight can be controlled by using seeds grown where these diseases do not occur—the Western states, largely. "If you live in the East, South, or central United States, where it gets humid, you should order fresh seeds each year," he says. "Do not save or plant your old seeds from one year to the next. Instead, by a fresh supply from a trustworthy dealer." Some GREAT NORTHERN varieties are resistant to bacterial diseases.

Beans are also susceptible to seed rot and damping-off. For control, don't put your beans in the same place each year. Rotate them around the garden with a cereal crop, grass, or nonlegume. That way the diseases can't get established in the soil. And try to avoid a peas-after-beans or beans-after-peas planting sequence because both crops can be infected by the same diseases.

Rust, though widely distributed along the East and West coasts, is generally not a problem in the North. According to Dr. Meiners, "Rotation will help a bit, as will careful applications of sulfur dust. But sanitation is the best tactic. Dispose of all bean crop residues—do not plow them back into the soil. In the fall, rust can form an overwintering spore that will germinate next spring. Do not work with the plants when the foliage is wet because the disease is readily spread from one plant to the next."

Common bean mosaic, which causes dwarfing and poor production in dry beans, can be prevented by growing resistant varieties. Check with your seed supplier.

Nutritional Value: Dry beans with as much as 23 percent protein make a perfect nutritional complement to all grains.

BEANS, SNAP
Phaseolus vulgaris

Beans are a favorite crop among home gardeners. In fact, a recent Gallup poll found them second only to tomatoes in popularity. They are heavy yielders and can be prepared in dozens of ways. Many people still refer to snap beans as "string beans," but nearly all modern varieties have had the fibrous string bred out of them.

Soil Preparation: Beans will do well in most types of soil, but are happiest when it's well drained and friable. Where the ground is heavy or compacted, the seeds are going to have a harder time breaking through and the crop will suffer. If your soil is heavy clay, lighten it up with some sand, compost, peat, or leaf mold.

A slightly acid soil encourages the best bean growth. A pH of 6.5 is ideal, although beans will survive in soil where pH is as low as 5.5.

Beans aren't very heavy feeders. Highly fertile soil may force the plants into lush leaf growth at the expense of fruiting. High fertility favors weeds, too. The best bean fertilizer is a green manure crop of alfalfa. It can provide all the food your beans will need. Plant it in the fall and plow it under in the spring. Use manure only if it's well rotted. Dig it 6 to 8 inches into the soil at least two weeks before planting.

Other materials will provide the nutrients a good bean crop needs. Dig a 2-inch layer of shredded leaves, compost, or cottonseed meal into the top few inches of the row prior to planting. If the plants seem to be developing slowly, side-dress with a very dilute solution of fish emulsion or manure tea when they are 6 inches tall.

How Much to Plant: A rough guideline is 10 to 15 plants (three to five hills for pole beans) per person. For preserving, 100 feet of row will yield approximately 50 quarts of beans, about enough for a family of three.

SNAP BEANS

Variety	Description	Sources*
Astro	50–55 days; bush type; cold tolerant	14
Blue Crop	55–57 days; high performer; less attractive to leafhoppers	13, 38
Blue Lake	55–66 days; pole bean; good for small gardens, limited space; stringless; canning and freezing	WA
Cherokee	49–58 days; bush wax bean; NY15 and mosaic resistant; AAS	WA
Contender	48–55 days; good late-season crop; mosaic resistant; suitable for all climates	WA
Dwarf Horticultural	65 days; 5–6" thick, flat pods; delicious green or dried	WA
French Horticultural	60–65 days; 14–18" bush; use as green snap or dried; canning and freezing	WA
Gold Crop	45–52 days; bush wax bean; good fresh, frozen, or canned; AAS	WA
Green Ruler	51 days; spreading bush; less susceptible to heat and drought; long, very flat pods	13
Honey Gold	40 days; early wax bean; dwarf, bushy plants to 14" high; very tolerant of common mosaic	33
Italian Romano	64–70 days; pole bean; good yields; ideal for small gardens; good for canning or freezing	WA
Kentucky Wonder	58–74 days; vining pole bean; good for small gardens; good yields of long pods	WA
Pencil Pod Wax	50–65 days; vigorous bush; resistant to common mosaic and rust; stringless	WA
Sungold	45–56 days; bush wax bean; tolerant to common mosaic; good flavor	33
Tendercrop	52–61 days; bush bean; less attractive to leafhoppers; heat and drought resistant; good freezer	WA
Tendergreen	45–57 days; vigorous, erect plants to 20"; resistant to mosaic; extended season; good freezer	WA
Top Crop	48–52 days; bush bean; mosaic resistant; heat and drought tolerant; good for freezing	WA

*Listings correspond to seed companies listed under Sources of Seeds at the back of the book.

Planting: Bush beans do well in fairly crowded conditions. Whether you plant in rows or beds, don't be afraid of close spacings. Dense planting shades the soil, and that conserves moisture and keeps down weeds. Tests conducted at the University of Tennessee found that snap beans grown commercially did best when planted 1 inch apart in rows 12 inches apart. You may not want to jam plants this closely together at home, since it can lead to disease.

Plant snap beans no earlier than two weeks after the last predicted frost date (you can get that information from your local weather service). The soil temperature should never be any lower than 55°F. Somewhere between 60 and 85°F is preferable. In northern climates you'll find that the soil won't warm up to these temperatures much earlier than late May or early June. Applying a black plastic mulch to the soil several weeks before planting will heat it up faster.

Field tests at the USDA's research station in Beltsville, Maryland, have shown that snap beans planted on June 1 actually grew more quickly and yielded better than beans sown two weeks earlier. The seeds planted in May just waited for the soil to warm up before germinating, and in the meantime, many of them succumbed to rot and disease.

Gardeners who plant all their beans at once often find themselves with more than they know what to do with. Try succession planting, once every two weeks from early June until midsummer or about 60 days before the first predicted frost.

Most of the legume family, of which the snap bean is a member, fix atmospheric nitrogen in their roots. This is done with the help of soil bacteria (*Rhizobia*) that form nodules on the plant's roots. However, snap beans aren't as effective at this as other legumes. Commercial inoculants designed to help beans fix nitrogen were found to be mostly ineffective in tests at the University of Idaho.

"Beans don't develop very effective nitrogen-fixing nodules," says Dr. Jack P. Meiners of the USDA. "They're a short-season crop and aren't in the garden long enough to fix much nitrogen." Dr. Meiners suggests that if you've never grown a green bean crop in your garden, treating the seeds with an inoculant might help. Otherwise, he says, it's unnecessary. Inoculants are available through most major seed companies. Just soak the seeds in water, and dust with the powder. Unused seed is good for three years.

Growing Guidelines: Beans need plenty of sunlight. They'll produce, but grow tall and weak, in partial shade.

Keep the soil moist, but not wet, throughout the entire season. Beans are very sensitive to both too much and too little water. Dry conditions will cause pods to drop or shrivel, and waterlogging for even a few days can also lead to pod drop and stunted plants. If your area gets an average of 1 inch of rain per week, there's no need to water the beans at all. If it gets less than that, water sparingly with a soaker hose or drip-irrigation system. Avoid spraying water directly on leaves, since it can disturb flowering and spread disease. If you don't have a soaker hose, dig a trench down the space between rows and fill that with water once weekly. A heavy mulch of straw or grass clippings will help preserve moisture in dry climates and control weeds.

If you live in an area of heavy rainfall, consider planting in raised beds to facilitate good drainage. The beds will also help avoid soil compaction.

LIMA BEANS

If you've been tempted to grow lima beans, but your garden space is limited, you might automatically choose a bush variety from the seed catalog. But for most gardeners, pole beans are the better choice, whether their gardens are large or small. Bush varieties are not the space-savers most people believe them to be. Pole limas typically yield at least twice as much food per foot of row in return for the slight inconvenience of erecting poles or a trellis and a 10- to 14-day longer wait.

Bush limas are determinate plants and behave something like determinate tomatoes. After the plant produces a certain number of leaf nodes, the growing tip ends in a cluster of flower buds. The side shoots that spring from each node also end in flower trusses. More or less simultaneously, the buds burst into bloom. Six weeks later the crop starts ripening and finishes in ten days.

Dr. Charles Thomas, a plant breeder at the USDA research station in Beltsville, Maryland, is trying to develop bush lima varieties that are resistant to downy mildew. Partly because he is curious and partly because he knows that valuable traits may lie within older or wilder varieties, Dr. Thomas also grows some pole varieties. He loves to eat lima beans too, and the ones he prefers to take home are the big beans, succulent and full-flavored, the kind that grow only on poles.

"Lima beans are one of the finest-flavored things you can bring in from your garden," says Thomas. For gardeners, he strongly recommends pole types, saying their most important advantage is that they extend the picking season. A row of pole beans will bear right up to frost. Pole beans also offer a wider range of types. "There's no true bush SIEVA, which is a small-seeded, fairly heat-tolerant type popular in the South," Dr. Thomas says. "There aren't any bush beans that are really large like PRIZETAKER. No bush bean comes close to producing that size of seed."

Because all lima bean varieties must be planted late, at least two weeks after the last frost date, and because the pole bean harvest needs at least 30 days before the first fall frost to be worthwhile, don't plant pole varieties unless you have at least a 130-day season. Bush limas need at least 85 days of hot weather. Most places that get 100 frost-free days should produce a good crop. Figure that each foot of row will yield about a half-pound of shelled beans. For best quality, plan to pick twice, about a week apart.

LIMAS

Variety	Description	Sources*
Christmas	88 days; pole bean; heavy crops from mid-season until frost; high quality, butter-flavored beans	17
Improved Baby Bush	75 days; pods in clusters of 5 and 6; broad, slightly curved; thick-walled pods are easy to shell	5
King of the Garden	88 days; pole bean; climbs to 8' or more; 5" pods with 3 or 4 seeds each; good fresh or frozen	32
Prizetaker	90 days; pole bean; 6" pods with 3 or 4 giant seeds each; excellent quality	5
Sieva	78 days; quick to bear; pods to 3½" with 3 or 4 beans; beans small, flat, smooth; reliable; also good dried	5

*Listings correspond to seed companies listed under Sources of Seeds at the back of the book.

Don't let weeds get a jump on your beans when they're young. The shallow-rooted beans don't compete well with weeds for water and nutrients. Cultivate plants as soon as weeds appear, but don't dig too deeply with your hoe because the roots grow close to the surface. Better, scrape weeds away at the surface, leaving the roots in the soil if you have to. Never cultivate your beans when they're wet, or you'll risk spreading disease. Cultivate in the driest part of the day, when the bean leaves are turned up.

To support the beans, make a teepee of six to eight poles, allowing beans to grow up each pole. To start them on the poles, remember that runners grow in a counterclockwise direction.

Keys to Top Yields:
Frequent harvesting, before seed formation, will encourage more blossoms, which in turn means bigger yields. The plant is trying to produce mature seeds and finish its life cycle. If you keep picking the immature pods, new flowers will form. Plants that are well tended should bear right up until the first frost.

Harvesting and Storing:
Harvest should begin 50 to 60 days after planting. When blossoms appear, the beans will be ready in another week. Pick them when they are about pencil-width and the seeds are barely visible. Test one by breaking it in two. If it "snaps," the beans are ready (that's how they got their name).

Pick as carefully as you can to avoid damaging the plant and knocking off immature blossoms. And, again, don't harvest when the leaves are wet. Peak harvest time lasts only a few days, and if the pods are allowed to ripen after that, they tend to become tough and stringy and the plant will stop fruiting.

Beans will keep for up to two weeks in the refrigerator if sealed in plastic bags.

Pests and Diseases:

By far the worst bean pest is the Mexican bean beetle. This distant cousin of the ladybug is 1-4-- to ⅓-inch long and copper-colored, with 16 black spots on its back. A voracious eater, it usually attacks leaves first, giving them a lacy, skeletonized appearance. Both adults and larvae of the beetle feed on pods and stems, too. The beetles usually appear before the beans start to blossom and feed for a week to ten days. They then lay eggs—up to 400 each—and pass the winter in the bean refuse.

The best way to keep this pest in check is to continually turn over leaves and pick off the yellow egg clusters. If the beetles become uncontrollable, strip the plants of any mature beans and dust with rotenone. This problem can be prevented by cleaning up and composting all bean refuse each year.

The potato leafhopper often gives eastern and southern gardeners headaches. The small, wedge-shaped insect is green with white spots on its head and thorax. If your bean leaves whiten and curl, chances are there are leafhoppers about. Since the bug prefers open spaces, planting in an area bordered by trees or weeds can help. Cheesecloth or plastic netting will also help keep leafhoppers off the plants.

The disease that strikes down beans most often is anthracnose. It causes black or brown sunken spots on, and often eats through, the plant until it keels over. Your best defense is to buy clean seed. Today, almost all commercially grown varieties are anthracnose-resistant. If you live in the East, avoid locally grown seed.

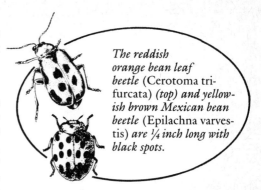

The reddish orange bean leaf beetle (Cerotoma trifurcata) (top) and yellowish brown Mexican bean beetle (Epilachna varvestis) are ¼ inch long with black spots.

Bacterial blight, another common disease, can also be controlled with clean seed and by rotation. Its symptoms are large, dry, brown spots on leaves, often encircled by a yellow border. Rotate your beans with corn or cole crops.

Rust is a problem throughout the East and on the Pacific coast. It causes lesions and a rustlike coloring of leaves.

Other Problems:

Scientists are finding that ozone pollution, a byproduct of auto and industrial emissions, can severely stunt bean plants. The symptoms are a "bronzed," or burnt, look and spots that go through the leaf. Ozone injury can kill the plant in two or three days.

More than 200 bean varieties were tested for ozone tolerance at the Beltsville, Maryland, USDA research center. Types that were found to be resistant include FRENCH HORTICULTURAL, ASTRO, BLUE CROP, PENCIL POD WAX, TENDERGREEN, SUNGOLD, and TENDERCROP. Among the varieties found particularly susceptible were DWARF HORTICULTURAL and HONEY GOLD.

A zinc deficiency can sometimes show up in snap beans, especially those grown in alkaline soil (above pH 7). If seeds mature slowly or irregularly, or if small, reddish brown spots appear on young leaves, a lack of zinc may be the trouble. It can be corrected with liberal applications of rock phosphate, shredded cornstalks, hickory leaves, or ground oystershells.

Nutritional Value:　　Most beans are good sources of vitamins A, B_1, B_2, and C, as well as calcium and iron.

Choosing Varieties:　　Bush bean varieties can be planted earlier than pole beans, are somewhat less susceptible to drought and extreme heat, and are a little easier to grow in that they don't require any structures to climb on.

Pole beans have a lot going for them, too. In general, the larger plants produce more beans while taking up less garden space and yield over a longer period of time. They dry off faster after a rain, thereby thwarting disease, and are less susceptible to damage by animals.

BEETS
Beta vulgaris

Beets' shapes adapt them to pickling, canning, slicing, or just plain baking. Canners prefer the round, ball-like roots that look like a child's top. Long, carrot-shaped beets, like the FORMANOVA variety, are popular for slicing. Other long-season beets grow to the size of grapefruits. All-time favorite eating greens are produced by the LUTZ GREEN LEAF (long season) variety.

Soil Preparation:　　The best beets are cultivated in soils that allow them to make rapid and uninterrupted growth. They favor light, well-drained soil that is well tilled to a depth of 10 inches. Rocks

and other obstructions should be removed, and the 10-inch zone should be lightened with sand and well-rotted manure. If you plan to dig heavy soil in late autumn, leave it rough. Winter's freezes and thaws will smooth it out. You won't end up with marble-sized beets if you create an environment where they can swell with minimal resistance.

Since the ideal pH level for beet cultivation is from 6.5 to 8.0, you are actually striving for a slightly alkaline soil. On the pH scale, 7 is neutral. Less than 6.5 is too acidic for beets. If your soil is too acidic, raise the pH by working in dolomite—most often recommended—or plain ground limestone. The best time to make these treatments is in fall, early winter or, at the least, two weeks before sowing. To increase pH by 1 unit (e.g., from 6.0 to 7.0) on an area of 100 square feet, use the following amounts of dolomite or ground limestone: sandy soil—3 pounds; sandy loam—5 pounds; loam—7 pounds; or heavy clay—8 pounds.

If you must apply more than 5 pounds of limestone per 100 square feet, spread out the dosage. It is better to make several applications over a six-week interval, incorporating lime into the soil each time, than to dump it on all at once.

How Much to Plant:　　A rough guideline is 5 to 10 feet per person for fresh beets, or 10 to 20 feet per person for canning. From 100 feet, an average yield is 150 pounds.

Planting:　　Since beets thrive in cooler weather, the normal spring planting time is three to four weeks before the average date of the last killing frost. Usually you can make succession plantings every two weeks after that. Beets can be sown anytime until six weeks before the average date of the first autumn frost, unless it is still very hot. Beets will germinate at soil temperatures ranging from 40 to 80°F, the optimum being 65 to 75°F.

According to Dr. George Abawi of the N.Y. State Agricultural Experiment Station in Geneva, New York, "The best climates for beets are in New York and Wisconsin, where the summers are not too hot and the spring and fall are cool—although beets can be grown anywhere." In warm regions of the country, beets must be sown at least two months before average daytime temperatures reach 80°F. Hot, dry weather produces tougher roots with low sugar content and uneven coloration, or "zoning."

Beet seeds are unique—each is actually a cluster of one to eight seeds from which clumps of seedlings emerge. The MONO GERM is an exceptional variety that comes as a single seed. Thomas Longbrake, Extension horticulturist at Texas A&M University, advises, "Before you start planting, it's a good idea to give the large beet seeds an overnight soaking for quicker, more uniform germination." When you're ready to plant, space the seeds an inch apart, burying them no deeper than ½ inch in fine-textured soil, ¾ inch in loam, and 1 inch in sandy soil. Allow 12 to 20 inches between the rows. Within one to two weeks, the seedlings should begin to appear. Unused seed is good for four years.

Handling Seedlings:

If you want to get a head start on the beet season, get seed flats going indoors three or four weeks before you'd ordinarily sow outdoors. When planting weather comes around, make holes deep enough for the taproot and water the seedlings immediately. While they're getting in gear, water them every few days, cutting back to once a week as they start to look perky. When seedlings are 3 inches tall, thin the thickest clumps to about 4 inches apart for best root development. But don't discard those you remove—if disturbed as little as possible, many can be successfully transplanted, making a double row.

Growing Guidelines:

Keeping the soil properly moist for beets requires half an inch of water every five days, the equivalent of applying about 1 gallon to each square foot of soil. In arid regions, 2 inches of water per week is required.

Mulching with organic matter after the seedlings have a good start will decrease the loss of soil moisture and keep the weeds down. If you're using grass clippings, pull back the grass from around the seedlings to avoid rot. Apply hay or straw mulch as the season progresses.

When weeds start to appear, carefully hoe them out, hand-pulling any that grow close to the beet plants. Deep cultivation is a mistake, since many of the beets' roots are near the soil's surface.

Harvesting and Storing:

Harvest beets when they're approximately 2 inches in diameter. (The long-season LUTZ GREEN LEAF beets don't fit into this harvesting category. If they are planted around April or May, you can expect to harvest them from summer through fall, when they've plumped out. They tend not to get woody, even when large.)

Remember to pick mature beets before killing frosts set in. Beets that are still growing toward maturity can survive frost and mild freezing while they're in the field, but it's a good idea to cover them with mulch for the winter.

After you've pulled the beets, cut

off the tops, leaving 1-inch stubs of stems. If the full leaves are left on the beet, considerable moisture will be lost from the roots through the leaves, causing shriveling of the roots. The 1-inch stub of stem prevents roots from bleeding and slows deterioration.

Beets that have been harvested in late fall can be stored in a cold, moist spot in your cellar or storage area. Keep them at temperatures no higher than 45°F, and as close to 32°F (without crossing the freezing mark) as possible. They need 80 to 90 percent relative humidity, and should be packed in damp organic material like sand, moss, leaves, or damp sawdust to prevent shrinkage. When kept sufficiently cool and damp, beets can last three to five months.

Pests and Diseases:
The insect that most often attacks beets is probably the beet leafminer, the larva of a little fly that lays small white clusters of eggs on the undersides of the leaves. The larvae burrow into the leaf, leaving a rambling track as they eat their way through it. The best way to deal with them is to simply snip off all the affected leaves and burn them.

"All beets are very subject to root-knot nematode invasions as well, so you must rotate them at least every four years with corn, hay, wheat, grains, alfalfa, or soybeans," says James Fischer, manager of the Sugarbeet Development Foundation. "The nematode is stimulated by a secretion from the roots. If an alternate crop is planted that does not excrete this substance, the eggs will not hatch." On the other hand, don't plant beets after snap beans, limas, peas, tomatoes, or carrots. These plants have a tendency to build up nematodes that would, in turn, attack the beets.

Aphids are always a problem, but one that's easily washed away with a strong spray of water. Another bug to look out for is the beet webworm. Usually yellow or green, with a black stripe and black spots along its body, it chomps on the leaves and constructs webs amid the foliage. Handpicking and pyrethrum are the recommended controls.

In rainy, colder climates, beets tend to be infected with a warmer mold fungus called root rot. It disfigures the beet and creates an internal rot that can't be detected until harvest time.

Cercospora leaf spot is another common beet disease, causing circular spots with reddish brown or purplish margins. Eventually, the infected areas turn gray and deteriorate, leaving holes. Deep tillage will usually destroy plant remains that harbor the fungus. Otherwise, rotate crops every three years.

Other Problems:
Under acid conditions, beets become very sensitive to boron deficiency. You can avoid potential problems with black spot, bitterness, and stunted growth by insuring that your soil makes this trace element available to the plants. Simply incorporate plenty of organic matter. Compost, vetch, sweet clover, and cantaloupe leaves are good sources of boron.

The clues of boron deficiency are reddish leaves, with a purplish tint that initially affects the margins or tips. The abnormal color then spreads to the entire leaf surface, including the veins, while the first leaf tips to be affected die. Finally, when the red pigment has disintegrated, the leaves turn dark brown. Older leaves may become abnormally crinkled, wilted, and scorched.

Black spot, a condition common to

BEETS

Variety	Description	Sources*
Albino White Beet	50 days; round white beet; plain green tops; smooth skin; delicious flavor; always tender	31, 33
Baby Canning	54 days; cylindrical roots	12
Burpee's Golden Beet	55 days; rapid growing; tops excellent when boiled; best eaten when small	5, 12
Crosby Egyptian	49–60 days; early bunching; flattened, heart-shaped root; 17" greens; holds shape longer	36
Cylindria	46–80 days; long, smooth; good shape for slicing; small, reddish green tops; uniform	4, 12
Detroit Dark Red	55–60 days; 12" dark, glossy tops; DM resistant; sweet; excellent for canning and freezing	WA
Early Wonder	48–55 days; deep red, oval roots; especially good greens; stores well; good for canning	WA
Formanova	55–60 days; long, cylindrical root; excellent for slicing; smooth, dark red flesh; good freezer	15
Little Ball	42–56 days; quick-forming roots; remains small; sow spring or late summer; good canned or pickled	5
Little Mini Ball	54 days; round roots; short tops good for greens; good used for whole, pickled beets	33
Long Season	78–80 days; dark red, cylindrical roots; very good greens; sweet and tender; good storer	12
Lutz Green Leaf	60–80 days; purple-red roots; long, 14–18" tops; high yields; excellent flavor	WA
Mono Germ	45 days; only one sprout per seed; uniform; size, shapes, and tops similar to Detroit varieties	33
Perfected Detroit Dark Red	58 days; early; darker inside than outside; large dark green tops; heavy yield; good canner	WA
Red Ace	55 days; very vigorous; adaptable to all areas and short-season areas; deep red globes	19
Ruby Queen	52–55 days; deep red, round roots; short greens; excellent for pickling and canning; AAS	WA

*Listings correspond to seed companies listed under Sources of Seeds at the back of the book.

boron-deficient beets, causes scattered brown or black corky spots that usually appear at the surface of the beet or near its growth rings. These cavities frequently show up in the first half of the growing season.

Early and short-season beets have a tendency to become woody late in the season. A fibrous, tough texture is usually brought about by bad timing: either the plants had too much nitrogen, which caused them to grow too rapidly, or they were left in the soil more than ten days after they attained an edible size. Careful harvesting and mulching with well-rotted manure should control woodiness.

Zoning, otherwise known as "white ring," is usually caused by drought or heavy rains which follow an extended period of high temperatures. The best flesh color is generally created by a combination of damp weather and cooler temperatures.

Nutritional Value: Beet leaves are among the most nutritious greens— richer than spinach in iron and minerals.

BROCCOLI
Brassica oleracea,
Botrytis Group

The secret of an extra-long broccoli harvest is to give the plants exactly what they need from seedling tray to final cutting. Planted at the proper time, broccoli will produce a central head 8 to 10 inches across. After the head is harvested, the plant generally makes numerous tender side shoots—each 3 to 5 inches across—for as long as six weeks afterward. Gardeners in most areas can enjoy this production in both spring and fall,

and can coax a third crop of broccoli in California and the Deep South, by growing a slow-maturing variety in winter.

Soil Preparation: Broccoli likes a rich soil that drains well. Make sure your transplants are furnished with ample nutrients, especially the calcium and magnesium supplied by dolomite. The fall before a spring planting, spread 3 to 5 inches of manure over the plot and allow it to rot over the winter. Turn it under in the spring about three weeks before setting out your transplants. Just before planting, add 6 pounds of cottonseed meal, 2 pounds of bonemeal, and a pound of kelp meal or wood ashes per 100 square feet of garden space.

How Much to Plant: A rough guideline is three to six plants per person.

Planting: Space plants 18 inches apart. Given optimum soil fertility, head size is a direct function of plant spacing. At commercial spacing (7 inches, normally), a typical variety will yield heads that are 5 or 6 inches across. But if you plant the same broccoli 1½ feet apart, you'll get 10-inch heads. Never try close spacings if you want side shoots. Unused seed is good for five years.

Handling Seedlings: Although broccoli can be direct-seeded, you will get the most from your garden space and produce hardier plants by raising seedlings. But the health of those transplants is all-important. "Too large or too old a transplant usually gets you a lot of premature heading," warns Dr. H. J. Mack of Oregon State University. A few years ago,

Dr. Mack studied broccoli transplant vigor and found that four-week-old seedlings, each with two to four leaves and a stem half a pencil's thickness, have the greatest chance of survival and high production.

The temperature at which you raise your seedlings is another important factor. "Keep the temperature in the 60 to 65°F range," says Dr. Ronald D. Morse of Virginia Polytechnic Institute. Colder or warmer temperatures in the early phase of plant life encourage vernalization: plants rush to seed while still very small.

Broccoli tastes best when matured and harvested in cool weather with cool nights. Start plants from seed about three months before the harvest date. "Vigorous transplants can be set out two weeks before the last average frost-free date in your area," says Dr. Morse. But don't set out transplants too early. Prolonged periods of cool weather (35 to 50°F) can cause the plant to form "buttons"—tiny, immature heads.

Fall broccoli should be transplanted considerably earlier than fall cauliflower. Unlike cauliflower, late broccoli can give you several cuttings. To allow time for the regrowth of side shoots, plan the harvest to begin at least a month before killing frosts halt production.

Growing Guidelines: Keep broccoli growing rapidly and evenly with good soil preparation and timely side-dressings. Once you put a plant in the ground, you want it to grow as quickly and as smoothly as possible. Any condition—including a nitrogen deficiency or other nutrient stress—which causes a prolonged cessation or checking of early vegetative growth can trigger the onset of buttoning.

"The most critical time for nutrients is when the broccoli plant is in the early stages of development—especially during the first half of its life," explains Dr. Ronald E. Voss of the University of California. Joseph Stern, plant breeder for Goldsmith Seed Company in Gilroy, California, agrees. He recommends supplemental feeding for broccoli plants (fish emulsion or manure tea are good choices) two or three weeks after you set out your transplants. "You want good vegetative growth before your plant initiates a head. Once the head is initiated, it is too late to change its eventual size," he says.

A second feeding during the plant's middle age will help stimulate side shoots. Dr. Raymond Webb, chief of the USDA's vegetable lab in Beltsville, Maryland, believes that this feeding can make a big difference in the length of productive life of a broccoli plant. "The seed-production phase of the plant is one of its most demanding," he says. "One week to ten days before you cut the center head, side-dress the plant. That will keep it growing and heading up. Side shoots should be larger and more tender with this late boost."

Broccoli is more sensitive to temperature than to daylength. Nighttime temperatures should average between 60 and 70°F, and daytime temperatures should not exceed 80°F. "Broccoli likes sun, but it doesn't like [heat]," says Stern of Goldsmith Seeds. "It will grow well in 80 and 90°F days, but it just won't head up."

"At these temperatures, the plant puts its energy into the leaves," notes Ken Bixby, a plant breeder at the Asgrow Seed Company in San Juan Battista, California. If temperatures drop below 85°F again, the plant might revert to the reproductive (bud-producing) stage, but the quality would be lost. "The buds on the head tend to get brown, die, and fall off," Bixby adds.

"A young plant 4 inches tall can withstand a light frost of 25 to 27°F," says Bixby. "It will experience some leaf burn, but the plant can still recover. Sometimes, though, such cold temperatures can cause the stalk to rupture and split." As a broccoli plant gets older, it also gets more frost-tolerant. "By the time it matures to the heading stage, it can withstand frosts of 20°F, but only for an hour or two," Bixby says.

Harvesting and Storing:

Broccoli heads are immature flowers, a thick cluster of blue-green buds. The central head is compact at first, but if it isn't harvested at the peak of maturity, it gradually separates and the individual florets begin to open. "You can still harvest and eat it then," says Stern of Goldsmith seeds. "But it won't be as tender as broccoli harvested before the buds open." Two or three days make all the difference between mature and overly mature broccoli. In the spring, the florets will open quickly. In the fall, they will hold in good condition a few days longer because of the cooler temperatures.

To encourage maximum side shoot production, harvest the main head by cutting 10 inches to 1 foot of stalk with the head. If you cut low on the plant, eliminating some of the potentially productive nodes on the stalk, the remaining nodes will send out side shoots with added strength. "You'll get fewer branches from the stalk, but the heads that form on those branches will be larger," says plant breeder Ken Bixby. Four to six cuttings are possible from each stalk for up to six weeks.

Broccoli can be canned, frozen, or pickled. It can be kept fresh in the refrigerator for up to two weeks.

Pests and Diseases:

Cutworms chew through the stems of young broccoli plants, dropping them like felled trees. Removing all mulch from your garden, tilling just after harvest time, and keeping the area free of weeds and grass until spring can greatly reduce the number of cutworm larvae wintering underground. Still, most broccoli growers have to deal with them anyway. The easiest method of control is simply to fasten a piece of stiff paper, 3 inches wide, around the stem of the broccoli seedling, pushing some of the "collar" into the soil. By the time the plant has outgrown its collar, it will be hardy enough to withstand cutworm damage.

Aphids can be controlled by weekly sprays of insecticidal soap. *Bacillus thuringiensis* (Bt) is a bacterial disease that can be purchased in powdered form, and attacks moth larvae. Loopers and other cabbageworms stop feeding soon after they have nibbled a little of the stuff, and die within a few days. Mixed with water, the Bt should be sprayed on broccoli plants as soon as you notice small holes in the leaves.

Because the spaces between the florets make a convenient hiding place for tiny caterpillars and aphids, some invariably find their way into the kitchen. Plunge broccoli into warm water with a little white vinegar, and any stowaways should float to the top. Never soak the shoots more than 15 minutes. Use warm water, since hot water destroys nutrients and cold water doesn't clean as well.

Diseases that attack broccoli also attack other members of its family, including cabbage, Brussels sprouts, and cauliflower. To discourage diseases like black rot, black leg, and rhizoctonia, a fungal soil disease, avoid planting broccoli for at least four years where other crucifers have grown.

Nutritional Value: Broccoli has large amounts of vitamins A and C, as well as lesser amounts of the B vitamins, calcium, and iron.

Choosing Varieties: Commercial broccoli varieties like PREMIUM CROP and GREEN HORNET have been specially bred to produce heads 5 to 8 inches across that all ripen at once. Home gardeners would do better to choose fast-maturing vari-eties that produce multiple side shoots as well as large central heads. For an almost certain six-week-long cutting period, plant a variety like DECICCO, an Italian favorite which has prolific side shoots but matures unevenly. BRAVO gives a nice 6- to 8-inch head, with a good yield of side shoots after the main head is cut.

A sudden spring heat wave can work against a great crop of early broccoli. Planting quick-maturing varieties minimizes this problem. At 45 days to maturity, CLEOPATRA is an extra-early strain that forms abundant side shoots. In addition, it shows some resistance to both cold and drought, making it versatile as either an early or late crop.

BROCCOLI

Variety	Description	Sources*
Bravo	83 days; medium compact plant; medium-large head to 8"; good choice for northern areas	22
Cleopatra	45 days; vigorous; abundant side shoots; cold and drought resistant; good for freezing	29
DeCicco	70–80 days; compact; flat heads to 4" across; abundant side shoots; excellent for freezing	15
Green Comet	55 days; blue-green heads to 7" with firm, small, tight beads; AAS	38
Green Hornet	78 days; bright green heads to 8"; good once-over crop—no side shoots; good freezer	33
Premium Crop	58–65 days; large, blue-green heads to 8"; heads hold tight longer; disease resistant; good freezer; AAS	WA
Spartan Early	58 days; short, compact plant; dark green heads to 7"; heat resistant; sow spring or midsummer	23
Waltham 29	74–85 days; low, compact plant; blue-green heads to 9"; few side shoots; best as a fall crop	WA

*Listings correspond to seed companies listed under Sources of Seeds at the back of the book.

For a fall harvest in most of the country and an excellent winter crop in the South and coastal California, plant WALTHAM 29. It's at its best when sown during the long, warm days of early summer, so it can mature during the shorter days of late summer and fall. Where winters are mild, it can also be planted in the fall. Able to tolerate a modest frost (27 to 30°F), WALTHAM 29 is noted for both its side-shoot yields and 8- to 9-inch heads.

BRUSSELS SPROUTS
Brassica oleracea, Gemmifera Group

Brussels sprouts are distinctive-looking plants in the garden. The stem, up to 3 feet tall in some varieties, is covered along its length with miniature cabbage heads that appear to be so many green balls stuck on a stick. These sprouts develop at the points where the leaves join the stalk. Each plant produces somewhere between 60 and 100 sprouts, which are 1 to 2 inches in diameter. The cluster of leaves at the top of the stem looks like a bunch of collard leaves, and can be prepared and eaten as a cabbage substitute.

Brussels sprouts are a long-season crop that ties up garden space for a large portion of the season. However, they are suitable for small gardens because they produce a lot in return for the space they take up. While the Brussels sprout plants are still small, quick-maturing vegetables like lettuce and radishes can be grown between them. Once the sprouts at the bottom of the stalk begin maturing, they may be harvested over a period of six to eight weeks. This prolonged harvest can even continue well after the first killing frost, when the sprouts will hold up well and taste better for the nip in the air.

Brussels sprouts can be grown anywhere there is a cool season in which to mature them. They can withstand frost very well, but are averse to extreme heat. They are not suited to areas that have long, hot, dry summers, unless they are grown as a fall and winter crop. The best average temperature range for growth is 60 to 65°F.

Soil Preparation: Brussels sprouts need rich, well-drained soil with lots of organic matter to hold in moisture. They prefer heavy soil to light, sandy soil. Lay down 6 to 10 inches of compost or well-rotted manure and work it into the soil as deeply as 12 inches. Put in ample amounts of potassium- and phosphorus-rich materials, such as wood ashes and rock phosphate. Adjust the pH to between 6.0 and 6.8; lime toward the higher pH if clubroot disease is known to be a problem.

How Much to Plant: A rough guideline is five plants per person.

Planting: The common practice is to sow seeds directly in an outdoor seedbed 10 to 12 weeks before the first killing frost. Unused seed is good for five years.

In the outdoor seedbed, sow 1/2 inch deep and cover seeds with fine, friable soil. Space seeds about 2 inches apart. When the plants are 5 to 7 inches tall, transplant them to their permanent place in the garden.

Plant seedlings deeply, so that the lower leaves are just above the soil. Place the transplants 18 inches apart in a growing bed and 18 to 24 inches apart in a conventional row. Space rows 30 to 36 inches apart. Firm the soil around the roots, otherwise the sprouts will be loose and leafy instead of firm and overlapped.

Handling Seedlings: In areas with extremely short growing periods, the seed can be started indoors to gain time. Plants need 5 to 6 weeks to reach transplant size, and can be set out at the same time recommended above for seed sowing.

Growing Guidelines: Brussels sprouts need even moisture and good fertility. Keep the soil moist during hot weather, and feed the plants with a high-potassium fertilizer such as wood ashes or seaweed extract. If you're setting out plants in warm weather, mulch them as soon as they are transplanted and provide shade to prevent transplant shock. All transplants need cutworm collars. Keep the area free of weeds, but be careful of the shallow roots as you cultivate. In windy regions, these top-heavy plants benefit from support stakes.

Keys to Top Yields: Sprouts begin to form at the lower leaf axils first and then develop up toward the crown of the plant. When the sprouts have begun developing, the leaves turn yellow. Break or cut these yellow leaves off, gradually working up toward the crown. Leave about 2 inches of leaf stem on the stalk. This gives the sprouts more room to grow, resulting in rounder, neater sprouts. Trimming off the leaves also seems to stimulate growth in the sprouts.

Harvesting and Storing: Warm weather will cause the sprouts to become

BRUSSELS SPROUTS

Variety	Description	Sources*
Captain Marvel	85–95 days; small, very hard sprouts; good for colder areas; harvest October through December	35
Catskill	85–95 days; compact plants to 18"; small, 1¼" sprouts; best as a fall crop	8
Fortress	85–90 days; large yields; December through March harvest; very hardy	35
Jade Cross Hybrid	90 days; heavy yields; adaptable to many areas; sprouts to 1¾"; AAS	15
Long Island Improved	95–115 days; plants to 20" tall; sprouts to 1½"; best for fall harvest; freezes well	8
Lunet	90–105 days; high yields; medium-large sprouts; harvest November and December	35

*Listings correspond to seed companies listed under Sources of Seeds at the back of the book.

loose-leaved and strong-flavored, but these same sprouts will firm up and improve in flavor as soon as the weather cools and they are touched by light frost. The first sprouts of the season are usually not the best tasting.

Harvest by cutting 1- to 1½-inch sprouts from the bottom of the plant and gradually work up as the sprouts develop. The harvesting can go on for several weeks until the sprouts are finished.

In areas where winters bring severe cold that would freeze and destroy the sprouts which have yet to be harvested, lift the plants with root ball intact, and bring them into a protected place where they will stay fresh and edible until all the sprouts are harvested. The protected area can be a pit, a cold frame, a root cellar, or an unheated greenhouse. Pack earth around the roots so that they will not dry out.

Fresh sprouts plucked from the stem can be stored in a cool (30 to 42°F), moist place for three to five weeks. Sprouts are easily frozen after blanching.

Pests and Diseases: See Cabbage.

Nutritional Value: Brussels sprouts are very nutritious. They have high amounts of vitamins A, C, B_1, and B_2, and they are rich in calcium, potassium, and iron.

CABBAGE
Brassica oleracea,
Capitata Group

Like other members of the cole family, cabbage develops best when matured during the cool weather and shorter days of fall. Cool weather at maturity also produces milder cabbages. According to Dr. Michael Dickson, plant breeder at the state Agricultural Experiment station in Geneva, New York, frost sweetens cabbages. Temperature changes affect the amounts of starches and sugars in the plants, and there are more sugars in later varieties, brought about by cooler weather during the plants' critical growth stages.

Soil Preparation: Summer, fall, and early winter plantings do best in heavy fertile loams, while spring crops thrive in sandier loam. But cabbage will grow in just about any soil type, as long as it is rich in organic matter and contains a hefty amount of nitrogen. Cabbage needs soil with good drainage.

Cabbage grows best in slightly acid soil with a pH range of 6.0 to 6.5. If your soil is more acidic than 5.5, apply ground limestone. A general rule of thumb is to apply 50 pounds of limestone to every 1,000 square feet of soil to increase the pH by one unit (from 5.8 to 6.8, for instance). About two weeks before the plants are set out, spread well-rotted manure at least 3 inches thick over the garden area to be used, then till it under.

How Much to Plant: A rough guideline is four to five plants per person of early cabbage and ten to twelve plants per person of storing cabbage.

Planting: To sow cabbage directly into the garden, open shallow furrows and drop in seeds about 1 inch apart. Partially cover the seeds with soil and tamp it down, then finish covering with loose soil to a total depth of ½ to 1 inch. If the soil is dry, water immediately.

Fall crops can be sown directly into the garden and later thinned. The plants that are thinned out can be used as transplants, if carefully dug. Reset them immediately, and they'll be ready to harvest 10 to 14 days after the undisturbed plants. Unused seed is good for five years.

Handling Seedlings:
While cabbage seed can be sown directly into the garden, most gardeners will find it to their advantage to sow cabbage in flats, seedbeds, or containers for transplanting later. Starting seedlings indoors gives you two to three weeks more growing time in the garden.

Sow seeds ½ inch deep in flats indoors or in a greenhouse (with a maximum day temperature of 65°F and a minimum night temperature of 60°), four to six weeks before setting outside. In the North, early crops can be set out as soon as hard freezes are over, while late cabbage is set out at the end of June or the beginning of July. From coastal Virginia to Florida, on the coast of Texas, and on the mild West Coast, plantings for spring crops are set out in late fall or early winter. In Alabama, Louisiana, and Mississippi, plants are seldom set out before January for spring harvest. In California, spring crops are set out in the fall, while winter crops are set out in midsummer.

In the South, and for a late crop in the North, seeds for transplants can be sown outdoors in a seedbed. Sow seed thinly in rows about 12 to 14 inches apart. Thin the plants to 2 inches apart in the rows when they show their first true leaves.

When the seedlings grow their first true leaves (about two weeks after sowing), transplant them into another container, leaving about 2 inches between each plant. Harden-off the seedlings before setting them out in the garden by putting them out a little while each day and by watering sparingly. After a week of hardening, leave them outside overnight for two or three days. Your seedlings will then be ready to withstand the shock of transplanting. The best transplants are four to five weeks old with three to five true leaves, and are free of diseases.

Prepare the rows by digging holes about 2 inches deep. Take the seedlings from the flat or bed and leave as much soil around the roots as possible. Put the plant in the hole, then firm the soil around the roots. Water each hole, wait for the water to drain down, then pile more soil around the plant so the stem is covered slightly higher than it was in the flat or bed. Try to transplant in the evening or on a cloudy day to prevent the seedlings from drying out.

Growing Guidelines:
Never plant cabbage where it or any other brassica was grown the year before. Crop rotation is vital to prevent disease and discourage overwintering pests.

If you're setting out seedlings in regular garden rows, plant early varieties about 14 inches apart within the rows, midseason varieties about 16 inches apart, and late varieties about 24 inches apart. Rows are usually spaced between 28 and 36 inches apart. If you're planting in a raised bed, you can plant in equidistant, or staggered, spacings, maintaining planting distances within rows, but spacing the rows 12 to 15 inches apart. Seedlings can be planted closer, but smaller heads will result. Miniature or dwarf varieties, such as MORDEN DWARF, or the more compact-headed varieties such as JERSEY WAKEFIELD or HYBRID EMERALD CROSS, are ideal for close planting.

Cabbage roots are shallow and spread out over a fairly wide area, so use caution when cultivating. The Oregon State Extension Service recommends that you hoe soil just under the surface, and don't hoe under the cabbage leaves. If cultivated early in the morning when the plant is turgid, leaves may break off.

Cabbage grows best with adequate moisture and in a humid atmosphere. A mulch of hay, straw, or leaves helps provide a cooler, more moist soil when the weather is hot. (Do not mulch with plastic because it retains heat.) Give your plants about 1 inch of water per week. It is important to maintain a uniform moisture level so the heads do not split or crack. (Splitting is also caused by overmaturity.) But if your plants go through a dry spell, don't try to compensate by drowning them.

Heavy rains may leach calcium out of your garden soil, and the resulting calcium deficiency will cause the leaf margins of your cabbage heads to brown. Additions of limestone, bonemeal, or wood ashes will replenish the soil.

Some cabbage growers, eager to get things under way, set out their plants too early and later are dismayed to see them bolt (go to seed). Small plants (with leaves 1 to 1½ inches wide) can withstand cold for up to six months without bolting. However, many larger plants (with 2- to 3-inch-wide leaves) will shoot seed stalks if exposed to continuous cold of 40 to 50°F for 30 to 60 days. So avoid setting plants out too early, and go easy on the nitrogen fertilizer when your transplants are set out to avoid stimulation of early plant growth.

Keys to Top Yields: You can help your early plants produce another head or two before calling it quits. Wisconsin gardener Michael Goc explains, "We cut the head off the stalk with a knife and leave the stalk and roots of the plant undisturbed. It will resprout in several places. We rub off all but one of these buds. With the mature roots nurturing it, the young sprout develops into a head of cabbage before winter." These heads are usually smaller than the parent, but taste just as good. Some gardeners leave all of the buds to sprout, ending up with four or five tiny cabbage heads.

Harvesting and Storing: Cabbage heads are edible as soon as they become fairly firm. Early varieties should reach harvest stage 55 to 70 days after transplanting, while later varieties may take up to 120 days or more. In warm weather, heads may split soon after reaching maturity, so watch them closely. In cooler regions, harvest your cabbage before hard freezes.

Late varieties of white cabbage can be pulled up in mid-autumn and hung upside down by the stalk in a shed or garage, where they will keep well for months. Red cabbage can be saved in the same way. You can also store cabbage by pulling up entire plants and stacking them upside down in a protected corner of the yard. Cover the cabbages with a 1-foot layer of leaves or straw.

Pests and Diseases: Very early plantings in the North and very late plantings generally have little or no pest problems because the plants are maturing during cool weather, before or after the bugs are out in full force. And according to plant breeder Dr. Dickson, red cabbage appears to be more insect-resistant than white because moths are repelled by the color, and thus lay fewer eggs.

The cabbage aphid is a tiny greenish

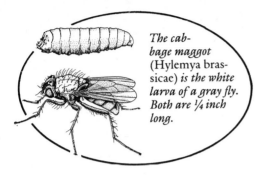

The cabbage maggot (Hylemya brassicae) *is the white larva of a gray fly. Both are ¼ inch long.*

blue insect that clusters on the undersides of leaves, causing them to curl. Affected plants are stunted and seedlings may die. When the aphids appear in cool weather, a fine, forceful spray from the garden hose or an insecticidal soap spray will dislodge them. Finely ground limestone sprinkled over the cabbage plant will keep the aphids away, and diatomaceous earth will kill them. Plants may be saved by simply removing the affected leaves, but keep an eye out for signs of further infestation.

The cabbage looper, a pale green worm with light stripes, emerges from eggs laid on the surface of the leaves by the cabbage looper moth. According to Dr. Dickson, moths search out healthy plants. If you rip off leaves and drape one on the head to decay,"you may make the plant unattractive to moths." The greatest breakthrough in cabbage looper control has been the use of *Bacillus thuringiensis* (Bt). Used as directed, Bt will clean up infestations and prevent their reappearance. Bt will also take care of imported cabbageworm problems.

The cabbage maggot attacks stems of early cabbage, causing plants to wilt and die. Place a tablespoon of wood ashes around each stem, mix with soil, tamp it down, and water. When setting out winter cabbage in early August, mix wood

ashes, lime, rock phosphate, and bonemeal (4:1:1:1) and stir 2 cups of this mixture into the soil in a 2-foot radius for each plant.

The adult imported cabbageworm is the familiar white cabbage moth which has wings marked with black spots and tipped with gray. She deposits her eggs at the base of the cabbage plant, and about a week later, green caterpillars emerge and eat ragged holes in the foliage. Later, they bore into developing cabbage heads. In cabbageworm tests at the Rodale Research Center, researchers found sprays of Dipel (a Bt trade name) and rotenone to be most effective in eliminating the cabbageworm. You may also want to try companion planting by surrounding your cabbage patch with tansy, tomatoes, sage, rosemary, catnip, hyssop, onions, or garlic.

Plump, variously colored cutworms attack cabbage plants by chewing through young plant stems at ground level. Larger plants suffer from serious foliage loss. The most effective barrier is a cutworm collar placed around the seedling at transplant time. Push 3-inch-high collars of cardboard or tar paper an inch into the ground and fasten them around the stems to protect your plants.

The harlequin bug, which is black with red and orange markings, feeds

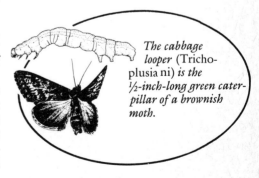

The cabbage looper (Trichoplusia ni) *is the ½-inch-long green caterpillar of a brownish moth.*

heavily on cabbage. Keep down weeds in and near the garden to discourage the bugs. You may also want to use sabadilla or pyrethrum to get rid of them.

Northern gardeners would be wise to buy only yellows-resistant varieties. Yellows is a disease caused by *Fusarium oxysporum* f. *conglutinans,* which turns plants yellow soon after transplanting. The leaves fall off, and the plants soon die.

Black rot can appear in your cabbage patch at any stage of growth. It is primarily a wet-weather disease. The first indication of this bacterial disease is a yellowing of leaves and blackening of the veins. Plants will later become dwarfed and may produce one-sided heads, if any. The bacteria live in the soil, in plant refuse, or in the seed. You can control the problem by treating the seed with hot water before it is planted. Place the seed in a cheesecloth sack and immerse it in water held at a constant 122°F for 15 to 20 minutes. Keep the water agitated. Then immerse the seed in cold water, drain it, and spread in a thin layer to dry. Seed that is produced in areas with little or no rainfall, such as California and other Pacific Coast regions, is free of black rot infection and need not be treated.

Black leg, like black rot, is a seed-borne disease. It attacks the stems of young plants, causing dark, sunken areas. The plant wilts and dead leaves adhere to the stem. The controls for black rot are effective against this disease as well.

The clubroot fungus attacks cabbage roots, causing clublike swellings. The roots become unable to absorb nutrients and water, leading to yellowed leaves and stunted plants. Crop rotation and a slightly alkaline soil (pH 7.2) will help control this disease.

Root knot is caused by a nematode that attacks plant roots, forming knots on them. Rotation with small grains, corn, velvet beans, and soybeans is recommended for control. There is much evidence that increasing the content of organic matter in the soil reduces crop loss from this disease by encouraging growth of fungi that prey on nematodes.

Nutritional Value: Cabbage leaves are high in vitamin C, as is the core. Cabbage is also high in vitamin A and the B vitamins, and supplies a fair amount of other important nutrients such as calcium, potassium, and protein.

Choosing Varieties: The variety you choose will depend on where you live and when you want to harvest your cabbage. Dr. Dickson of New York's Agricultural Experiment Station recommends that gardeners who want to grow cabbage for an extended season, or year-round, should keep planting a succession of varieties.

One of the earliest cabbage varieties is GOLDEN ACRE, followed by the small, conical-headed JERSEY WAKEFIELD. Mid-season types include GLOBE, MARION MARKET, and WISCONSIN ALL SEASONS. HOLLANDER and DANISH BALLHEAD types are grown in the North for winter storage, along with late SAVOY varieties that stand up to cold weather.

Flowering cabbages are beautiful and practical, and just as easy to care for as their vegetable relative. Ornamental cabbage does not reach its full glory until fall. That's when beautiful red, white, and pink heads emerge against green leaves. You can plant these cabbages for visual variety in the regular cabbage patch, or use them in the flower border. They are not only colorful, but edible as well, and perk up any salad.

CABBAGE

Variety	Description	Sources*
Chieftan Savoy	80–90 days; sweeter than regular cabbage; flat heads up to 5 pounds; white inside; crinkled leaves; stands well	WA
Danish Ballhead	110 days; round, blue-green heads; adapted to the Northeast, mountain areas; high yields; resists bolting, splitting	WA
Earliana	60 days; very early; round, compact 4–5″ head; small frame of uniform size	5
Globe Yellows Resistant	85 days; spreading, uniform; heavier head with unusually short core; yellows resistant	8
Glory of Enkhuizen	75 days; old Dutch variety popular in North America; round, blue-green 7½″ heads; dense and solid	22
Golden Acre	60 days; early; short-stemmed, compact, and erect; heads to 7″; yellows resistant; does not stand long in hot weather	WA
Hollander	100 days; very tight heads, no hollow spaces; medium-sized globe; excellent storer; good for the North	8
Hybrid Emerald Cross	63 days; early, vigorous, uniform; compact, good for close spacing; heads to 9″; resists cracking; AAS	5
Hybrid Ruby Ball	65–72 days; early; red, ball-shaped heads to 5 pounds; good raw, cooked, or pickled; AAS	7, 20
Hybrid Savoy King	80–120 days; vigorous; semi-flat heads to 6 pounds; crinkled, flavorful leaves; AAS	WA
Hybrid Stonehead	60 days; compact, good for close planting; dense, hard heads; yellows and heat resistant	WA
Jersey Wakefield	62–65 days; small, compact plants with 6–7″ pointed, compact heads; uniform maturity	WA
Late Flat Dutch	100 days; large frame with short stem; very flat, round head with white interior; good winter keeper	8, 22
Marion Market	70–90 days; short-stemmed; midseason; large, solid 6–7″ heads; yellows and bolt resistant	WA
Morden Dwarf	60 days; small plants with 4″ heads; resists cracking; good for small gardens; sweet and tender	9

(continued)

CABBAGE—*Continued*

Variety	Description	Sources*
Penn State Ballhead	90–110 days; large, spreading plant; very hard, uniform, flattened head; excellent for storage and kraut	WA
Red Acre	74–90 days; small, compact; red heads; sure heading; yellows and cracking resistant; best for keeping	WA
Wisconsin All Seasons	76–95 days; spreading plant; large, hard, flattened globe to 12"; resistant to yellows and wilt; hardy; good keeper	WA
Wisconsin Hollander	90–110 days; deep blue-green head up to 8"; very prolific; excellent keeper	WA

*Listings correspond to seed companies listed under Sources of Seeds at the back of the book.

CARROTS
Daucus carota var. *sativus*

Gardeners expect a lot from their carrots. It's not enough that they taste good, they've got to look good as well. A carrot that's split, forked, or hairy isn't likely to make its grower proud, no matter how it tastes. and what good is a perfectly formed carrot if it's bitter and woody?

The goal is big sweet carrots that look and taste great. The secret is in careful planning that starts with choosing the best carrot variety for your garden and ends with careful soil preparation.

Soil Preparation: As with most root crops, the key to good carrots, no matter which variety you choose, is soil preparation. The carrot has a delicate root system during its early stages of growth and is poorly adapted to penetrating stiff, hard soil or heavy clay. Compacted soil will make it difficult for the taproot to

penetrate, and the hairlike feeder roots won't be able to find enough oxygen for optimum growth. In a study conducted at the University of London, carrots raised in a well-aerated medium grew nearly twice as large as those grown in unaerated conditions. The ideal soil for carrots is a fertile, well-drained sandy loam. Forking is often caused by rocks. If the tender taproot encounters a stone, no matter how small, as it grows down into the soil, it will form a branch and grow around the obstruction.

Plow or spade your carrot bed 8 to 10 inches deep. Break up large clods of dirt with a rake or hoe and remove as many rocks as you can find. Avoid walking on the bed after you've prepared it to prevent unnecessary compaction. When the soil is free of obstructions, add lots of organic matter in the form of compost, leaf mold, seaweed, peat moss, or well-rotted manure to lighten it and help it retain moisture.

If you use manure, work it in during

the previous fall to ensure that it's fully decomposed before the carrots are planted. The high levels of nitrogen in fresh manure will almost always cause branching and hairy, rough skins in carrots. If rotted manure isn't available, a fertilizer composed of one part dried blood, one part rock phosphate, and four parts wood ashes can be worked into the soil before planting at a rate of 7 pounds per 100 square feet.

Carrots do best in a slightly acidic soil with a pH level of 6.0 to 6.5. If your soil tests out at a lower pH, adding dolomite at a rate of 7 pounds per 100 square feet should raise the pH by one full point (for example, from 5.8 to 6.8).

Improving the tilth of your soil could take several seasons, but there's no reason why you can't grow winning carrots in the meantime. If you're not planning on growing a lot of carrots, try digging a v-shaped trench 8 inches deep and 3 inches wide and filling it with a 50-50 mixture of compost and sand or peat moss and sand. The trench will provide a perfectly shaped growing medium in which your carrots can mature unobstructed. A top dressing of well-rotted manure will give the crop an extra boost after planting. Raised beds are also well suited to carrot growing. They reduce the chance of soil compaction, are easier to weed, have better drainage, and the soil is usually loose enough to give carrots room to stretch. The bed should be a least 6 to 8 inches high and filled with sandy loam.

How Much to Plant:

A rough guideline is 30 plants per person. As a rule of thumb, figure on about a pound of carrots for every foot of row. For a small family, sow a 10-foot row and follow it every three weeks with another 5- or 10-foot row for a continuous supply of fresh carrots all summer.

Planting:

Carrots are a cool-weather crop that can stand light frosts at either end of its growing cycle. For the earliest carrots, plant seeds as soon as the ground can be worked. Many gardeners make a major sowing of carrots two or three weeks before the last predicted frost in their area. If you want to be precise about it, use a soil thermometer and plant when the daily average soil temperature is about 55°F.

Carrots germinate in 7 to 20 days. Keep the soil moist, especially in the first week or so, but don't overdo it. Waterlogging the soil can lead to poor germination and fungal disease. You can get a head start in the spring by planting under a cold frame or cloche, but because of their fragile root systems, starting carrots indoors and transplanting them to the garden isn't a good idea.

Carrot seeds are very tiny (about 23,000 to the ounce), so waste from too-heavy sowing is often a problem. You can sprout seeds indoors between two sheets of damp paper towel. Plant them as soon as the tiny roots appear. Another good trick is to place the seeds in moist sand until they swell to a more easily manageable size. Pelleted seed, coated with soil or vermiculite and a binder to increase its diameter five to tenfold, is also available from some suppliers. These seeds are more expensive, but can cut down on waste through more precise planting.

The choice of whether to plant in single rows or wider beds really depends on your preference: the orderliness of neat, straight rows or the dense compactness of beds. A study conducted at the

National Vegetable Research Station in England concluded that there is no significant difference in the size of carrots grown in rows and those grown in beds. Your total yield may be slightly higher in beds, due to the dense planting. On the other hand, rows are easier to weed.

If you're planting in rows, make them 10 to 24 inches apart with string and stakes. Use a dibble or rake handle to dig a shallow furrow by dragging it along the length of the row, pressing lightly into the soil. You'll have better control while shaking seeds from the packet if you're careful to tear only a tiny hole in its corner. Plan on about ¼ ounce of seed for every 100-foot row.

If you choose to broadcast seeds over a bed, prepare the area first by marking it off with stakes and string. The bed shouldn't be much more than 3 feet wide, or reaching weeds in the middle will become a problem. Try to get thin, even coverage—it will mean less thinning later. Mix the seeds half-and-half with dry sand or coffee grounds with some radish seeds thrown in. The quick-growing radishes will be up and out of the way before the carrots need the space.

Once they're sown, cover the seeds with a ¼-inch layer of soil or compost. If you're planting in midsummer and conditions are hot and dry, you can probably stretch the covering to ½ inch but not much more, as the tiny carrot seeds can't take deep planting. A light mulch of sawdust, just enough to cover the surface, will help keep the soil from drying out or caking. Or cover the bed with sheets of burlap, held down with rocks or bricks. The burlap helps keep the shallow-planted seeds from washing away and also retains moisture. Water as soon as you put the burlap down and check in a few days to see if the soil is dry. As soon as the seeds sprout, remove the covering, preferably late in the day so the young plants won't be subjected to the hot sun their first day out. Unused seed is good for three years.

Growing Guidelines: No matter how carefully the seeds have been distributed, there are probably going to be too many seedlings and you'll have to thin. Crowding can cause stunted growth and twisted, intertwined roots. Thin the seedlings to about 1 inch apart. About two weeks after the first thinning, thin again to about 3 to 4 inches apart.

Carrots grow slowly and are not very good at competing with weeds. Mulching will help keep weeds in check. Start with a light covering of grass clippings, and add more each week or two as the seedlings grow. Pine needles, straw, leaves, and hay are also good mulch materials when the plants get bigger. Mulching will prevent the sun from turning the exposed "shoulders" of mature carrots green and bitter.

If you don't mulch, you'll have to hoe or pull weeds by hand. In either case, be careful; cut off weeds just below the surface to disturb as few of the carrot's feeder roots as possible. The tiny roots are the most dense in the top 2 to 4 inches of soil, and deep cultivation will disturb many of them—the carrot will have to send out new feeders instead of growing a fatter taproot. Pulling large weeds can also disturb carrot roots, so get the weeds while they're young.

Season Extending: If you can keep the carrot bed from freezing, you can keep carrots in the ground all winter. Clip the tops and cover the plants with a deep mulch, such as leaves or hay bales. Bags of autumn leaves are easy to work with and do the job. Dig carrots as needed. Alternate hard freezings and thawings will ruin carrots, so cover them with mulch a foot deeper than your ground freezes.

Harvesting and Storing:

Most varieties mature in 70 to 80 days, but they're usable anytime from pencil-size on. According to Dr. Frank Eggert, professor of horticulture at the University of Maine, sweetness increases until the carrot is mature but doesn't decrease after that time. "I don't think there's any optimum time to pick carrots," he notes. "Gardeners should pick them at whatever size they prefer." The darker the foliage, the bigger the carrot.

To harvest carrots, grasp the greens near ground level and pull. A good watering beforehand will make this easier. If the soil is hard or the greens break off, dig around the root with a fork or trowel and pull the top of the carrot.

Carrots keep very well, so there's no reason why you can't enjoy your summer crop throughout the year. They're good canned, freeze nicely, and can be kept crisp and tasty in a root cellar for six months or more.

When harvesting for storage, cut off the tops of the greens, leaving about an inch of stem. Leave the harvested carrots out in the sun for a few hours to kill the root hairs and make the plants go dormant. It's best not to wash carrots before storing, as the water may encourage a new growth of root hairs. Instead, give them a good scrubbing to wash off soil as you use them.

The ideal conditions for storing carrots are a temperature of 34° F with 90 to 95 percent humidity. To store carrots in a root cellar, line a cardboard box or plastic trash can with peat or sphagnum moss or sawdust. Make sure that none of the carrots are touching and never store bruised, broken, or diseased carrots. Also, studies have shown that ethylene gas, released by stored apples, can cause a bitter taste in carrots, so don't store the two in the same area.

Pests and Diseases:

Rabbits or other rodents may take a liking to your crop. A well-made fence discourages them. Gophers demand underground fencing; that is, lining the carrot bed with hardware cloth to keep the varmints out.

In general, most carrot diseases and pests can be kept under control with a good system of rotation. Try a three-year pattern, alternating peas, carrots, and lettuce. Preceding carrots with peas is a good idea because the peas loosen the soil with their roots and enrich it as they decay.

The carrot rust fly is a significant problem in many parts of the country. The yellowish white larvae hatch from eggs laid in the carrot's crown and burrow down into the roots, leaving rusty-looking tunnels. If the damage isn't extensive, the affected parts can be cut away and the carrots used. Carrot fly larvae are attracted by the smell of the leaves. Sowing onions next to your carrots will help baffle the insects. A light sprinkling of wood ashes over the soil at planting time will also help deter them. But the best control is to skip your early planting, breaking the fly's life cycle. By early summer, the larvae will probably have died of starvation. Avoid replacing the early carrot crop with celery, though, because the insect has a taste for that, too.

The small, dirty-white larvae of the

carrot weevil are a gardener's headache from Colorado to Georgia to New England. The grubs tunnel into the roots and injure the plants, especially early crops. The adult spends the winter near the carrot patch and makes its way back to the garden in the spring. Rotate carrots with crops other than parsley, celery, and parsnips, and you'll deny this pest a home. If you cultivate your garden deeply in the spring, it will also help destroy grubs in the soil.

Nematodes, microscopic worms that live in most soils, are responsible for a malady known as root knot. The knots form pimplelike swellings on taproots which enlarge and roughen the surface. If crops are rotated so that a susceptible crop is grown in a given spot only once every 12 years, nematodes won't be a problem. Some gardeners have also had success rotating carrots with members of the French marigold family such as TANGERINE, PETITE GOLD, and PETITE HARMONY. The marigolds allow nematodes to enter their roots but prevent them from completing their life cycle. Interplanting these marigolds won't do the trick. You'll have to plant a solid crop of the flowers and allow them to grow at least 90 to 120 days, then use the bed for carrots next season.

According to Dr. Clinton Peterson, professor of horticulture at the University of Wisconsin, alternaria blight is the biggest disease threat to carrot growers in the United States. It usually shows up as yellow or white spots on leaf margins. The spots soon turn brown, take on a water-soaked look, and will eventually kill the root. Seeds can be treated by soaking for 10 minutes in 126°F water before planting.

Vegetable soft rot attacks carrots. Characterized by its strong sulfurous odor and gray or brown discoloration, this bacterial disease favors hot, humid weather. Making sure your crop is stored in a cool, well-ventilated place insures against soft rot.

If your soil is poorly drained and becomes waterlogged, your carrots may fall prey to cavity spot. Symptoms are black or brownish areas near the crown of the roots which break down, leaving a cavity or depression in the root.

Other Problems: A deficiency of boron or manganese can turn the cores of carrots black. The best remedy for this is the liberal use of compost. Rock phosphate and limestone also contain adequate amounts of these trace minerals.

Nutritional Value: There's more than a grain of truth in the common belief that carrots are good for your eyes. Carrots are loaded with carotene, which the body can convert into vitamin A, which helps us see in reduced light at night. In addition to being good for your eyes, carrots may be good for your heart. In a recent study published in the *American Journal of Clinical Nutrition,* it was found that eating four raw carrots per day decreased the serum cholesterol level of four subjects by 11 percent in three weeks.

Choosing Varieties: When we talk about a carrot's taste, what we're really discussing is its sweetness. The higher the sugar content, the better-tasting the carrot. It seems that carrot sweetness is mostly a matter of breeding. "There's very little that the gardener can do to grow a sweeter carrot," says Dr. Peterson of the USDA. "The sugar content has pretty much been determined. That's

CARROTS

Variety	Description	Sources*
Chantenay	68–72 days; quick-maturing; distinct core; yields heavily; good keeper	WA
Coreless Nantes	68 days; uniform shape to 6"; good quality; smooth, fine-grained, and exceptionally sweet; always crisp	11
Goldinhart	70–72 days; slow to mature; uniform; good for canning and freezing, but best eaten fresh	9
Gold Pak	70–80 days; smooth, slightly tapered cylinder; almost coreless; tall bushy tops; good keeper	WA
Imperator	85–95 days; long, slender, tapering to 11"; requires deep, light soils; usually commercially grown	WA
Kinko	55 days; small, conical, stump-rooted; good for heavy or shallow soils; crisp, sweet; best harvested young	15
Nantes	65–70 days; quick to mature; medium length; cylindrical; high sugar content; good for home gardeners	WA
Oxheart	70–80 days; blunt, short root to 3"; suited to heavy soils; tender; good keeper	8
Scarlet Keeper	85 days; heavy yields; cylindrical; only for fall harvest, winter storage; non-bitter even after long storage	15, 31
Short 'N Sweet	68 days; shorter Goldinhart type to 4" long; good in heavy or shallow soils	5
Spartan Bonus	70–77 days; Danvers type with hybrid vigor; medium-long, tapering root; good quality and flavor	27
Tendersweet	69–80 days; tapers to almost pointed tip; nearly coreless; heavy yields; good for freezing	24
Touchon	60-75 days; quick to mature; cylindrical; needs good soil, but very disease resistant; good for northern areas	WA

*Listings correspond to seed companies listed under Sources of Seeds at the back of the book.

why it's important that gardeners experiment with the new hybrid varieties."

He suggests growing one of the popular NANTES varieties. These cigar-shaped carrots, which grow 5 to 7 inches long, don't look quite as nice as the long, tapered IMPERATOR and GOLD PAK varieties that most commercial farmers grow, but the taste is stronger and the roots are less prone to forking. Dr. Peterson also recommends SPARTAN BONUS, a uniform, high-yielding variety that was developed at Michigan State University.

Stump-rooted varieties like OX-HEART, KINKO, and SHORT 'N SWEET grow only about 3 inches long. They won't win any beauty contests, tending to look more like beets than carrots, but they're particularly well suited to heavy soils.

CAULIFLOWER
Brassica oleracea, Botrytis Group

Cauliflower is finicky. If its needs aren't met, it will disappoint. Briefly, those needs are a rich, well-drained, loamy soil, high in nitrogen, with a slightly acid or neutral pH; a rapid, vigorous growth period with mild temperatures; and an ample supply of water, especially during dry spells. Because spring-planted cauliflower runs a greater risk of failure due to a sudden rise in temperature, most gardeners settle for a fall crop. But, with a little extra care, you can raise two crops of cauliflower—one early and one late.

Soil Preparation: Cauliflower demands well-drained, nutrient-rich loam with a pH around 6.5. Both spring and fall crops need large doses of nitrogen, so work in plenty of compost and rotted manure, and water with manure tea. Green manuring with deep-rooted crops like sweet clover and alfalfa, or applying rock powders like greensand, will help guarantee your cauliflower its share of potash. If a recent pH test indicates your soil is too acidic for the crop, incorporate

natural ground limestone. If it shows your soil is too alkaline, work in cottonseed meal, acid peat moss, or leaf mold. Dig in the neutralizing substances as deeply as possible. To insure proper drainage, grow your cauliflower in raised beds.

How Much to Plant: A rough guideline is four to six plants per person.

Planting: If you want firm, round heads of cauliflower, start about four months before harvest with disease-free seed and special care of seedlings to ensure steady growth. You must follow a rigid schedule to plant your crops for an early summer and a late fall harvest. Unused seed is good for five years.

Handling Seedlings: Unless you live in California or in the South, where plants can be started in open beds, sow seeds four to six weeks before transplant time in separate 3-inch-wide plastic or peat containers. "Without a doubt, raising seedlings in containers is better," says Dr. Ronald D. Morse of Virginia Polytechnic Institute. "Because their root systems are completely surrounded by the growth medium, they aren't disturbed when you transplant young cauliflower, and the plants don't suffer shock. Raised in small individual containers, transplants grow faster and produce more hardy and better-yielding cauliflower than those raised in seedbeds or flats."

Soil should be a fine, easily pulverized loam that does not crust on top. To prevent lush growth or legginess, it should not be too fertile—many gardeners choose a sand-and-compost mix for good drainage. The soil temperature of the containers or seed flats should average around 70°F.

Pay close attention to seedling development—if stunted at this early stage, heads will be small and tasteless. Given plenty of light, seeds should germinate in about a week. If you can, set the containers under grow lights 12 to 14 hours a day for two weeks after germination, then move them to a sunny porch for another three or four weeks. The temperature should now be warm and relatively stable. Cauliflower seedlings raised at 68° F produce higher yields than those raised at 58° F, so a small temperature difference can make a difference in your harvest. At no time should the temperature drop below 60° F.

Keep the soil moist. To safeguard against transplant shock, Pennsylvania gardener Nancy Bubel uses a fish emulsion spray to help sustain seedlings. "Small, frequent feedings—weekly, at half strength for the first three weeks—are more effective than less frequent larger feedings," she says.

Early cauliflower should be transferred to the garden no sooner than two weeks before the last average frost date. You'll know it's time when each seedling is 6 inches tall and has six leaves and a stem width one-half that of a pencil. Be sure to keep a ball of soil around the seedling's roots when you move it.

Dr. Morse of Virginia Tech cautions gardeners to handle young cauliflower with care. To avoid buttoning, he recommends setting out young, healthy transplants that have not yet begun to form heads and to delay planting until weather conditions are favorable for growth. Season-extending structures, such as cloches, clear plastic enclosures, and cold frames, effectively help harden-off newly transplanted seedlings and allow them to adjust to their new environment gradually. If possible, transplant on a cloudy day or when rains are expected.

Set seedlings every 20 inches in rows 30 inches apart. Studies in Sweden and Scotland prove that exact spacing is important for two reasons. First, uniform planting produces more uniform and compact heads. Second, a small difference in spacing can affect the earliness of the crop—the more space each plant is given, the quicker it reaches maturity. Water each seedling before planting the next one and firm the soil well around the roots. To prevent clubroot disease, the plot should not have been sown in brassicas for at least five years.

Growing Guidelines: Cauliflower demands care while it's growing. Give the leaves a good misting as often as every other day. Once a week, water the crop heavily—the best time is two hours before the sun goes down so the water will have at least 12 hours to soak into the ground, acting as a water reservoir. Keep the plants cool and the soil moist.

All things considered, nothing conserves soil moisture and controls weeds better than mulch. "When my cauliflower has been set out, I lay down an inch of rotten sawdust, and water lightly," veteran gardener James Jankowiak says. "Then when the radish, upland cress, mustard, or other fast-growing, cool-weather crop that I've interplanted sprouts, I lay on an additional 6-inch mulch around all the plants."

If weeds become a problem despite your best mulching efforts, cultivate shallowly. Even though cauliflower roots extend deeply into the soil (as far as 3 feet in mature plants), deep cultivation can damage them, especially late in the season. And whenever you work around cauliflower, don't disturb the leaves. Even minor leaf damage can cause buttoning.

Blanching cauliflower. Tie the leaves over the developing curds.

Sunlight turns cauliflower curds an unappetizing brown but doesn't affect their flavor, according to Dr. Michael Dickson, plant breeder at the New York State Agricultural Experiment Station. When the head first forms, small incurving leaves close around it, protecting it from the sun. But as the head gets bigger, these inner leaves are forced apart and away from the head. Some varieties, like SELF-BLANCHE, developed by Dr. S. Honma of Michigan State University, have very long leaves which shield the curd until it is ready for harvest. Predominantly purple varieties don't need to be blanched. But the leaves of other varieties, like the SNOWBALL types, must be tied for curd protection.

To blanch a cauliflower, gather the longest leaves together over the curd and tie them with soft twine, raffia, or tape. The best time to do this is in the afternoon when the leaves are dry and pliable. Never do it when the plants are wet or they may rot.

Keys to Top Yields:

Cauliflower does best in a cool, moist climate where temperatures are mild. These requirements mean planting the first crop in the garden no sooner than two weeks before the last spring frost and the second crop no later than August, so it can reach maturity before the first killing frost. According to Dr. Dickson, "the main thing is to keep your cauliflower growing fast and to harvest it early."

About a month after the plants are set out, substitute one of the usual irrigations with a feeding of fish emulsion fertilizer or manure tea, spraying it directly on the plant and pouring it around the base after temporarily pulling back the mulch. This can be followed with a foliar feeding two weeks later.

Harvesting and Storing:

Examine the heads frequently to determine their harvest readiness. If the weather is warm, heads may mature in as little as three days after blanching. In cooler weather, it may take as long as two weeks. The color and size of the curd is your best guide. Mature heads are fully developed, compact, clear white and firm to the touch. Avoid any overmatured open heads (called "ricey" because they begin to separate and resemble rice grains). Six-inch-diameter heads are prime for harvest.

Harvest cauliflower early rather than late. What you sacrifice in size by cutting early, you gain in quality. Use a large knife to cut the heads from the plants, leaving one or more whorls of leaves attached to protect the curds. Pulled up by its roots, cauliflower can be stored for a month if it is suspended upside down in a cool root cellar. It's safe to eat heads that freeze during fall nights unless they thaw and refreeze.

Pests and Diseases: Several species of caterpillars injure cauliflower by eating holes in the leaves or buds, and by tunneling into the heads of older plants. The cabbage looper, probably the most destructive pest your crop will come up against, can be controlled with *Bacillus thuringiensis* (Bt), sold under the trade names Dipel, Thuricide, and Biotrol. Mix the powder or liquid with water and apply in a spray during the evening or very early morning. Sprinkling diatomaceous earth over the growing plants will also help control the looper. Where cutworms are a problem, protect plants with cardboard collars.

The most troublesome pests in James Jankowiak's cauliflower plot are the cabbage maggots that burrow into the roots just under the soil surface and can actually cut down a plant. He sets each plant out in a wood-ash-and-compost-filled planting hole and dusts a mixture of pyrethrum around the roots after each watering until the plants get established.

Many home gardeners claim that purple-headed cauliflower varieties don't attract pests as readily as white-curded ones do. The insect resistance of purple cabbage-type plants was tested by the New York State Agricultural Experiment Station's Dr. Dickson. "We found that purple-headed varieties have fewer insect problems than green types," he confirms. "The color of the leaves discourages insects from laying their eggs on the purple plants."

Diseases include black rot, clubroot, downy mildew, and yellows. For controls, see Cabbage.

Nutritional Value: Cauliflower is one of the best vegetable sources of vitamin C; one serrving has more than the RDA. Purple cauliflower is even richer in vitamin C, as well as vitamins B_1 and B_2, calcium, and iron.

Choosing Varieties: Because of cauliflower's need for a short, consistent growing season, choose the most fast-maturing, heat-resistant varieties, especially when you plant an early crop. Some, like SNOW CROWN, produce bigger and whiter heads than others, while ROYAL PURPLE and PURPLE HEAD produce curds that aren't white at all and don't need to be blanched. WHITE SUMMER, DELIRA and SNOWBALL SELF-BLANCHING provide their own curd protection, or are "self-blanching." Look for varieties that yield uniform, milky white, dense curds with a delicate flavor in as short a time as possible—between 50 and 60 days. (Keep in mind that the time to maturity for all brassicas, including cauliflower, is from the date of transplanting, not seeding.)

California growers can plant extra-slow-maturing cauliflower as a winter crop, especially if they live on the coast. Generally, they rely on hardy strains of SNOWBALL-Y, which produce compact white curds in 70 to 90 days, depending on the variety.

By planting SNOWBALL-type cauliflower along with the quicker-maturing varieties, gardeners in other parts of the country can enjoy fresh-picked cauliflower long after the second planting has been harvested. "SNOWBALL-Y makes a perfect late crop in the East when the nights are getting quite cool," says Dr. Vincent Rubatsky of the University of California's Extension Service. "By timing your planting so the crop matures after the first frost but before the killing frost, you can grow it right up to the very end of the season."

CAULIFLOWER

Variety	Description	Sources*
Abuntia	45 days; earliest maturing; crisp, white, medium head; excellent quality; good for freezing	36
Burpeeana	58 days; upright, vigorous plants; well-rounded, compact heads with smooth curds; excellent fresh or frozen	5
Delira	67 days; self-blanching; very short harvest period; heavy, white heads	33
Early Abundance	47 days; early, vigorous; self-blanching; large, tender heads; good for muckland or well-fertilized highland	33
Early Snowball	55–80 days; very short plants with pale green leaves; compact white heads to 6"; great for small gardens	33, 38
Early Super Snowball	60 days; large head with generous protection of leaves; heads remain nice and white	24
Purple Head	80–85 days; large plants need room; easier to grow than white; purple head turns green when cooked; freezes well	16
Royal Purple	95 days; compact, 6–7" purple heads; green when cooked; easy to grow; excellent for freezing	9
Self-Blanche	71 days; 6" heads; leaves curl around head to self-blanch; fall crop only	37
Snowball Self-Blanching	67 days; leaves grow upward to surround well-domed head; no need to tie to blanch; tender, high quality heads to 8"	24
Snowball-Y	70–90 days; vigorous; large plants; erect outer leaves; heads to 7"; long harvest period; good fall crop	6
Snow Crown	50 days; very quick to mature—beats hot weather; bigger, whiter heads; also good for fall crop; good fresh or frozen	5, 15
Snow King	45 days; shorter plants; flat heads with creamy curds; heat and disease resistant; AAS	16, 23
White Summer	62–65 days; uniform; tall, erect leaves provide self-blanching; suitable for summer or fall crop; heat tolerant	33, 35

*Listings correspond to seed companies listed under Sources of Seeds at the back of the book.

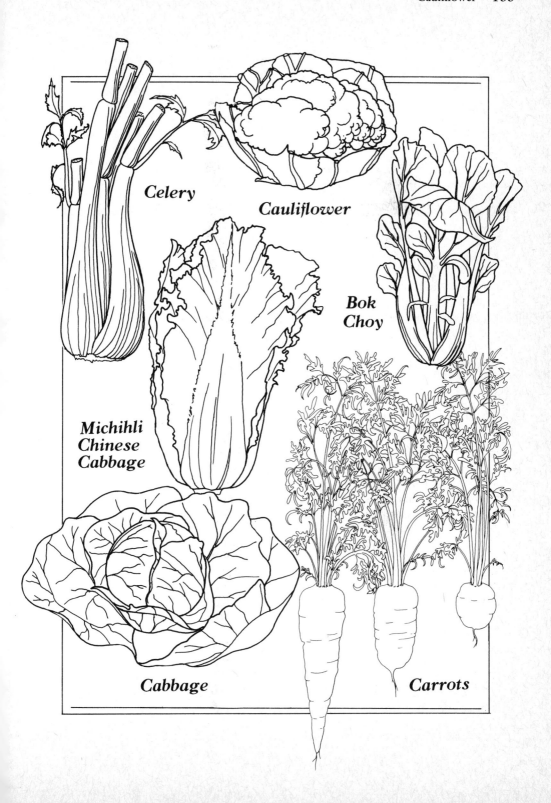

Celery

Cauliflower

Bok Choy

Michihli Chinese Cabbage

Cabbage

Carrots

CELERY

Apium graveolens
var. *dulce*

Even though celery is one of the country's favorite vegetables, it has been shunned by most home gardeners because it has a reputation for being hard to grow. In order to to bring in good-looking bunches of celery, it's important to understand the nature of the plant. A mild climate is essential because celery, a biennial, will respond to a cold snap the same way it responds to the cold winter that marks the beginning of its second year of life: it will send up a flower stalk and begin to make seeds—a phenomenon called bolting. Water also is a key factor, because the plant itself is 94 percent water and simply can't grow without an abundant and constant supply.

You must be very, very patient during seed germination—which is slow, erratic, and often frustrating to the first-time celery grower. If you don't have the right disposition, you can always buy started plants from a local nursery.

Soil Preparation: To create the cool, moist environment in which celery flourishes, dig trenches 12 to 14 inches deep. Because celery is a very heavy feeder, you will need to enhance the soil in the trenches by filling the bottom third with compost, well-rotted manure, or a combination of both. Mix the compost and manure with some of the dirt dug from the trenches and fill them about 8 inches deep with the mixture.

If you are serious about your celery crop, have your soil tested for boron and pH. Celery grows best in soil with a pH of 6.0, but a range from 5.0 to 7.0 is acceptable. The test should also show the presence of at least 0.5 parts per million of boron in the soil.

Boron is a key element for celery. A deficiency will result in cracked stems that look as though they were scratched by a cat. The stalks eventually become brittle, and brownish spots appear on the leaves. If you find your soil is low in boron, you can give the plants fish emulsion. The addition of good compost to the planting hole, however, should prevent a deficiency.

How Much to Plant: A rough guideline is six plants per person. Since one packet can produce 400 to 500 plants, you won't need to spend much on seed.

Planting: Start your seeds ten weeks before the final frost date in your area. They will take anywhere from 15 to 21 days to begin to germinate.

To speed germination, soak the seeds overnight. Putting them in 118°F water for 30 minutes hastens germination and also kills fungus spores that later might cause blight. But don't let the water get much hotter than that or you could kill the seeds. Unused seed is good for five years.

Handling Seedlings: Before sowing the seeds, fill flats or flowerpots with compost and water them thoroughly. To make spreading easy, combine the seeds with an equal amount of dry soil. Sprinkle them evenly on the compost, then cover with a light dusting of soil. With a houseplant mister, gently mist the soil. (Be careful not to force the seed deeper into the soil with water pressure.) Cover the flats with clear plastic or glass and set them in a dark place where the temperature stays a steady 65°F. If your temperatures are higher than 70°F, exposing the flats to some light will help stimulate germination.

Make sure the flats are uniformly moist at all times. If the seeds don't germinate in three weeks, wait another week or two. As the seeds sprout, transplant them to a flat kept in direct sunlight and where temperatures are in the 50 to 60°F range. To prevent damping-off, it's important to keep the developing plants at least 2 inches apart. Because their root systems are rather skimpy, you can lift the small plants from the soil with a dinner fork, easily transporting them to their new, prewatered location. When the plants are 3 inches tall, they should be transferred to individual pots. Keep the pots evenly moist, but provide good drainage and air circulation to prevent damping-off. You can keep the celery in a greenhouse or cold frame provided the temperature does not dip below 45°F.

When the plants are 5 or 6 inches tall, they're ready for the garden. Before putting them outside, harden them off. Instead of exposing them to cold temperatures (which can cause them to bolt), simply withhold water for five or six days. Although the plants may wilt during the day, they should revive in early evening. If they don't recover, give them a minimum of water.

The day before the celery is to be planted in the garden, water the planting trenches thoroughly, soaking the soil deeply. Plant the celery about 6 inches apart in the trenches, and water again. Then, gather grass clippings or any mulch that will not mat and tuck it around each plant so that only the leaves at the top of each stalk are in the sun. Finally, cover the entire trench with a deep layer of mulch. The mulch helps keep the celery from becoming dark, stringy, and bitter. It also keeps the ground cool and damp.

Growing Guidelines:

During the summer, add mulch so that only the celery's leaves peep out of the trench. Each time you add mulch, check the soil beneath for dampness. If it has begun to dry out, water the base of each plant thoroughly, but be sure to keep the water from running down the stalks and into the crown where rot can get a foothold.

If you prefer not to drag a hose or watering can to your garden each day, try placing cans with small holes punched in the sides and bottoms between the celery plants. The cans will hold water for several days, slowly soaking the trench soil.

When cultivating the soil around the celery, use an onion hoe, or any instrument that will not dig deeply into the soil. Celery roots are spread in a 6-inch circle around the base of the plant, but they are in the top few inches of the soil and can be easily damaged by vigorous and deep cultivation.

Keep the area free of weeds. Celery needs all the garden's nutrition, and there's none to spare for plantain or ragweed. With a deeply mulched trench, however, weeding shouldn't be a problem.

Harvesting and Storing:

You can begin to harvest the plants as soon as the stalks are tall enough to suit you. Most gardeners harvest plants as they need them.

To harvest, cut the root 1 or 2 inches below the crown of the plant. Store the stalks in a plastic bag in the refrigerator. Should the celery wilt, you can revive it by standing it in a pitcher of cold water on your refrigerator shelf—it crisps very quickly. Save the leaves for soups and sauces, or cut them in small pieces and sun-dry them for six hours. They are a tangy addition to winter stews and soups.

To store a large amount of celery that has been harvested all at once, dig up complete plants—roots and all. Plant them in boxes of earth so that the crowns are level with the soil's surface, then water the roots. Rewater when the earth dries. In a cool, dark cellar, the celery should keep for three to five months.

Pests and Diseases:

Weeding can keep leafminers from becoming a problem. These bugs are lured to an area by weed hosts, but once they discover the celery, they'll abandon their wild homes for your succulent stalks.

Bacillus thuringiensis (Bt) is a bacterial disease that will control celery loopers and variegated cutworms. Check for variegated cutworms in late spring. The larvae feed on the celery stalks near the heart of the plant. The looper is a light green caterpillar with a white stripe down the center of its back and matching stripes down each side. Loopers feed on celery leaves and tender stalks. You often will find them inside rolled leaves that have been tied with a filmy web. If the infestation is serious, you can also use pyrethrum. Apply it undiluted. The first dusting will make the larvae sick, and a second dusting will finish them off.

Carrot weevils stunt or kill celery plants. These beetles are $1/4$ inch long, brownish in color, and sport six speckles on their backs. They emerge from the soil in early spring and will attack young celery plants. They lay their eggs right on the celery stalks. In just a week, the eggs hatch and the larvae move down to the crown of the plant. There, they feed for six to eight weeks, and then migrate to the surrounding soil to pupate. A second generation emerges in mid-July to repeat the cycle. Rotation of your celery bed will control these weevils. Since the adult beetles walk, they won't travel very far in your garden. If you've had an infestation, clean your garden before winter. Because the weevils will be unprotected by plant debris during the cold weather, they won't survive for another season.

If you soaked your seeds in hot water before planting them, you probably won't have to worry about blight. Green celery varieties used to be resistant to blight, but commercial growers in California recently found that their "resistant" stands of UTAH green celery had succumbed to blight. Symptoms include a lag in growth, yellowing leaves, and discolored roots and crowns. Blight comes in two waves. Early blight, one of the most destructive celery diseases, is caused by a fungus that lives both on seeds and on plant debris in the garden. It requires high temperatures and humidity to really get a foothold, and generally does its worst damage in midsummer. But in Florida and occasionally in southern California, it often follows—rather than precedes—late blight. Early blight causes circular yellow spots on the plant's leaves. As the spots grow larger they turn gray, with spores developing at the center.

Late blight is caused by two species of fungus. The disease appears as small, pale spots on leaves and stalks. As the fungus grows, these spots become brown lesions. Eventually, tiny black specks appear on the plant's dead tissues. Late-blight fungus is spread by wind-driven rain, sprinklers or any splashing water,

CELERY

Variety	Description	Sources*
Cornell 6-19	95–100 days; self-blanching, golden yellow stalks; resistant to fusarium yellows; good for Northeast, short seasons	2
Fordhook	130 days; compact, dark green stalks; tender and mostly stringless; holds well in storage; stalks to 18"	8
Giant Pascal	120–140 days; dark green stalks to 18"; medium length, overlapping; blight resistant	8, 12
Golden Detroit	85–100 days; self-blanching; compact to 22" high; crisp, solid, stringless; adapts to all areas	10
Golden Plume	85–118 days; early; self-blanching; full, compact hearts	33
Golden Self-Blanching	90 days; self-blanching; stocky, compact, yellow stalks; relatively stringless; blight resistant; good keeper	12, 16
Summer Pascal	120 days; compact, bright green stalks to 26"; vigorous; blight resistant; heavy heads with well-developed hearts	8
Utah	125 days; stocky, compact; medium-broad and well rounded; thick stems; good for late use and storage	8

*Listings correspond to seed companies listed under Sources of Seeds at the back of the book.

and even by animals and garden tools. The fungus can survive over the winter in garden refuse. Growing celery in a different part of the garden each year and a thorough fall cleaning also aid in control.

Another potential problem is blackheart. It affects the young leaves at the center of the plant, causing brown spots that gradually spread to the stalks. It can eventually kill the plant. Studies have revealed that blackheart affects plants which have a deficiency of calcium in their leaves. It is not calcium, however, that prevents or cures blackheart. Instead, the solution lies in proper watering. Scientists have concluded that regular watering prevents blackheart, and that alternate drying and wetting is most harmful to celery. To keep your celery safe, be sure the soil is evenly moist beneath the mulch around the plants.

Nutritional Value: High-fiber celery contains significant amounts of vitamin A.

Choosing Varieties: Though most gardeners select green varieties of celery, golden varieties—preferred by Europeans—are also available. These golden types are self-blanching, while the green ones must be blanched in the garden before harvest. While golden celery requires less work in the garden, it is not as hardy as the green varieties and is more susceptible to disease. The self-blanchers also lack the snap and zing of green celery; instead, they are bland and tender.

CHINESE CABBAGE
Chinese celery cabbage, nappa, wong bok
Brassica rapa, Pekinensis Group;
Bok choy, Chinese mustard cabbage, pak choi
Brassica rapa, Chinensis Group

The name Chinese cabbage is a catchall term for a number of plants which have distinctive appearances. Basically, there are two types—heading and nonheading. The Pekinensis Group contains the heading plants, which are the most familiar and are known as Chinese celery cabbage. Certain varieties (MICHIHLI for one) form torpedo-shaped, cylindrical heads that are self-blanching, while other varieties (the wong bok types) form slightly squat, rounded heads. The nonheading plants of the Chinensis Group slightly resemble Swiss chard. They produce loose bunches of green, spoon-shaped leaves with a thick white midrib. These plants go by the common names of bok choy, pak choi, or Chinese mustard cabbage.

The term "cabbage" is something of a misnomer for all these plants, for they are botanically more closely related to mustard than to cabbage. However, they all thrive under the same growing conditions as cabbage.

Home gardeners who have tried to grow these oriental brassicas and have not had good results have usually broken one of the rules for growing them successfully. They need a superior soil, rich in moisture-holding organic material; they must never suffer stress from lack of water; they need a fertilizer boost to speed their growth; and they are highly sensitive to daylength. Long days in combination with fluctuating temperatures (especially during the four weeks following germination) cause stalks of insignificant yellow flowers to develop before a good head of leaves has formed. This is particularly true for spring-grown crops. Crops planted in midsummer for fall harvest are less prone to bolt. The gardener who has the knowledge to provide for these needs will find that Chinese mustard cabbage and Chinese celery cabbage are easy to grow.

Anyone who has grown standard cabbage would do well to consider adding one or all of these oriental brassicas to the garden plot. They are quicker to mature than most cabbages, and some varieties mature as quickly as eight weeks after seed is sown. They are generally more delicate and mild than cabbage, with a slight mustardy flavor; they can be used before they have reached maturity; they are more digestible than cabbage; and they do best in late fall, when many traditional occidental vegetables have long been harvested. These advantages more than offset the extra effort their culture requires. Moreover, they are admirably suited to the small garden.

Chinese cabbage can be prepared like traditional Western cabbage and Chinese mustard cabbage like mustard greens, but many choose to use them as the Chinese and Japanese do. The Asian tradition is to stir-fry or add them to soups. They are also delicious when used fresh in salads.

Chinese cabbage is a cool-season crop that makes the best growth when average temperatures are between 60 and 65°F and days are becoming shorter. In northern areas, it is generally grown as a fall crop. In mild-winter areas, it grows well as a winter and spring crop. Plants withstand heavy frost (down to 20°F) with little damage. Hybrids have been developed to tolerate long days and heat without bolting, which opens up a wider range of growing conditions.

Soil Preparation: Chinese cabbage will grow in a wide range of soil types, and will do well as long as adequate moisture is present. It prefers a moderately rich soil but will still grow fairly well in less fertile soils, although growth may be somewhat slower and the plants smaller at maturity. To prepare for spring planting, lay down fresh manure in the fall. Work this manure deeply into the soil right away if weather permits, or in the spring as soon as the soil can be safely worked. If planting in the spring or summer without having previously manured the ground in the fall, apply 3 to 4 inches of well-rotted manure or compost and dig in before seeding. Soil pH is acceptable in a range from 6.0 to 6.8.

How Much to Plant: A rough guideline is three to six plants per person.

Planting: Direct-seed the fall crop about 12 weeks before the first expected frost. Sow the seed about 2 inches apart in raised beds and in conventional rows. Space rows 18 to 24 inches apart. Cover seeds with $1/2$ inch of fine soil. Unused seed is good for five years.

Handling Seedlings: Chinese cabbage can be started indoors or in the garden, depending on the season it is grown. For spring planting, unless the variety is bred to tolerate lengthening days, start plants indoors four weeks before setting out, which can be done four to six weeks before the frost-free date. To further ensure that these plants don't bolt, protect them in the garden by covering them in the late afternoon and making sure they aren't exposed to cool temperatures.

Growing Guidelines: Thin both rows and beds when the plants are four weeks old and have four to five true leaves. Use these tender thinnings in the kitchen. Thin nonheading varieties (Chinese mustard) to 9 inches apart. Thin heading varieties (Chinese celery cabbage) to 16 inches apart.

Keep the ground moist. Add a mulch during dry periods. Don't mulch in autumn when the sun's power is waning, in order to give the soil as much heat as possible. Watering from below is preferable to overhead watering. In areas of high humidity, overhead watering may promote pests and diseases in the interior of the plant. On soil that is not adequately enriched, plants may need a mid-season nitrogen boost. Side-dress with well-rotted manure after thinning, or water with manure tea every two weeks once plants are four weeks old.

Harvesting and Storing: The harvest can begin as soon as plants reach a stage which the gardener finds usable. Plants sown at the same time tend to mature at the same rate, so start taking

CHINESE CABBAGE

Variety	Description	Sources*
Green Rocket	70 days; Chinese variety improved MICHIHLI; tolerant to most diseases; tall, 18″ cylindrical head to 5 pounds	38
Michihli	75 days; tall cylindrical heads; tightly folded bright green leaves; sow for fall harvest; 18″ tall by 4″ wide	23, 24
Pak Choi or Bok Choy	50 days; dark green leaves fold out from thick, prominent, white midribs; to 12″ tall and 5″ wide	24
Spring A-1	60 days; short, round, thick heads with light green leaves; good for spring or summer sowing; bolt resistant; 10″ tall	38
Treasure Island	85 days; suited for mild-winter growing areas; cylindrical heads to 12″ tall, 8″ wide	21

*Listings correspond to seed companies listed under Sources of Seeds at the back of the book.

some early to stagger the harvest period.

To harvest, pull out the whole plant and cut the leaf growth from the root crown. Discard the outer leaves. The non-heading types can be also treated as a cut-and-come-again crop by harvesting a few outer leaves at a time from each plant. Make sure at least five leaves remain on the plant to promote continuous production.

Heading and nonheading cabbages store for one to four months under cool (32 to 40°F), moist conditions. The tall, cylindrical heading types should be placed upright to prevent them from growing into an L-shape during storage.

Nutritional Value: Chinese cabbages furnish potassium and vitamins A and C to the diet.

Pests and Diseases: See Cabbage. Pests may be common, while diseases are occasional problems.

CORN
Zea mays

Nearly 200 years ago, the settlers of the Northeast borrowed sweet corn—and all the ways we eat it—from the first corn breeders, the Indians. Ever since, with growing fervor, seedsmen have been at work. They had 6 varieties to sell in 1858, 6 more in 1866, 63 at the turn of the century, and 700 by 1921. Now, new varieties appear by the dozens each year, and corn breeders don't seem to be tiring of the search for ever-sweeter varieties,

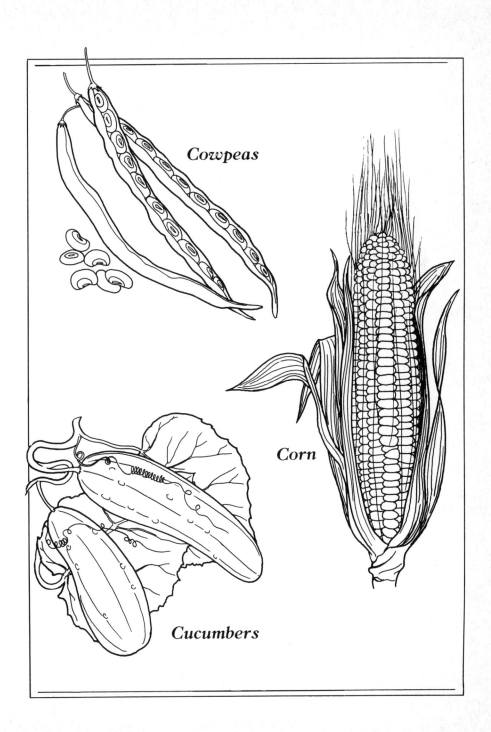

Cowpeas

Corn

Cucumbers

stronger stalks, earlier harvest, bigger ears, and more pest and disease resistance.

Soil Preparation:

Corn does well in most soils, but yields best in a loose, well-drained loam. In heavier soils, late varieties do best, while in sandy soils the early types are preferred. Corn needs heavy feeding, especially of nitrogen. For this reason, it does well where beans were planted the previous season, or when preceded by a cover crop of alfalfa, clover, or another legume crop that will add to the soil's nitrogen supply. The recommended pH range is 6.0 to 6.8. At planting time work the rows and beds to a depth of 6 inches, and add generous amounts of compost or aged manure, as well as bonemeal and wood ashes.

How Much to Plant:

A rough guideline is 30 to 40 plants per person.

Planting:

To plant corn closely, you need deep, fertile soil. The roots of one plant can fill a circle about 5 feet across and 2 feet deep. Try an equidistant spacing of 15 inches for open-pollinated varieties, and 18 inches for hybrid sweet corn, which is generally more vigorous.

If you want to make several plantings, keep in mind that corn growing in midseason matures far faster than corn planted either early or late in the season, when the weather is cooler. In one experiment, late corn took 2½ times as long as midseason corn to grow from silking to maturity, nearly two months instead of the usual three weeks or so. Corn grows fastest in full sunlight. Allow more time for your early and late plantings than the seed packet predicts, especially if your later plantings won't tolerate cross-polli-

nation. Corn stops growing at temperatures around 50°F.

The seedling leaf of most sweet corn can grow about 4 inches tall, even underground. For midsummer plantings, when the top few inches of soil overheat in the noon sun, put your corn seed that deep. When the soil is cool, plant the seed an inch deep.

The supersweets demand warm soil, and they should be planted less than an inch deep so the seedling leaf reaches the sun before it exhausts the kernel's meager supply of food. In cool soil, or constant damp, supersweet kernels are prone to rot. Research at Cornell University has shown that germinating corn seed before planting results in a better stand of plants. Plant the seed just as the root appears, when it's too short to break. Unused seed is good for up to two years.

Growing Guidelines:

Corn has a reputation as a crop for big gardens. However, it can be grown to perfection in small patches if you work to overcome the pollination problem—the most common reason for poorly filled ears. Even in large plantings, poor pollination often causes a disappointing crop. Corn is wind-pollinated, and for every strand of silk that doesn't get a grain of pollen, there will be a gap in the mature ear. Especially when the plants stand in only one or two rows crosswise to the prevailing wind, the pollen often wafts away, never reaching the silk. It's better to make your plantings square. Rather than two long rows, make five short ones. With the plants at equidistant spacings, the middle plants are sure to catch ample pollen.

A seedling's first root grows downward rapidly and soon pushes into the subsoil. In one experiment, a 16-day-old plant had a single root 18 inches long, with branches that spread 12 inches. Until they're about a foot tall, you can hoe as close as you like to corn seedlings. But after the first root is safely grown, the plant sends out rings of new roots, each ring above the last (the last ring of roots often appears aboveground). When the plant is a month old, its new roots are an inch or less underground near the stem of the plant, and only 1 or 2 inches deeper a foot away from the stem.

If you keep the soil hoed and weed-free for the first month, try scattering the seed of white or ladino clover among the corn. Research at Cornell showed that the clover did a good job of keeping down weeds without harming the yield of corn. And when the corn is harvested, you'll have a cover crop to turn under.

Keys to Top Yields: If you want full ears on every plant, try handpollinating. Mark Mikel, a student of corn breeding at the University of Illinois, tells one way to do it: "Go out about 9:30 A.M. or so, just as the dew dries off the tassels— when the pollen will come loose, but before it blows away. Take a brown paper shopping bag, bend the stalk gently— don't crack it or jar it—hold the tassel inside the bag and shake. Then let the stalk straighten up. You'll get a thimbleful of pollen. When you have enough, sprinkle a little on all the silks. You can do this every day until the silks begin to brown, but once or twice should be enough. Don't shake the plants before you take pollen—just walking down a row can send pollen flying."

Harvesting and Storing: Once an ear of sweet corn is picked, the sugars rapidly change to starch. Gardeners used to say that the way to pick corn is to start the water boiling first—that's still good advice, at least for the standard varieties. STOWELL'S EVERGREEN, introduced in 1851 and the oldest variety still grown commercially, will lose nearly half its sugar over 24 hours when kept at 104°F. Promptly cooling the ears helps. Stored at 32°F, it loses only 8 percent of its sugar in a day. Many of the new varieties are much sweeter, and they also hold their sugars long after picking.

Pests and Diseases: The corn earworm and the sap beetle both feed on silk, then follow the silk into the husk. Both find it hard to attack corn varieties with husks that grip the ear tightly and extend beyond its tip, making a narrow channel for the silk. Sap beetles are especially apt to infest an ear whose husk does not cover it completely, or one already damaged by earworms.

Resistant varieties include STO-WELL'S EVERGREEN, COUNTRY GENTLE-MAN, SUGAR LOAF, and SILVER QUEEN. Resistance in these varieties is far from perfect, but they are more resistant than strains that suffer heavy damage, such as JUBILEE, GOLDEN CROSS BANTAM, PLATI-NUM LADY, and AZTEC. (Along with the damaged ears, though, AZTEC can produce a heavy crop of good ears.)

Researchers at North Carolina State University fixed clothespins over the silk channel of some ears when the silks had just emerged, and were rewarded with undamaged ears. Try cinching a few ears with rubber bands, too.

One other measure promises some protection from earworms. Corn breeders working in Hawaii found that a bit of *Bacillus thuringiensis* (Bt) and *Baculovirus heliothis,* another biological caterpillar control sold under the trade name Elcar, killed earworms. One of the researchers, M. S. Zuber of the University of Missouri, says the two controls are worth trying. "I don't see why you couldn't just sprinkle them on the silk," he says. If you try it, start early. The earworm moth lays its eggs on the silk shortly after it emerges.

Sometimes you can blame poor pollination on damp weather, which sticks the pollen to the tassel, or intense heat, which quickly dries the silk. But if you can't blame the weather or your planting pattern, suspect a pair of viruses called maize dwarf mosaic and maize chlorotic dwarf. Joe McFerran of the University of Arkansas says that in the Fayetteville area the viruses are inescapable, overwintering in Johnson grass, a common weed. The infection is spread by leafhoppers, and the only sure way to have sweet corn is to plant early, before the hopper population swells. "We tell growers to get sweet corn planted no later than mid-April, and downstate we tell them the first of April, without fail," McFerran says. "Any later and the disease gets going. Late plantings sometimes have no ears at all." Mark Mikel, of the University of Illinois, says corn planted there in late May is sure to be infected.

Nutritional Value: Corn offers moderate amounts of vitamins A and B, along with some minerals and protein.

Choosing Varieties: If you want a standard sweet corn variety such as SILVER QUEEN, look for certain words in the catalog description—conventional, normal, sugar, standard, traditional.

Among the nonstandard sweet corn varieties, the closest in taste to standard sweet corn are the three-to-ones. For every three normally sweet kernels, these have one sweeter kernel with the creamy feel of standard corn but a higher sugar content. The sweeter kernel is caused by one of two genes. When it is due to the so-called shrunken gene, the catalog is apt to describe the variety as a bi-sweet or a sugary supersweet. SUGARLOAF and HONEYCOMB are in this category. If the gene at work is the so-called sugary enhancer, the catalog may say sugary extender, sugary enhanced, or EH (a trademark, standing for Everlasting Heritage). Some varieties are WHITE LIGHTNING, PLATINUM LADY, GOLDEN SWEET EH, KANDY KORN EH, SENECA SENTRY, and EARLIGLOW EH.

In varieties where every kernel is altered by the sugary-enhancer gene, the sugars are twice as high as in standard varieties and comparable with the supersweet varieties. When harvested, the ears are slower to become starchy than those of standard varieties. MIRACLE belongs in this category.

All the altered sweet corn varieties described so far revert to standard sweet corn if they are pollinated by standard varieties. Instead of sweeter kernels, you get sweet kernels, so the loss is not complete. But if you want to reap what you sow, separate the two kinds by 250 feet (you'll still get a few cross-pollinated kernels) or arrange your plantings so they mature at least two weeks apart.

Finally, there are corn varieties that have no sugary gene. The most common substitute is the shrunken gene, which blocks the conversion of sugar to starch in the kernel. About twice as sweet as standard varieties, shrunken-gene corn types are generally known as supersweets, and stay extra-sweet days longer after harvest. Dry kernels have almost no starch and are shriveled and shrunken, so they need careful handling to germinate and grow. Some varieties are HOW SWEET IT IS (white), SUCRO, FLORIDA STAYSWEET, and EARLY XTRA SWEET.

CORN

Variety	Description	Sources*
Aztec	69 days; stalks to 6½'; 7–8" ears with glossy green husks; deep, rich, golden kernels	33, 39
Country Gentleman (Shoe Peg)	88–100 days; open-pollinated; ears to 8" with non-rowing kernels; heavy yields of 2 ears per stalk; good for freezing	WA
Earliglow EH	72 days; uniform, yellow ears to 8"; tender and sweet; holds 10 to 12 days after harvest	38
Early Xtra Sweet	71 days; supersweet; needs to be isolated for maximum sweetness; holds sweetness for a long time	WA
Florida Staysweet	87 days; yellow ears to 7½"; twice the sugar content; resistant to northern leaf blight	13, 24
Golden Cross Bantam	85 days; hybrid; popular for home growing; stalks to 7'; ears to 8" with rows of light, golden yellow kernels	38
Golden Sweet EH	87 days; excellent holding ability and disease resistance; good for home gardeners; extremely tender kernels	33
Honeycomb	79 days; ears to 8"; high sugar content; good husk cover; excellent quality	6
How Sweet It Is	87 days; white supersweet; ears to 7½"; uniform; excellent eating quality and holding ability; AAS	15, 37
Jubilee	85 days; hybrid; stalks to 6'; 8" ears with deep, narrow kernels; good fresh, canned, frozen, or creamed	1, 16
Kandy Korn EH	89 days; stalks to 8½' with 8" ears; heavy yield; excellent quality with high sugar content	38
Merlin	84 days; ears to 10"; longer keeping quality; light butter color; good sugary taste	33
Miracle	78 days; ears to 9½"; good producer; gourmet sweet corn; extra tasty	19
Platinum Lady	81 days; midseason sweet corn; ears to 8½"; popular with home gardeners; good taste	38
Seneca Sentry	89 days; good yields; ears to 8½"; extra-sweet, yellow kernels	24
Silver Queen	92 days; hybrid; tall stalks produce 8–9" ears; pure white kernels; very popular late variety	WA

(continued)

CORN—*Continued*

Variety	Description	Sources*
Stowell's Evergreen	90–100 days; open-pollinated; deep, sweet kernels; oldest variety still available	31
Sucro	90 days; good yields; ears to 9"; sweet, long-lasting flavor; freezes well	26
Sugar Loaf	83–85 days; hybrid; stalks to 6'; ears to 8" with yellow kernels; main crop variety	13
White Lightning	92 days; late-maturing, large, white ears; good tip cover; good disease resistance	16

*Listings correspond to seed companies listed under Sources of Seeds at the back of the book.

POPCORN

What makes a gourmet popcorn? Not taste. Most hybrids taste pretty much alike. Orville Redenbacher's vote for the chief characteristic of great popcorn goes to tenderness. "It's got to be tender," he says. "Good popcorn shouldn't be chewy or have hard centers."

In most instances, "gourmet" is another word for "hybrid." That's not to say there aren't some great open-pollinated types. JAPANESE HULL-LESS and SOUTH AMERICAN DYNAMITE are excellent standard varieties.

There are two basic types of popcorn: white and yellow. There's not much difference between them, except that the white types have a slightly thinner hull. Better kinds of popcorn are "hull-less." Technically, there's no such thing, since all popcorn types have a hard outer skin. But in the popper it should shatter into tiny pieces that you won't notice. If the "hull" breaks up into only two or three pieces and sticks to the flakes, the popcorn will be chewy and tough.

Crockett Seeds (P.O. Box 237, Metamora, OH 43540) specializes in popcorn. Owner David Crockett grows 17 varieties on 9 acres. He says his two best hybrids are P-305, a hull-less white popcorn that's early maturing and has good popping volume, and P-410, a large-

POPCORN—Continued

kerneled yellow that's not quite as tender. Crockett is also partial to some older, open-pollinated varieties. STRAWBERRY, which gets its name from its deep red kernels and strawberry-shaped ears, pops up into very small but very tender flakes. TINY TENDER BLACK has narrow teardrop-shaped kernels that pop up bigger than STRAWBERRY, but still much smaller than most hybrids. Both are white after popping.

All types of gourmet popcorn, says Orville Redenbacher, should pop into big, fluffy kernels. That's mostly a matter of controlling the amount of moisture, since moisture is what makes the popcorn explode. Getting the right moisture content is all in the drying and storing. The ideal moisture content is 14 percent, but that's pretty hard to determine without special equipment. The easiest way to tell is to rub off a few kernels and try them. At least eight out of ten should pop.

The best way to dry popcorn is right on the stalk in the field, where the leaves and stalk can wick moisture out of the corn. If your winters are mild, you can leave the corn in the field until it's fully dried. But in most places it's too cold. Frost can crack kernels that aren't completely dried and hardened. Once the shells are toughened, though, only a heavy freeze will damage them. If you have to harvest early, a month or so indoors will finish things. Redenbacher suggests hanging the unshelled ears in an onion bag in a warm, dry spot.

Shell the ears by twisting each one in your hands, or by rubbing two ears together. If the papery bits of husk that cling to the corn bother you, they can be winnowed out by running an electric fan over the corn as you mix it up with your hands.

The moisture in popcorn is unstable, and the kernels can quickly get too dry. Don't put popcorn in plastic bags—plastic "breathes" and will change the moisture content. Use glass jars and seal them tightly. If air is allowed to leak in and out, the corn can lose as much as 1 percent of its moisture every two days. In less than a week, it won't be worth much. If this happens, you can partially salvage a batch by putting a tablespoon of water into the container for every quart of popcorn. One last storage tip, straight from Orville Redenbacher: "Don't put your unpopped corn in the refrigerator. It'll pop much better if it's at room temperature."

POPCORN

Variety	Description	Sources*
Burpee Peppy	90 days; stalks to 6'; 2 or 3 4" ears per stalk	5
Japanese Hull-less	110 days; well-filled ears to 4½"; narrow, hull-less white kernels; tender when popped	38
Pretty Pops	95 days; ears to 5"; bright kernels of red, blue, black, yellow, purple, and orange; superb flavor; never tough	24
South American Dynamite	100–105 days; high yields; 2 or 3 9" ears per stalk; large yellow-orange kernels; buttery flavor when popped	12
Strawberry	100 days; hybrid; ornamental as well as for popping; ears to 4"; mahogany-red kernels; straw-colored husks	16

*Listings correspond to seed companies listed under Sources of Seeds at the back of the book.

All these supersweet varieties turn as starchy as field corn if they are pollinated by standard sweet corn, and standard varieties suffer the same fate if they are pollinated by supersweets. If you grow the two together, you risk having no sweet corn unless your varieties mature at least two weeks apart or grow at least 250 feet apart.

COWPEAS
(Blackeye peas, China beans, protopeas, southern peas)
Vigna unguiculata

The cowpea is actually a bean, both botanically and according to its use. The most popular cowpeas generally fall into one of three groups: blackeye, crowder, or cream.

Cowpeas can be used in any of their three stages of growth: as a green snap bean, picked while immature and tender; as a fresh shell bean; and as a dry bean for storage. They are a popular soup ingredient and are often simmered with salt pork or a ham hock. Cowpeas are also grown as livestock feed or as a green manure crop. Since they are legumes, they enrich the soil's nitrogen supply, and they act as good soil conditioners, making sandy soil more compact and loosening heavy soils.

Cowpeas are now available as bush or semivining varieties, in addition to the standard vining varieties. All cowpeas produce slender pods varying in size from 3 to 12 inches. The seeds are small but of good quality, and there are many different flavors among the varieties.

Cowpeas will do well in any region that offers long, hot summers with temperatures averaging between 60 and 75°F. These tender plants are very sensitive to frost.

Soil Preparation: Cowpeas are not particular about soil, as long as it is well drained. Slow-draining, waterlogged soil will damage the plants, as will flooding, so avoid low-lying areas that collect runoff. Phosphorus and potassium are important nutrients, but excess nitrogen will encourage foliage growth to the detriment of pod and seed formation. They tolerate a pH of 6.5 to 7.0.

How Much to Plant: A rough guideline is 37 plants per person.

Planting: Cowpeas are sown directly in the garden at least one week after the frost-free date. Wait until the soil is at least 60°F. They can be grown through the summer even in very warm areas, with successive plantings made three weeks apart. Plant the seeds 1 inch deep. For conventional rows, space seeds 2 to 3 inches apart in the row, with rows set 24 to 42 inches apart, depending on the variety (refer to the seed packet). Pole types may be planted in rows or hills like pole beans. Bush varieties are suited to planting in wide rows. Unused seed is good for three years.

Growing Guidelines: Treat cowpeas the same as other beans (see Beans). They need no supplemental feeding during the growing season, and they withstand drought even better than soybeans, which are noted for that quality.

Harvesting and Storing: For use as a green snap bean, pick cowpeas while they are young and succulent. As a green shell bean, wait until the seeds are nearly mature in size and harvest before the pods have yellowed and begun to deteriorate. Green shell beans can be canned or

---

COWPEAS

Variety	Description	Sources*
Brown Crowder	74–85 days; high yield of long pods; good quality, buff-colored seeds; seeds turn brown upon cooking	17
California Blackeye	75 days; high-yielding; vining with long pods; disease resistant	24
Mississippi Silver	64–70 days; high-yielding, bushy plants; Crowder variety; multiple disease resistance; silverish pods easy to shell	38
Pink Eye Purple Hull	50–85 days; semi-vining plant with purple pods; abundant white seeds with pink spots; very good for freezing	38

*Listings correspond to seed companies listed under Sources of Seeds at the back of the book.

frozen. For dry use, cowpeas may be treated like dry beans. Because of their small size, cowpeas dry fairly rapidly.

Nutritional Value: Cowpeas are high in protein (up to 20 percent), low in fat, and provide a large amount of vitamin B$_1$.

Pests and Diseases: Both insects and diseases have always plagued cowpeas, especially in very warm regions, although breeders are continually working on new disease-resistant varieties. The plants attract cornworms, Southern green stinkbugs, and weevils. The cowpea curculio is especially attracted to the developing pods. Diseases include root knot, wilt, and others caused by viruses. See Carrots and Corn for insect controls.

CUCUMBERS
Cucumis sativus
While most hybrids and all standard, open-pollinated cucumbers are monoecious—producing both male and female blossoms—there are new gynoecious hybrids which produce only female blossoms, and that means early, heavy yields. Their first six or seven flowers will set fruit, but the first blossoms on the monoecious types are male and won't set fruit until the females arrive farther out on the vine. The all-female plant can set about one-third of its yield without being pollinated, but needs male blossoms to pollinate the rest. Seed packets will contain a few monoecious seeds, usually dyed a different color.

Because of the greater number of female blossoms, gynoecious varieties will bear more fruit. But studies have shown that their yields diminish as the season progresses. If you want early yields and also want vines that go on producing late in the season, plant both gynoecious hybrids and monoecious or open-pollinated varieties.

Soil Preparation: Cucumbers prefer a slightly acidic to neutral soil with a pH of 6.5 to 7.0. Although cucumbers will grow in almost any type of soil, it should easily absorb and retain water. One or two weeks before planting, till the soil to a depth of 6 to 8 inches and work in plenty of organic matter, such as compost, manure, old leaves, or grass clippings.

If your soil drains poorly, or if you live in an area of heavy summer rains, form your plot into a slightly raised bed. "You have poor drainage if water hasn't drained away within eight hours after a heavy rainfall," says Dr. Conrad Miller of North Carolina University. "Work the soil into a fine tilth and mound the top of the bed 3 to 4 inches from the undisturbed level of the soil. Raise it slightly higher in the middle. Then if you have a heavy rainfall, the excess water will drain off."

How Much to Plant: A rough guideline is two or three hills, or six to nine plants, per person.

Planting: Cucumbers are a warm-season vegetable and will not tolerate even a light frost. "The biggest mistake most gardeners make is to plant their seeds too early," claims Dr. Clinton Peterson, professor of horticulture at the University of Wisconsin. "Seeds planted later under optimum conditions will develop as well as seeds planted earlier under poor conditions, so there's no need to rush the season."

Two weeks after the last frost is usually a safe time to plant, but make sure that the average air temperature is at least 60°F. The best average soil temperature range is 55 to 95°F. The higher the soil temperature, the faster the seeds will germinate. To help the soil warm up quickly, pull back any mulch that's been protecting it over winter, and let the sun start warming it as soon as possible. Using black plastic, which absorbs rather than reflects the sun's heat, is the fastest way to heat the soil. Lay it down over moist soil. Cover the edges with dirt and rocks to hold it in place. Cut holes in it for plants and water to get through.

Give vines enough space to run in the garden. Four to 6 feet is the distance normally recommended between rows. For a 20-foot row, that's 80 to 120 square feet of garden space. Each hill that you plant can take up as much as 25 square feet. However, a 20-foot row of vines climbing 6 feet upward on a trellis instead of running on the ground will take up only 20 to 40 square feet, depending on the type of trellis you use.

If you use a trellis, put it up before you plant so it won't harm the plants' roots. Plant seed 6 inches from the trellis on the windward side so that when the prevailing wind blows, the fruit will be blown toward the trellis, not away from it. Guide the tendrils onto the trellis to get them started.

Plant in a very sunny spot—cucumbers need at least eight hours of sun every day. For a trellis, choose the north side of the garden so it doesn't shade other plants. Don't plant where squash, pumpkins, or melons, which are susceptible to the same soilborne diseases, have grown in the previous three years.

When planting seed, dig a hole 1 foot deep and 2 feet in diameter. Place 2 to 4 inches of compost or rotted manure in the bottom, replace the soil, and form it into a 5-inch mound. Round off the top and plant seeds in the center. Planting in small mounds like this will concentrate cucumbers' favorite fertilizer near the roots, provide for extra drainage, and keep the soil warmer.

Sow four or five seeds per hill, 2 inches apart in a circle. When two or three true leaves appear, thin to the strongest two plants. If you're planting an all-female variety, you'll notice a few green seeds among the cream-colored ones. These are pollinating seeds. Sow one of these to every five or six of the others for good pollination of the female flowers. Sow seeds $1/2$ to 1 inch deep. Unused seed is good for five years.

Handling Seedlings:
You can also start cucumbers indoors and transplant when you're sure soil and air temperatures are warm enough, but be careful— their sensitive roots won't recover well if injured during transplanting. Sow in 2- to 3-inch peat pots that can be planted right in the ground. Sow one or two seeds per pot, $1/2$ inch deep, on edge. Later, thin each pot to the best-looking seedling. Put them in a warm spot out of direct sunlight until seedlings emerge (in about seven to ten days), then move them into the light.

When the first true leaves are $1/2$ to 2 inches wide, set the pots outside for two to three days to harden them off before planting. When you transplant, make sure the top of the pot is below the soil surface or it will dry out. The soil should be almost up to the cotyledons. Feed with a liquid fertilizer such as manure tea or fish emulsion. From seeding to transplanting, keep the soil moist but not wet.

Growing Guidelines: Controlling the amount of water cucumbers get throughout the growing season is also critical. The shallow root system must feed a vine that grows over 6 feet long and bears fruits that are 90 to 95 percent water. "The cucumber vine has a unique plumbing system," explains Dr. R. L. Lower, horticulturist at the University of Wisconsin. "Water travels up the vine in one direction to supply soil nutrients to leaves and fruit, then carries nutrients manufactured by photosynthesis back along the vine to wherever they're needed. There's a high demand for water—especially after fruit develops."

Too little or irregular watering causes misshapen, bitter, or tasteless cucumbers. Too much causes stunted plants. When the plants are small and have not yet set fruit, they need about ½ inch of water a week. Once fruit sets and temperatures start to climb, they need 1 inch or more. If the soil is dry 4 inches below the surface, you need to water. If it's moist, even if the surface is dry, you don't. The plants themselves are the key—water if they look wilted before 11 A.M. (Wilting is normal, though, in the hot afternoon sun.)

If you use an overhead sprinkler or hose, water in the morning so foliage and fruit can dry off by evening and disease organisms will have less opportunity to grow. Using a soaker hose will avoid this problem. A heavy layer of mulch—clean, dry straw, hay, or sawdust—will prevent moisture from evaporating.

When the vines are about 18 inches long, feed them a moderate amount of bloodmeal, well-rotted manure, or a mix-ture of bloodmeal and compost. Place it 4 to 5 inches to the side of the plant in a furrow 2 inches deep and water it in. You also can pour fish emulsion or manure tea on the ground around the plants instead of a regular watering.

Flowers form within ten days from the appearance of the first true leaves. The first blossoms are male (unless, of course, you're planting an all-female variety), and about a week later the females appear on the same vine, usually at alternating nodes.

There are enough bees in most gardens to pollinate the flowers, but if you have a prolonged stretch of rainy, cloudy weather, they won't be very active. Check your vines daily. Unpollinated cucumbers are distorted little things—twisted and c-shaped. Cutting them lengthwise will show the absence of seeds, which means pollination has not taken place. You will have to hand-pollinate the rest of the blooms to make sure you get a crop.

Use flowers that are in full bloom. In the center of the male blossoms are anthers which contain the pollen. In the center of the female blossoms are stigma which receive it. Carefully tear off the petals of the male blossom, but be careful not to injure the anthers. Hold the flower between the middle and forefinger of the left hand. Touch the anthers to the stigma so the pollen will adhere to it. The best time is in the morning, when blossoms are open at their widest and dew helps the pollen adhere.

Keys to Top Yields: "Trellised vines stay healthy for a longer period of time, so they produce fruit for a longer period of time," according to Dr. Thomas Konsler of North Carolina State University. Studies done there compared

yields from normal field production of cucumbers with yields from vines supported on trellises. The amount of fruit acceptable for fresh market tripled.

One reason they stay healthy longer is better air circulation. Cucumbers are susceptible to several diseases brought on by a combination of high humidity and either high or low temperatures. The canopy of leaves formed by vines on the ground creates its own humid environment—a good breeding ground for disease.

However, Dr. Norman Oebker from the University of Arizona cautions against trellising in hot, dry areas where humidity is low. "The canopy of foliage protects the fruit from an overexposure to sunlight during dry conditions. Low humidity and greater sunlight could cause the cucumber to become bitter and the skin to turn a lighter color."

Another reason for increased production during the North Carolina study was the pruning of the first five or six lateral shoots. "These appear as small growing points in the leaf axils," explains Dr. Konsler. "Pinching them off encourages more vegetative growth in the early stages of plant growth, rather than fruit set. The plant then has a good framework for producing more fruit later on in the season." Early yields will be lower, though, so you may want to leave a few unpruned.

Trellised cucumbers also have a good, uniform, dark green color and a better shape because they hang freely. They're easier to find when ready for picking than cukes hidden by vines on the ground. Bees have better access to the blooms, too, so pollination is better.

Harvesting and Storing:

"You must pick the fruit right away," warns Dr. Henry Munger, a horticulturist at Cornell University in Ithaca, New York. "You can't go on vacation just as they're starting to set fruit. When you get back, you'll find a lot of overripe cucumbers and a plant that has stopped producing altogether." A single ripe cucumber left on the vine will stop production.

You can store cucumbers in a cool, moist place (40 to 50°F) for a week or two, but after that, they'll start to shrivel and lose flavor. The best long-term storage technique is pickling.

Pests and Diseases:

Cucumber beetles, both spotted and striped, and the bacterial wilt they carry, are probably the biggest threats to your cucumber plot. Young plants are the most vulnerable. Just as they're poking through the ground, large numbers of beetles fly in to feed on them. The bacteria spread by their mouthparts clog the water vessels with sticky white ooze that's visible when you cut across the stem. The leaves and stems droop at first, then wilt, and the plant eventually dies.

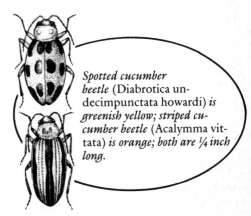

Spotted cucumber beetle (Diabrotica undecimpunctata howardi) is greenish yellow; striped cucumber beetle (Acalymma vittata) is orange; both are ¼ inch long.

Look for yellow-winged bugs with three black stripes down their backs, or yellow-green wings and 11 or 12 spots. Both pests are only about ¼ inch long. But don't wait until you see them to try to stop them. As soon as the plants are up, cover the plot with cheesecloth or Reemay. Bury the edges in at least 1 inch of soil so the beetles can't get beneath them. A couple of weeks later, remove the cloth—if beetles return, spray both sides of the leaves with rotenone. If you don't mind a later crop, delay planting until the beetles have come and gone. A local entomologist can tell you when it's safe.

The beetles are homing in on the cucurbitacins in your cucumbers. These are the chemical compounds responsible for cucumber bitterness. Several varieties, such as SWEET SLICE and COUNTRY FAIR, have had the bitter principle bred out of them, and therefore are less attractive to cucumber beetles. "But," says Dr. Munger of Cornell, "although nonbitter varieties are less damaged by cucumber beetles, they are more subject to damage from rabbits, woodchucks, and spider mites, so you have to weigh the advantages against the disadvantages."

Two other insects that you may have trouble with are the melonworm and pickleworm. The green melonworm has two white stripes down its back. It feeds mostly on foliage, but may find its way inside a cucumber, especially in the early part of summer. You can control them and pickleworms by handpicking.

Young pickleworms are pale yellow with black spots that disappear as the insects mature. When full grown, they're ¾ inch long and turn green or copperish. You will see them burrowing into all parts of the plant. Keeping your garden free of weeds and cleaning up refuse at the end of the season will help keep them under control.

The tiny melon aphid can be washed from plants with a forceful jet of water. These green, louselike bugs form small colonies on the undersides of leaves, depositing a sticky substance which attracts ants, bees, and flies. They can spread throughout the garden if unchecked, especially when cool, wet spring is followed by a hot, dry summer.

Mosaic virus is another serious disease which northern gardeners, especially, should watch for. It overwinters in common perennial weeds such as milkweed, ground cherry, catnip, ragweed, pigweed, burdock, various mints, and horse nettle. Mosaic is spread by the striped cucumber beetle and the melon aphid. Curled green and yellow blotchy leaves, warty fruit, and malformed blossoms are all symptoms of mosaic virus. The plants become dwarfed and yields will be low, or the plants may die.

Other diseases that can seriously damage your cucumber crop if allowed to gain a foothold in the garden include anthracnose, scab, downy mildew, powdery mildew, and angular leaf spot. Check with your county Extension agent to find out which, if any, are prevalent in your area, since there are resistant varieties for each.

It's also wise to stay out of the patch after a rain or watering to avoid spreading disease to other plants. Remove any diseased plants as soon as you spot them, without letting them touch any others, and thin out weak and scrawny plants that make good targets for infection.

Nutritional Value: The skin of the cucumber contains vitamins A and C.

CUCUMBERS

Variety	Description	Sources*
Burpeeana Hybrid II	55 days; gynoecious; productive; fruits to 9" long	5
Burpee Hybrid	55 days; gynoecious; heavy yields; vigorous; straight fruits to 8"; resistant to cucumber mosaic and downy mildew	5
Burpless Hybrid	62 days; monoecious; curved fruits to 10"; resistant to downy and powdery mildew; non-bitter	WA
Burpless Tasty Green	62 days; monoecious; fruits to 10" long; crisp and non-bitter	7, 36
Country Fair	50 days; gynoecious; heaviest pickling variety; resistant to many cucumber diseases; non-bitter	33
Gemini	60 days; gynoecious; heavy yields; vigorous vines; resistant to most diseases; good length and quality	13
Marketer	60 days; very attractive 9" fruits; not high in disease resistance; especially suited to southern gardens; AAS	WA
Marketmore 70	55–67 days; high yields throughout summer; fruits to 8"; scab and mosaic virus resistant; good for northern areas	5
Marketmore 76	58–75 days; dark green, straight fruits to 8"; does well even in hot weather; resistant to many diseases	10
Poinsett 76	65–70 days; heavy yields of dark green, cylindrical fruits; resistant to many diseases; especially suited to the South	WA
Spartan Valour	60 days; monoecious; high yields of dark green, 8" fruits; mosaic and scab resistant; ideal for slicing	WA
Straight Eight	52–75 days; early, prolific, and vigorous; smooth, straight fruits; excellent quality	WA
Sweet Slice	62 days; gynoecious; 10–12" slightly tapered fruits; burpless; tolerant of many diseases	WA
Triumph	60 days; gynoecious; heavy yields; vigorous vines; fruits tapered, to 8"; good under poor conditions; AAS	38
Victory	50 days; gynoecious; very early, heavy yields; fruits to 8"; tolerant of many diseases; AAS	WA

*Listings correspond to seed companies listed under Sources of Seeds at the back of the book.

Choosing Varieties: If you find it difficult to eat the thick skin of some of the more common varieties, try a Japanese "burpless" type, such as BURPLESS TASTY GREEN or BURPLESS HYBRID, which not only have thin, easy-to-eat skin, but also have a reputation for being easy to digest.

EGGPLANT
(Aubergine)
Solanum melongena var. *esculentum*

This attractive member of the nightshade family is related to the tomato, pepper, and potato. The plants grow from 1 to 3 feet tall, depending on the variety, and produce pretty, star-shaped purple blossoms. The fruits, too, are pleasing to the eye. Because both flowers and fruits are so attractive, eggplant may be worked into the landscape as an edible ornamental.

The most popular varieties available in North America offer glossy, deep purple to black, plum-shaped fruits weighing from 1 to 5 pounds each. The Italian white eggplant varieties, which are rarely seen in North America, are considered by those who grow them to be the best-tasting of all.

Eggplant is a warm-weather crop and produces the best harvest in a long, hot summer. Although early-maturing varieties have been developed for short-season gardens, even these will bear poorly during an extended cool and damp period. Ideally, each plant of the common varieties should yield from four to eight fruits. More often, however, the home gardener will harvest two or three.

Most eggplant varieties are classified according to the shape of the fruit, either oval or elongated. Many gardeners, having always grown the large, oval varieties, are surprised to find that the smaller slices of the elongated fruits are more convenient to use in recipes. The fruits may be peeled, sliced, and broiled, or dipped in batter, then fried.

Eggplant is a very tender crop which grows best in average temperatures between 70 and 85°F. Long-season varieties are best grown in regions that offer a hot summer and a mild fall. Early-maturing varieties may be grown in all temperate regions, although it must be realized that all types of eggplant are harmed by chill (extended temperatures below 50°F) and destroyed by frost. Also, the fruit won't set when temperatures dip below 60 to 65°F.

Soil Preparation: Eggplant will do well in an average loam that is well drained, deeply prepared, and well supplied with organic matter. Avoid low-lying areas and heavy soils. The pH should be in the range of 5.5 to 6.8.

How Much to Plant: A rough guideline is two to three plants per person.

Planting: Eggplant is usually started in the garden from transplants, although it can be direct-seeded in very warm climates with a long growing season. (Sow seed according to spacings given below for transplants.)

Handling Seedlings: Start plants eight to ten weeks before transplanting time. Seedlings can be set out two to three weeks after the frost-free date when the soil is warm. Set plants 2 feet apart in conventional rows with 2 to 3 feet

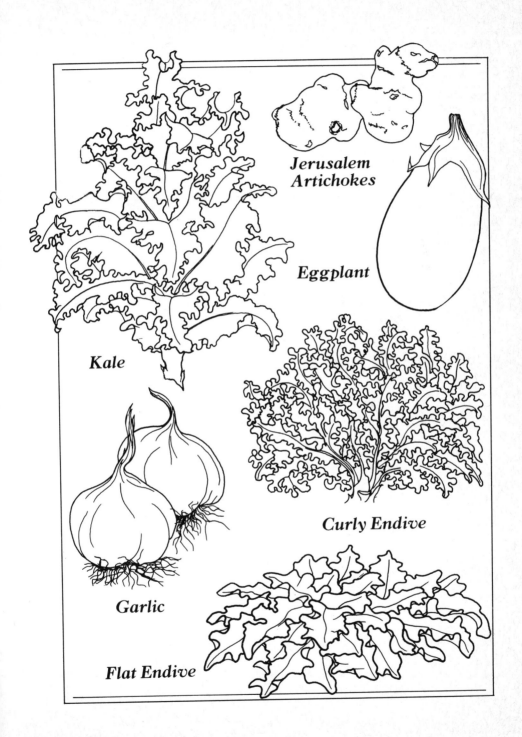

Jerusalem
Artichokes

Eggplant

Kale

Curly Endive

Garlic

Flat Endive

between rows. Growing bed spacing is 24 inches. Unused seed is good for five years.

Growing Guidelines: Eggplant requires plenty of moisture for best growth. Apply a mulch as soon as the soil has warmed up thoroughly and the plants are established. Keep the area free of weeds. On less than fertile soil, eggplant may benefit from a nitrogen and potassium boost one month after planting. Side-dress with well-rotted manure or compost and wood ashes, or water with a solution of manure tea and seaweed extract.

Harvesting and Storing: The common practice has been to delay the harvest until the fruits are of nearly mature size, which means the entire crop is picked during a short period of only a few weeks. To extend the harvest period, begin picking whenever the eggplant is large enough to use, around 3 to 5 inches, depending on the variety. These immature fruits are more tender and generally of much better quality than those left to grow to full size. Young fruit has glossy skin, while older fruit past its prime has a dull sheen. When eggplant slices reveal seeds that have turned brown, that fruit has passed its peak of quality. Since the fruits are difficult to remove from the plant, use a sharp knife or pruning shears. The fruits may be kept for about one week in any location that

EGGPLANT

Variety	Description	Sources*
Black Beauty	73–83 days; plump, oval, dark purple fruits; tolerates drought; dependable producer	5
Burpee Hybrid	70–75 days; plants spread slightly; medium-sized, oval, dark purple fruits; drought and disease resistant	5
Burpee's Jersey King Hybrid	73–75 days; elongated, dark purple fruits to 10"; should be harvested at 7" for best flavor	33
Casper	70 days; medium-size plant; fruits have ivory white skin; mild, snow-white flesh; grow to 6"	33
Dusky	55–62 days; extra early; compact plants; slender, oval, black fruits; good for short-season areas	5
Ichiban	65 days; very high yields; elongated, slender, purple fruits; especially suited to oriental recipes	38
Little Fingers	68 days; long, slim fruits to 7"; borne in clusters of 5 to 10; easy to pick; excellent for frying, oriental recipes	13

*Listings correspond to seed companies listed under Sources of Seeds at the back of the book.

offers high humidity and a warm temperature. Eggplant does not can or freeze well.

Pests and Diseases: Eggplant may be bothered by a wide range of common insects, including aphids, Colorado potato beetles, cucumber beetles, cut-

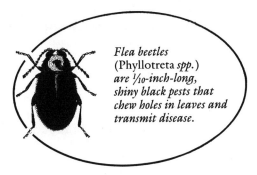

Flea beetles (Phyllotreta spp.) are ¹⁄₁₀-inch-long, shiny black pests that chew holes in leaves and transmit disease.

worms, flea beetles, leafhoppers, potato tuberworms, and tomato hornworms. Diseases include fruit rot and verticillium wilt (the latter in cool-climate areas especially). See Potatoes and Tomatoes for insect controls.

Nutritional Value: Although eggplant is not rich in nutrients, it has a moderate amount of dietary fiber and is very low in calories—only 27 per cup of boiled eggplant.

ENDIVE
(Curly endive; also escarole or broad-leaved endive)
Cichorium endiva

There are two types of endive from which the gardener can choose. The most common is the curly variety, which produces a loose head of notched, frilly leaves. Curly endive is the most cold-tolerant and is best for planting in early spring and late winter, though it makes a fine fall crop as well. It's good in salads and as a garnish. Another form of endive, commonly marketed as escarole, has broad, thick, smoother leaves of a lighter green. Broad-leaved endive really shows its stuff when the hot weather comes, and is good for late spring and summer plantings. It's good in salads but can be cooked in soups, too. Although the two look quite different, both are grown in exactly the same way. An unrelated plant, Belgian endive, is forced in winter for high, creamy heads. Belgian endive is delicious in salads, but one of the nicest ways to eat it is braised with a little butter and lemon juice.

Soil Preparation: Endive will grow in almost any kind of soil, but it does best when there is lots of humus. In southern New Jersey, where much of the East Coast's endive is raised, many farmers dig in a layer of chicken manure several months before planting. The high nitrogen level in the fresh manure promotes lush leaf growth. Since it seldom puts down roots deeper than 18 inches, endive needs its food close to the surface. A 2-inch layer of manure or compost dug 6 inches into the row or bed should do the job. Although endive prefers a neutral or slightly acidic soil (about pH 6.0), it is quite tolerant of acidity as low as pH 5.0.

How Much to Plant: A rough guideline is five endive plants for every adult in the family. A quarter-ounce package has over 100 seeds, so you are going to have some left over. Properly stored, however, endive seed will be good for five years.

Planting: July is the time to plant a fall crop of this hardy vegetable. In fact, endive that matures in cool weather is said to be the best-tasting of all. A few light frosts seem to improve flavor and reduce bitterness. To determine the right planting time for a late fall harvest, count back 90 days from the first killing frost in your region. In the South, you can plant endive year-round. Stagger your plantings every two weeks to spread out the harvest. Thin the plants in the garden to 12 inches apart.

Plant endive seed no more than $1/4$ inch deep in a humus-rich soil that's been watered thoroughly beforehand. Plant two or three seeds per inch and cover them with a light sprinkling of sand, soil, or peat. Germination usually takes place in 10 to 14 days.

Nearly all endive varieties available to the gardener take at least 85 to 95 days from seed to salad. Don't be tempted by a variety that promises a significantly shorter season. There are a few of them, favored by many commercial growers. But vegetable-growing experts warn that those varieties are bred to store and ship well, not to taste good. That's the reason that so much supermarket endive is tough and very bitter.

Handling Seedlings: Summer and early fall endive crops can begin life right in the garden, but seedlings for the spring crop should be started indoors. A study at Rutgers University found that cooler temperatures during germination caused endive heads to bolt before they were mature. The tests showed that 68°F was optimum for the first two weeks of growth. After that, the endive was ready to face the cold.

To get an early summer harvest in colder regions, you should start endive seed indoors about eight weeks before the last frost date. Seedlings growing in flats should be thinned to 6 inches apart. Transplant those seedlings outdoors when they are four weeks old. You could risk transplanting even earlier with success in most years, especially if you use cloches or hotcaps. Once they're 4 to 5 inches tall, endive seedlings will withstand anything short of a hard freeze.

When you're ready to set plants out, pick a spot in the garden that gets direct or partial sunlight. In the hottest months, shade transplants with a board or sheet of cardboard stuck into the ground on the southern side. Plants should be spaced no closer than 12 inches in all directions. Endive will take a little crowding, but the heads will be smaller and rot can start if the maturing leaves overlap.

Growing Guidelines: Endive needs plenty of moisture. It can take some water stress, but if the roots are allowed to dry out for a prolonged period, the leaves will become tough and bitter. Make sure the plants get an inch of water a week. According to Brad Johnson, New Jersey Extension specialist in vegetable crops, "The way a person waters is more important than how much he waters. Overhead sprinkling traps moisture inside the endive heads, and that can lead to rot."

Johnson recommends drip irrigation and soaker hoses, which wet the roots deeply while the leaves stay high and dry. Otherwise, dig a trench between rows and run water down it with a hose. A mulch of straw, leaves, hay, or grass clippings will help conserve moisture and protect the fall and winter crops from freezing.

With such a shallow root system, endive doesn't compete well with weeds. Mulch is the best way to keep weeds down. If you must cultivate, however, be careful not to damage roots.

To tame endive's somewhat bitter nature, most gardeners blanch it before harvest. Blanching—excluding light from the heart of the plant until it turns creamy yellow—does give endive a milder taste, but it also robs it of vitamins, particularly A and C.

Blanch endive about 60 days after planting, or when it's two-thirds grown. The preferred method is to gather up the outer leaves and tie them over the top of the plant with a rubber band or heavy twine. Placing a bucket or flowerpot with its drain hole plugged over each plant also works well. If you want to blanch only the heart, put a saucer over each, or lay a board along the center of the row and prop it up with bricks at each end.

You'll be inviting rot if you cover or tie up a wet plant. Untie blanching plants after rainstorms to let them dry out for a day. Complete blanching takes about two weeks in warm weather and three weeks during the cooler months.

For the earliest possible spring crop, dig up a few heads in mid-fall complete with a ball of earth covering the roots, and place—but don't plant—them in a cold frame or unheated greenhouse. Moisten occasionally if dry. Return the plants to the garden in late winter and you'll be eating endive in April.

If you are raising one of the varieties known as Belgian endive, grow it like a leaf crop in the spring and summer. The summer leaves are edible but extremely bitter. It's the roots, about the size and shape of a large carrot, that you're after. Dig them up when autumn's killing frosts come. Cut off the leafy head about 2 inches above the crown.

To "force" the endive, place it upright in a box or a bucket and fill with enough sandy soil to cover each root. Pour an 8-inch layer of sand or sawdust on top of that and put the container in a dark spot that stays about 55°F. Douse the sawdust with water once a week, and in about 21 days the roots will sprout pale, tear-shaped heads. After you slice these off, the roots will produce smaller side shoots.

Harvesting and Storing: Your plants can be harvested anytime during their growth, either a leaf at a time or by cutting the entire head. Once the endive is mature, though, it should be picked soon or it will grow tough, especially in warm weather. When the head is full and about a foot across with a heart that's well formed, the endive is mature. Cut off the plant at ground level. If you leave about an inch of stem and all the roots undamaged, new, smaller heads may form in warm weather. Should you find yourself with a few extra heads, wrap them in plastic and store them in the coldest part of the refrigerator. Keep them away from apples, which release a gas that hastens spoilage.

Pests and Diseases: To help prevent aphid attacks, clear the garden area of chickweed, which attracts the tiny green insects. Interplanting endive with garlic, sweet basil, chives, and anise can also help to repel this pest. Slugs can be controlled by sprinkling a circle of wood ashes at the base of each head.

Cutworms are fat, light-colored larvae that chew through plant stems at night, cutting them off at ground level. A line of ashes will keep cutworms at bay, but the best way to protect plants is to fasten a 3-inch-high cardboard collar

ENDIVE

Variety	Description	Sources*
Elodie	70 days; dense plants; lacy outer leaves; crisp ribs; closely bunched, blanched hearts; heat tolerant; long season	32
Full-Heart Batavian (also Florida Deep Heart)	85–90 days; plants upright to 14″ wide; slightly crinkled, dark green leaves with white midribs	WA
Green Curled	80–90 days; very frilly, crisp leaves with white midribs; grows to 9″ tall and 18″ wide	WA
Salad King	80–100 days; finely curled leaves with light green midribs; vigorous and slow to bolt; tipburn and frost resistant	WA

*Listings correspond to seed companies listed under Sources of Seeds at the back of the book.

around each stem at planting time.

If your crop is rotated each year, and water isn't allowed to stand in the crowns of plants, disease should never be a problem.

Other Problems: Air pollution damage in endive shows itself in a silvering of the undersides of leaves and in small black specks. It can kill the plant in a very short time, and, unfortunately, the symptoms often don't show up until it's too late. If you notice that your endive leaves have a silvery cast, douse them with water and hope for the best.

Nutritional Value: Endive is a good source of vitamin A, and has as much vitamin C as lettuce.

GARLIC
Allium sativum

This relative of the onion is a perennial that is grown as an annual in temperate climates. The plant produces a compound bulb made up of as many as 12 individual sections (called cloves), and a leaf stalk, 8 to 24 inches high, which produces both seeds and bulblets (which may be planted). Although garlic may be grown from seed, most gardeners find it simpler to plant the cloves, each of which will grow into a whole new bulb.

Garlic is an essential ingredient in many recipes, especially those of southern European and central Asian origin. It is also reputed to have medicinal value, particularly in fighting the common cold and in preventing high blood pressure. It is used, too, in the garden as an insect repellent, either when interplanted among other crops or ground up and made into a spray.

Growing garlic is not difficult, although the plants are somewhat more sensitive to soil and climatic conditions than most onions. Since they take up so little room, the plants are often used in interplanting, to make best use of garden space.

In addition to common garlic, the gardener may come across references to elephant garlic. This is an entirely different species (*A. scorodoprasum*), producing large bulbs with a milder flavor than the more well known *A. sativum*. Elephant garlic is so mild, in fact, that it can be diced and used raw in salads. In all but extreme northern areas, this plant can be grown as a perennial, and any bulbs left at the end of the season can remain in the ground.

Garlic requires cool temperatures during the early stages of growth when the leaves are developing. Later in the growing season, warm temperatures and long days are needed for best bulb development. Garlic is among the hardiest of garden crops, and is not damaged by frost or light freezing. Elephant garlic is extremely hardy and can withstand lower temperatures than regular garlic.

Soil Preparation:
Garlic needs a fertile, well-drained soil that will supply ample nutrients and moisture during the growing season. A good soil is more important to garlic than to most alliums, and a sandy loam with lots of organic matter promotes vigorous, healthy growth. Till and rake the soil finely before planting. The recommended pH range is 5.5 to 6.8.

How Much to Plant:
A rough guideline is five to nine plants per person.

Planting:
A half pound of cloves will plant 100 feet of row, and will produce up to 5 pounds of mature bulbs, more than enough for the annual needs of most families.

Cloves can be planted directly in the garden, or sprouted indoors, than set outside. Plant cloves directly outdoors four to six weeks before the frost-free date, as soon as the soil can be worked. In warm climates, plant in the fall. In areas with severe winter temperatures, cloves also may be planted in the fall and mulched over the winter for early spring growing.

Set cloves 1 inch deep with the pointed end up and the blunt end down. Space them 3 to 4 inches apart in conventional rows set 12 to 16 inches apart. Spacing in growing beds is 6 inches. Garlic may also be grown in wide rows. Gardeners usually plant only small areas with garlic, since just a few cloves yield a bumper harvest. Many gardeners simply work garlic in among other crops.

Growing from Seed:
Garlic may be grown from seed, in the same way as onions (see Onions and Scallions).

Handling Seedlings:
Start cloves indoors four to six weeks before setting out, which can be done from two to four weeks before to one week after the frost-free date.

Growing Guidelines:
The greatest threats to good production are dry soil and weeds. Water the ground thoroughly after planting, and mulch between rows. Hand weeding is essential, especially

GARLIC

Variety	Description	Sources*
Elephant Garlic	100 days; produces bulbs 6 times larger than common variety; each clove weighs up to 1 oz.; mild garlic flavor	WA
Italian (pink) varieties	110 days; bulbs of better quality than Mexican (white) varieties; store very well	30
Mexican (white) varieties	90 days; early maturing; high yields; bulbs do not store as well as Italian (pink) varieties	38

*Listings correspond to seed companies listed under Sources of Seeds at the back of the book.

early in the season when plants are becoming established.

Keys to Top Yields: Remove flower heads as they appear; this produces the largest bulbs. For bigger bulbs next year, save the largest bulbs from this year's harvest for replanting.

Harvesting and Storing: Leaves can be snipped like chives and used wherever a mild garlic flavor is desired, although this practice slows down bulb formation. Garlic is ready for harvest when the tops begin to yellow and droop. At that time (approximately 90 to 110 days from planting), stop watering and knock down all the tops to hasten bulb curing. Three to five days later, loosen the soil around the bulbs before pulling, or use a fork to lift them. Leave them outdoors in a dry, shady location for several days until the tops are completely dry and the skin has become papery. If the weather is rainy, bring them indoors to spread on screens in a cool, dry spot. Once bulbs are completely dry, trim off the leaf stalks and trim the roots close to

the base. Hang them in mesh bags in a cool and dry storage area. Garlic can also be braided into decorative strands for storage; if this method is preferred, don't trim the leaf stalks. Garlic will keep for up to a year under proper storage conditions. Even braids hung in the kitchen will keep for several months.

Nutritional Value: Garlic is not a good source of nutrients but is highly prized as a seasoning.

Pests and Diseases: See Onions and Scallions.

JERUSALEM ARTICHOKES
(Girasole, sunchoke)
Helianthus tuberosus

The Jerusalem artichoke is not from Jerusalem, and it is not an artichoke. It is a native North American perennial sunflower with knobby stem-tubers that are eaten raw, added to salads, or used like potatoes. The crisp tubers, white with brown or reddish brown skins, have a sweet and nutty taste, although they will taste bland if harvested before the ground has started to freeze in autumn.

The Jerusalem artichoke is perhaps the easiest of all vegetables to grow—certainly the easiest of the perennials. A single tuber planted in a corner of the garden will soon expand to supply the needs of any family. In fact, the major problem with Jerusalem artichokes often is attempting to keep them from taking over the entire garden.

The tubers are delicious raw, and they can be used as crudités with dips, or sliced thinly into salads. Jerusalem artichokes can also be cooked—but just steam or sauté them lightly.

Jerusalem artichokes are extremely hardy and will grow in all regions. They are a long-season crop, requiring 120 days to mature. In frost-free areas the texture and taste of the tubers will be inferior.

Soil Preparation:
Any warm, well-drained soil will support good stands of Jerusalem artichokes. It's a good idea to set aside a separate bed for this crop so their rampant growth doesn't interfere with other garden crops. Till soil to a depth of 10 inches. Add some compost to poorer soils to give the plants a good start. The pH level should be close to 5.8.

How Much to Plant:
A rough guideline is three to five plants per person.

Planting:
Jerusalem artichokes may be planted four to six weeks before the frost-free date, as soon as the soil can be worked. In warm climates, plant them in the fall to provide a spring crop. They are planted like potatoes, using either an entire tuber or one that is cut up so that each piece contains an "eye." Plants have even grown from peelings placed in a compost heap. Many gardeners plant this crop in a row along the back of the garden, where the tall-growing plants will not shade other vegetables. Set the tubers 6 inches deep every 12 inches along rows spaced 36 to 48 inches apart. The tubers may also be planted in hills, one per hill, with hills set 12 inches apart.

Growing Guidelines:
Once planted, Jerusalem artichokes need little further care. They should be given moderate moisture until they have become established. A mulch—applied when the soil has warmed up thoroughly—will help to keep weeds down. However, since each tuber sends up from 1 to 12 stalks, the Jerusalem artichokes will most likely outrace the weeds and smother them. In windy areas, plants may need supports.

Keys to Top Yields:
If the top 12 to 18 inches of stem are cut off as flowers form, the size of the developing tubers will be increased. Do not cut the stems off completely—otherwise the yield of tubers will be decreased.

Harvesting and Storing:
For best taste and texture, tubers should not be dug until the foliage has died down and the ground has just begun to freeze, in late autumn or early winter. Then, the easiest harvesting method is to loosen the soil slightly with a garden fork, grasp the thick stem of the plant, and pull it out of the ground. Some tubers will adhere to the roots, and the others may be exposed easily with a hoe or garden fork. Rarely will all the tubers be recovered, and those that remain behind will ensure the following year's crop.

JERUSALEM ARTICHOKE

Variety	Description	Sources*
American	120 days; plants can grow to 8'; dig in fall and store in cool place; plants need to be confined	5, 12

*Listings correspond to seed companies listed under Sources of Seeds at the back of the book.

To clean the tuber surface of all dirt, soak in it water for five minutes, and scrub with a brush. Rinse and use at once, or store in a plastic bag in the refrigerator for three to four days.

Because of their thin skins, Jerusalem artichokes are difficult to store successfully indoors unless they are kept in a cool (32 to 40°F) location. In addition, stored tubers are less flavorful than those that are freshly dug. It is better to store them in the garden itself, and dig them as needed. In most temperate regions, a heavy mulch will keep the ground from freezing hard, enabling tubers to be harvested throughout the winter. In severe-winter regions, pack them in moist sand and store them in a box, barrel, or garbage can placed under the ground. Hard freezing will not damage the tubers.

Nutritional Value: The Jerusalem artichoke is unique among vegetable crops in that is has no starch content, storing its carbohydrate in the form of inulin. For this reason, it is often used by diabetics as a potato substitute. The tubers offer significant amounts of several vitamins and minerals and are especially rich in vitamin B_1 and potassium. They are also very low in calories, having only one-tenth the number found in an equal serving of potatoes.

Pests and Diseases: None are serious.

Choosing Varieties: The best variety is AMERICAN (formerly called IMPROVED MAMMOTH FRENCH), although many catalogs do not bother to mention a variety. Tubers are sold by the pound. A fraction of that will be enough to establish a lifetime planting.

KALE
(Borecole)
Brassica oleracea
var. *acephala*

Kale's true flavor is sweet and pungent, but many gardeners harvest it at the wrong time, when its eating quality is poor and its leaves are tough. Others buy kale at a market where its good flavor has been lost in shipping and storage. Unfortunately, a few bad experiences cause many people to give up on this beautiful, nutritious vegetable. If this has happened to you, give kale another chance. Garden-fresh kale can hold its own against *any* leafy green.

Soil Preparation: Plant kale in compost-rich soil with a pH of 6.5 to 6.8. Kale is hardy, but like all brassicas it does best in humusy soil, rich in nitrogen and calcium. Kale also tends to grow slowly at first, so it needs ample nutrients and moisture for healthy development. "Toughness is also related to slow growth," warns Dr. Edward Borchers, director of the Truck and Ornamentals Research Station in Virginia Beach, Virginia, so keep it growing steadily.

How Much to Plant:
A rough guideline is seven plants per person.

Planting:
The only way to get really delicious kale is to plant it at the right time. Kale isn't merely cold-tolerant, it actually prefers cool temperatures. It will keep growing at 40°F, thrive at 60 to 65°, then become tough and bitter at 75°. Don't make the mistake of planting kale in the spring and harvesting leathery leaves in the summer. Sow seeds ½ inch deep, 10 to 12 weeks before the first fall frost. Look for germination in five to ten days at a soil temperature of 68 to 75°F.

Planting kale so it matures in cool weather will ensure tender leaves, but cold makes it supersweet. Kale needs a sharp frost to change its starches into sugars. A few nights at 28°F or below will transform kale's flavor dramatically. And getting kale through the winter, eating it even as the snow piles up around it, isn't difficult. Kale is able to survive temperatures down to 10° below zero.

Grow kale in a raised bed. Traditional rows—18 to 24 inches apart—take up too much space. A 4-by-25-foot bed (100 square feet) of kale can yield 100 pounds of leaves, or 40 to 50 pints for freezing. You'd need 50 feet of row (200 square feet) for the same size harvest.

Kale is rated as fast-maturing in most catalogs, but the kale you plant 60 days before your first fall frost will probably be disappointingly small. Give it 90 days, at least, if you want big plants that will sustain pickings for weeks after frost. Remember, it grows well in heat—just don't pick it then. Unused seed is good for five years.

Handling Seedlings:
While most garden books say to seed kale directly, it's not difficult to grow seedlings. Summer is a busy time and gardeners are often rushed, unable to prepare the ground for a late crop. Growing kale as transplants allows the gardener to put them in as time permits. Seedlings can also be used as succession crops, placing them near tomatoes, summer squash, and corn. When these plants are killed by the first freeze, kale will take over the area.

Growing Guidelines:
Thin seedlings in conventional rows to stand 12 to 15 inches apart. Kale prefers damp, not soggy soil; keep well watered in dry weather. When plants are 4 to 5 inches tall, side-dress with nitrogen-rich fertilizer such as rotted manure or bloodmeal, or water with manure tea. Apply mulch once plants are well established. Kale is a very low-maintenance crop, requiring scant attention after sowing or transplanting.

Harvesting and Storing:
Even in cold-climate areas, kale can give you food for a good six weeks after frost has stopped the tomatoes and squash. Where winters are mild, you can pick it all winter. There are two ways to harvest kale. The commercial practice is to harvest the entire plant. Unless your plants are small and all tender, pluck leaves instead. The tougher leaves will not be tenderized by frost, only sweetened, so let them stay on the plant and harvest only those that have matured recently. Choose leaves from the middle of the stem. Let the young ones at

the top keep growing, fueled by the older leaves low on the stem. When freezeout threatens in the North, pick it all. If your kale winters over, plan on eating fresh leaves in the early spring. Don't eat wintered-over kale once the weather warms up.

Kale is delicious fresh as a pungent, hearty salad ingredient. But most kale-lovers agree that it's best when picked fresh and steamed lightly, served with a sprinkle of lemon juice or a pat of butter. Steamed kale is dark green, tender, sweet, and juicy, without the strong smell of cooked cabbage.

Pests and Diseases: Kale's worst insect pest is the flea beetle, which attacks the tender, slow-maturing seedlings. There are black and striped flea beetles, but their effect is similar—BB-sized holes in the leaves which, if extensive, can kill the plants. Covering the beds with Reemay and burying its edges in soil will keep the beetles away from your plants. It may be left on until harvest or removed once the plants are growing vigorously.

Cabbage moths also attack kale. *Bacillus thuringiensis* (Bt), a bacterial spray that kills only caterpillars, is effective against these moth larvae. Thoroughly wetting extremely crinkled kale leaves is a challenge. To make it easier, add a bit of detergent to the Bt solution and spray both sides of the leaves.

Cabbage aphids and, in the South, turnip aphids (also called "false cabbage aphids") may also bother kale. These pale-green specks with black heads cluster on the undersides of leaves. Wash them off with a fine, powerful spray of water. Some gardeners have controlled aphids by mulching plants with cut mint or by interplanting with mint. A dusting of ground limestone discourages aphids, while a sprinkling of diatomaceous earth

kills them. Aphid eggs overwinter on old brassicas, so cleaning up your garden in fall will help limit the next generation.

Diseases don't pose severe problems for kale, though it's subject to the same afflictions as other brassicas. Clubroot, a slime mold that survives seven years in the soil—particularly if it's acidic—may create problems for brassicas in the cool Northeast and Canada. But given good garden management, you're unlikely to have serious disease problems. The best disease control is rotation: never plant brassicas in the same place two years running. (A three-year rotation is best, but may be difficult in small gardens.)

Nutritional Value: Kale is rich in vitamin A, vitamin C, and calcium.

Choosing Varieties: Seed houses offer about 16 varieties of kale, though most of these fall into two major categories: the Scotch kales—dwarf green and dwarf blue curled—and Siberian kale. The Scotch types range from yellow-green to blue-green in color, with extremely curled leaves. They grow 12 to 14 inches tall, but remain compact. According to Dr. Borchers, plant breeders originally selected strains with extremely curled leaves because these would spring back after being packed for shipping. They also bred for slow bolting so spring harvesting could be extended before plants went to seed.

The VATES strain of dwarf blue curled kale was developed at the Virginia Truck and Ornamentals Research Station in 1950, and is considered an improvement over the older dwarf Scotch type. VATES is hardy, stands about 15 inches tall, and produces blue-green, finely curled leaves that may spread 2 feet wide.

KALE

Variety	Description	Sources*
Blue Curled Scotch	65 days; compact, low-growing to 12" tall; blue-green color; finely curled leaves	24
Blue Knight	45–55 days; earlier, stronger, uniform; deep blue, firm leaves; holds well after cutting; spring or fall harvest	37
Blue Siberian	65 days; hardy and vigorous; coarse, frilled leaves; 16" tall, 36" wide; a favorite in warm-climate areas	38
Chinese Kale	65 days; cut-and-come-again variety; harvest like broccoli; survives temperatures as low as 20°F; low nitrogen needs	21
Dwarf Siberian	65 days; thick head; frilled, gray-green leaves to 16" tall; withstands cold temperatures well	14
Ornamental Flowering Kale	80–90 days; plants to 15" tall; combinations of green, white, and purple; turns green when cooked	WA
Siberian Kale	60–65 days; short plants can spread to 36" or more; smooth, frilled, gray-green leaves	WA
Vates varieties	55 days; compact, low-growing; blue-green, curled leaves; withstands sub-freezing temperatures	38

*Listings correspond to seed companies listed under Sources of Seeds at the back of the book.

Siberian kale, a different species from dwarf kale, is more closely related to rutabagas. It has smoother, frilled gray-green leaves, grows 12 to 15 inches tall, and may spread laterally 3 feet or more. Cultural requirements for dwarf and Siberian kales are the same, though the flavors differ.

There is also an edible ornamental kale, which is beautiful in the garden and can even be used as a "cut flower." This kale forms tight rosettes of purplish, pink, yellow, or red leaves. Ornamental kale has a longer growing season than the other kales—80 to 90 days (dwarf and Siberian mature in 55 to 65 days). Plant it in spring to enjoy its color all season. It's especially striking as a border around vegetable beds.

KOHLRABI
Brassica oleracea,
Gongylodes Group

Kohlrabi has been described as a "turnip growing on a cabbage root." Indeed, the edible bulb (actually a swollen stem) of this unusual-looking

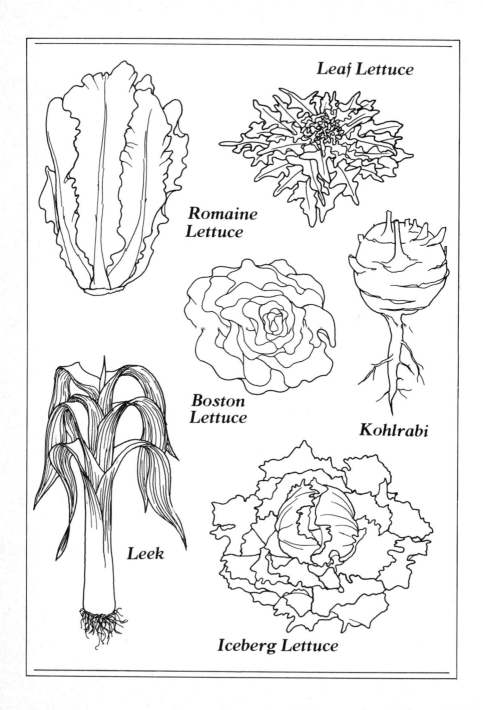

Leaf Lettuce

Romaine
Lettuce

Boston
Lettuce

Kohlrabi

Leek

Iceberg Lettuce

plant does resemble a turnip, but it has a delicate cabbagelike taste. True kohlrabi aficionados swear that it is the best-tasting member of the cabbage family.

Although the young tops of the plant are sometimes eaten as a steamed green, it is the white, green, or purple bulb that is the main attraction. It is often steamed with the skin on and eaten as a hot vegetable, or cooled for use in salads. Older bulbs should be peeled to remove the fibrous skin before eating. Sliced thinly or grated, the bulbs may also be used raw in salads.

Although kohlrabi is not difficult to grow, many gardeners fail, either because they do not give the plants sufficient nutrients and moisture to make quick, tender growth, or because they harvest the bulbs too late, after they have become woody and bitter.

Kohlrabi may be grown in gardens in any region that can offer a growing season of at least 80 days. It is a hardy cool-season crop which grows best in early spring or fall when the mild days and cool nights enhance its development. The average temperatures for best growth are 60 to 65°F. In warm regions, kohlrabi should be grown as a fall and winter crop. In an area where the growing days number between 120 and 140, two or three successive plantings may be made during the season.

Soil Preparation:
Kohlrabi grows well in any medium- to light-textured soil with an ample supply of organic matter and good water-holding capacity. Remove any rocks and other obstructions that may stunt the plants' growth, and work plenty of aged compost into the soil to a depth of 8 inches before sowing seeds. Also work in potassium-rich material like wood ashes or greensand. Kohl-

rabi tolerates soil with a pH from 6.0 to 7.0.

How Much to Plant:
A rough guideline is eight plants per person.

Planting:
Seeds of this crop can be sown directly into the garden four to six weeks before the frost-free date. If you're using transplants, plant them every 9 inches in conventional rows spaced 18 inches apart. In raised beds, space seedlings 9 inches apart.

For conventional-row plantings, sow ten seeds to each foot of row, burying them 1/4 inch deep, and space the rows as directed for transplants. Use the raised-bed spacing given above. For an especially fine-flavored and tender harvest, sow seeds about ten weeks before the first expected frost so that the bulb reaches edible size during the first cool days of autumn and experiences a few light frosts. Unused seed is good for five years.

Handling Seedlings:
In very short-season areas, plants may be started indoors six to eight weeks before being transplanted into the garden, which can be done from five weeks before to two weeks after the frost-free date.

Growing Guidelines:
Once seedlings have reached 4 or 5 inches tall, thin to stand 9 inches apart in the row. Keep kohlrabi well watered and mulch to conserve soil moisture. Tender, good-quality kohlrabi must be grown quickly, which calls for constant moisture and adequate nutrients. Deep cultivation is very likely to injure the shallow lateral roots. Avoid disturbing roots of young plants in any way, as they are very sensitive.

KOHLRABI

Variety	Description	Sources*
Early Purple Vienna	60–70 days; bulbs have purple skin, greenish white flesh; best variety for late summer, fall crops	33
Early White Vienna	60–65 days; smooth green skin covers creamy white flesh; good for freezing	38

*Listings correspond to seed companies listed under Sources of Seeds at the back of the book.

Harvesting and Storing: Kohlrabi must be harvested while the bulbs are immature, as small as 1½ inches in diameter and no larger than 2 inches. To harvest, slice through the stem an inch below the bulb. With the leaves removed, the bulbs will keep for several weeks in a refrigerator, and they may be stored for longer periods in a cool (32 to 40° F) and moist root cellar. Kohlrabi may also be diced, blanched, and frozen for later use, and can be substituted wherever turnips are called for.

Pests and Diseases: Kohlrabi is susceptible to the same pests and diseases that affect cabbage (see Cabbage). Harlequin bugs and imported cabbageworms can be especially bothersome.

Nutritional Value: Kohlrabi is a good source of vitamins A, C, and some of the B complex, plus calcium, phosphorus, and iron.

LEEKS
Allium ampeloprasum,
Porrum Group

Leeks offer big yields if the variety is chosen and cultivated with care. They have a long harvest season and provide fresh eating in the winter.

The part of the leek we eat is a false stem. Tightly layered, the bottom portions of its leaves form a tall, cylindrical sheaf, like the pages of a rolled-up newspaper. How much of the plant is edible depends partly on who cooks it, but mainly on who grows it. For leek and potato soup, the frugal French chef chops well beyond the stem. Some gardeners substitute tender bits of leaf for chopped chives. However, most of the edible portion is in the stem, and with proper care a gardener can double its length.

Soil Preparation: Leeks grow best in soils with a pH range of 6.0 to 7.0. Be sure the leek plot has a reserve of compost, well-rotted manure, or other organic matter that will last the season. A deep, well-aerated soil is important, too, because leeks need lots of water in the summer. Keep the nursery and garden plots free of weeds.

How Much to Plant: A rough guideline is eight to ten plants per person.

Planting: The shiny black leek seed is small and tough, germinating in two to three weeks in cool conditions."It's best to have the soil about 65 to 70°F by day and 10 degrees cooler by night," says John Gale, president of Stokes Seeds in St. Catherines, Ontario, Canada. "Most gardeners grow seedlings too hot." Wait until a week or two before the last spring frost to sow seed in the outdoor nursery. In areas with mild winters—the kind that don't kill broccoli—sow leeks in midsummer. Since the seed doesn't like hot soil, it helps to get it started indoors or in a shady nursery and then sow it deeper than usual.

Sowing leeks directly in the garden is probably more work than setting out well-started seedlings, given the weeding and mulching necessary in the garden. And it wastes space. In the nursery, the seedlings grow 1½ inches apart in rows 3 inches apart. There's room for 30 plants in one square foot of soil. In the garden, you have to space the plants 6 inches apart in the row, and to have room for hilling you can't squeeze the rows much closer than 18 inches. The same 30 plants take ten times the room they did in the nursery.

In Holland, leeks are as commonplace as onions. The Dutch use their fields efficiently and encourage leeks to grow as big as possible by deep transplanting. From midwinter until spring, Dutch growers sow seed, first in soil blocks kept in heated greenhouses, later in cold frames, and finally outdoors in nursery beds. When the seedlings are 8 to 12 inches tall and about twice as thick as a pencil, the growers lift them with a spade or fork, pull the plants free by their leaves, and take them to the fields. A leek has tough roots, and even treated this way it suffers less transplant shock than

Trench-planted leeks.

many vegetables. Of course, it's valuable to have light soil—it's no good pulling seedlings in heavy clay. When the leeks reach transplanting size, they are as much as three months old. It's a lengthy stay in the nursery, but the leek is a long-season crop, needing 120 to 150 days from sowing to harvest. Unused seed is good for one to three years.

Handling Seedlings: Use an oversized dibble to make holes 1½ inches in diameter and 6 inches deep. Then drop in a seedling and give it water, but don't pack dirt tightly around it. The tip of the plant should be only a few inches aboveground. Sheltered by earth, the plant readily roots. Then it stretches up for sun and soon the crown—the point on the stem where the leaves unclasp and spread apart—is above the soil. On some varieties the stem lengthens no farther. GIANT MUSSELBURGH, for example, makes a 5-inch-tall stem. But other varieties have the potential to grow taller—ALASKA to 8 inches, and KING RICHARD up to a foot.

Growing Guidelines: Give the plants a drink of manure tea or fish emulsion from time to time to satisfy their need for nitrogen. Hill soil around young plants, forcing the crown higher as long as it responds. Be careful not to cover the crown, or you'll have grit in the stem. This treatment elongates the stem—the edible part of the leek. Rob Johnston, Jr. of Johnny's Selected Seeds, in Albion, Maine, has grown the same variety of leek with and without hilling. "I haven't measured," he says, "but the difference is a least 50 percent."

Though it's often said that leeks are earthed up to blanch their stems, the blanching is incidental. Pale leeks are no tastier or milder than green ones. Some gardeners space the plants as close as 6 inches in all directions, leaving no room for hilling, but the leeks taste fine. (And what they lack in size, they make up in numbers.)

Rodale horticulturist Rudy Keller blanches his leeks by mulching them, but mulch does much more. "I hate to weed," he says, "and since leeks are such a long-season crop, I'd have to be in there cultivating all the time if I didn't mulch." Leeks are also a thirsty crop, and mulch keeps the soil moist between waterings. But its biggest advantage is that it keeps leeks clean by preventing dirt from splattering into the crowns during rainstorms or watering.

An early crop may suffer from heat during summer. The young plants of a late crop use water more slowly and are less susceptible to heat stress. Consider growing only a late crop in areas of high midsummer temperatures.

Harvesting and Storing: At harvest, as you struggle to unearth the plants, you'll see why the leek is a greedy feeder—its root system is rampant. One researcher found that four-month-old plants, still growing vigorously, had 50 to 100 or more main roots spreading as far as 21 inches and as deep as 2 feet.

For the biennial leek, "mature" is a relative term. The seed packet may say your plants will mature in 90 days, but if you leave them in the garden, they make significantly more growth, as long as they stay healthy—and as long as the weather holds.

As winter nears, give the late crop a foot-deep mulch of straw or leaves to insulate the soil and the stems. With the soil safe from freezing, you can dig leeks at will. The late varieties are rewardingly big. ALASKA and GIANT MUSSELBURGH have at least twice the volume of the early variety TITAN.

If you don't care for winter harvesting, dig up the crop in late fall, taking care to save some roots. Then heel in the plants in a cold frame. Pack them close together to save space. Standing on their roots, the leeks will last for months. Or pack the plants in a handy container with something to keep them moist—sand, soil, sawdust, vermiculite—and store them in a cool spot. You can get two dozen leeks in a 5-gallon pail. Trim the leaves so you can cover the leeks and they'll keep six weeks. Wrapped in plastic bags and put in the refrigerator, leeks keep about a month.

The leek goes to seed in its second year. Plants that overwinter start growing again before the soil is workable in early spring and stay edible until about mid-spring, when they send up a towering stalk topped with a globe of flowers. If you cut off the stalk when it appears and feed the leeks, they stay edible longer.

Pests and Diseases: Leeks have the same troubles as onions, and the

LEEKS

Variety	Description	Sources*
Alaska	105–150 days; thick white stems to 8"; hardy; keeps for months in ground; will not bolt; disease resistant	33
American Flag	120–155 days; hardy plants to 18"; well-blanched stalks; good variety for home gardeners	38
Giant Musselburgh	90–150 days; enormous stems; extremely hardy; tender, with mild flavor; good overwintered	WA
King Richard	75 days; fast-growing; white stems grow to 12" in good soil; upright leaves; susceptible to frost; mild flavor	15
London Flag	130–145 days; early and productive; long, broad stems; large green leaves; sensitive to cold	22
Titan	70 days; vigorous and extra long; for early summer or summer planting only—not winter hardy	33

*Listings correspond to seed companies listed under Sources of Seeds at the back of the book.

worst pest, the onion thrips, shows up in summer. Minute insects that feed on plant juices, thrips work their way into the crown and are hard to spot unless you part the leaves. On young plants, a daily spraying with the hose may control them. For mature plants, simply harvest the crop.

Nutritional Value: Leeks contain an ample amount of vitamins A, C, and E.

Choosing Varieties: Even though leeks are a long-season crop, some culti-vars mature earlier than others. But the fast growers tend to be the least hardy. For the early crop, sown in mid- to late winter in a cold frame and transplanted when the soil is first workable, use fast-growing varieties like KING RICHARD or TITAN, which are ready for harvest 70 to 75 days from transplanting. They tend to have less dry matter, lighter color, and taller stems than the slower varieties.

Sow varieties like ALASKA and GIANT MUSSELBURGH, which take as much as a month longer to mature, in early spring for harvest in fall and winter. Protected by mulch or snow, they will survive temperatures below zero and can yield fresh eating until spring.

LETTUCE
Lactuca sativa

With lettuce, the challenge is having a steady supply throughout the season. As a spring crop, it's easy. Lettuce grows quickly, but inevitably turns bitter soon after the plant reaches full size. Unless you make successive sowings, your lettuce harvest will last only a week or two. Keeping the July and August crops from turning bitter and bolting is even more work.

Fortunately, many lettuce varieties grow fast and well in cool weather, which means harvest follows soon after planting. And lettuce is a light feeder, so it is the perfect vegetable for interplanting, especially since you should replant it regularly and frequently through the season. These characteristics allow you to make good use of the fertile soil between plants like broccoli or tomatoes by planting it with individual lettuces. Spot lettuce here and there throughout the garden, instead of reserving a special place for one big planting, to conserve valuable garden space.

Soil Preparation: Lettuce grows well in a wide range of soils, preferring a pH between 5.8 and 6.8. Ground that grows good beets, peas, and lima beans should have the right pH for lettuce. Because of its limited root system, lettuce needs fertile ground even though it does not take much from the soil. If you are growing it as an interplant and the soil has been well fertilized for the main crop, the lettuce should do fine. Otherwise, work in 1½ pounds of fresh manure per square foot at least six weeks before planting. For an early spring crop, this is best done in the fall.

How Much to Plant: A rough guideline is seven plants of head lettuce and 15 to 20 plants of leaf lettuce per person.

Planting: If you have lots of space, you may prefer to direct-seed lettuce into the garden. Wait until the soil temperature reaches 50°F, and seedlings will emerge fast. Plant two or three seeds at the desired spacing, and thin each clump to one plant after the first true leaf stops expanding, a week or so after emergence. Lettuces should be spaced 6 to 12 inches from each other if planted in a bed, depending on the mature size of the variety.

Lettuce seed, especially fresh lettuce seed, does not germinate easily in hot weather. Very fresh lettuce seed has failed to germinate in tests at 68°F, near the ideal temperature. To break dormancy in hot weather, put the seeds in the folds of a moist paper towel and store them in the refrigerator (about 40°F) for three to five days. Germination will begin in the fridge, but the seedlings won't break out of the seed coat. Seeds treated this way have sprouted in 90°F soil. If the seed coat is still intact, you can even use these seeds in a seed planter. Unused seed is good for five years.

Handling Seedlings: To make the most of lettuce's strengths, start very early in spring. Lettuce will grow vigorously when it's cool. Ideal growth occurs when days are 65 to 75°F. Forty- to 45-degree nights don't slow the plant a bit. Seedlings that have been hardened properly and are protected at night can survive 20°F temperatures. You can set out young lettuce plants as soon as the average nightly lows approach 40°F. In cold-winter areas, that will be about the time the ground finally thaws deep enough to till.

Plant two or three seeds in 1- to 2-inch individual containers five to seven weeks before that time. Use a mixture of half compost and half vermiculite. The seeds germinate in two to four days if you keep them at 60 to 75°F. As soon as the seedlings break ground, put them outdoors in a cold frame because they need intense light. Bring them in at night. Thin them to one plant per container right away, and feed them with a weak solution of fish emulsion or manure tea once a week.

A week or so before transplanting them, begin the hardening-off process. Let the young plants dry to the early stages of wilting before giving water. Don't feed them. Leave them out in the cold frame at night and leave the cold frame completely uncovered during the day.

When you transplant, be sure to set the plant no deeper than it was planted in the pot. Soil heaped around the base of the plant can cause lettuce to rot. Be sure to straighten the taproot in the planting hole if the soil is knocked loose from the roots. If cutworms are a threat in your area, make collars with 1½-inch strips of newspaper.

Especially in small gardens, you can continue to raise successive crops of lettuce as individual plants in small containers. Container growing gives you a lot of control and conserves valuable garden space. It's also the best way to get good results in hot weather, since you can keep the seedlings out of the intense heat. When seedlings begin to need more than one watering a day, it's time to transplant them.

Growing Guidelines:

When the soil is cool in early spring and fall, microbial activity—which feeds the roots of

plants—is very slow. Your lettuce may benefit from a side-dressing of manure tea or fish emulsion, especially during the last four weeks of growth. The lettuce will grow fast, which makes the leaves large, yet tender and succulent—the ideal qualities for good eating.

Ample moisture is also essential for producing lettuce of the highest quality. Lettuce needs a steady supply of moisture for uninterrupted growth. It should get the equivalent of at least 1 inch of rain a week. One deep watering is better than several quick, shallow applications. Mulching lettuce is always a good idea, except on the Pacific Coast where slugs and snails use it to hide in, because it keeps the roots cool and the soil moist.

Lettuce turns bitter right before it starts to go to seed. Even before the plant begins to elongate and form a tiny cluster of flower buds, you can see the first subtle signs. The leaves lose their gleam and look slightly dull. If a torn leaf exudes a milky sap instead of the clear juice of lettuce in its prime, the plant is too far gone and nothing can make it taste right again. The primary trigger for the bitter flowering stage of growth is high temperatures for an extended period. For midsummer crops, you can delay the onset of bitterness either by planting lettuce in a very shady spot or by rigging an awning of shade cloth, laths, or burlap over your lettuce row.

Keys to Top Yields:

There's more than one way to stagger your lettuce crops through the season. The simplest is a new planting every two weeks from spring through late summer. You need to produce only 6 to 12 plants at each sowing, so a packet of 500 seeds will easily get you through one season. If you are growing only one variety, a loose-leaf lettuce is your best choice because it is the most resistant to both heat and cold. OAKLEAF types are the most heat-resistant of all.

A better way is to pick two or more varieties that mature at least a week to ten days apart. This method requires that you label the seedling trays and do a little more planning, but it streamlines the work.

If you choose one or two varieties from each lettuce type, you could get two months of harvest from one planting. For example, one sowing of BLACK–SEEDED SIMPSON, OAKLEAF, and BUTTERCRUNCH would give a month's worth of lettuce. Sow seed of all three once a month for steady harvests through the season.

Harvesting and Storing: Crisphead, romaine (cos), and butterhead lettuce are harvested when heads are firm and mature. Cut off the whole top at the root crown. For loose-leaf varieties, cut the outer leaves one by one when large enough to be of use, and allow the inner leaves to develop. All lettuces are at their best when picked as needed and used at once. If the harvest is more than can be used immediately, refrigerate it. Crisphead lettuce can be stored up to three weeks; romaine and looseleaf lettuces can be stored up to two weeks without losing quality; butterhead lettuce, which is the most fragile, shows signs of deterioration after only a few days of refrigeration.

Pests and Diseases: Cutworms and flea beetles are the bane of young plants. Aphids, cabbage loopers, leafminers, slugs, and snails all attack lettuce. For controls, see Broccoli, Cabbage, Celery, and Kale.

LETTUCE

Variety	Description	Sources*
Bibb	60–75 days; butterhead; medium green, soft leaves; bolts in hot weather	WA
Black-Seeded Simpson	40–65 days; looseleaf; quick growing; dependable; light green, frilly leaves; stands heat and drought well	WA
Boston	60–75 days; butterhead; medium green leaves with rippled edges; needs cooler weather to head up well	WA
Buttercrunch	75 days; butterhead; dense, heavy heads with dark green, soft leaves; larger and more heat resistant than Bibb; AAS	WA
Butterking	70–85 days; large butterhead; vigorous; light green, tender leaves; slow to bolt; excellent for Midwest, hot areas; AAS	WA
Citation	75 days; butterhead; good yields; thick, smooth, dark green leaves; excellent quality and flavor	35

LETTUCE—*Continued*

Variety	Description	Sources*
Green Ice	45 days; glossy, dark green savoyed leaves with wavy, fringed margin; slow to bolt	24
Green Wave	45 days; loosehead; large, long, deep green, frilled leaves; vigorous; disease and heat resistant	38
Iceberg	50-85 days; head lettuce; compact, medium-large heads; crisp hearts; tipburn and bolt resistant; good choice for the Northeast	WA
Oakleaf	50 days; looseleaf; compact plant; oakleaf-shaped leaves; suited to early summer sowing; resists heat; long standing	WA
Parris Island	75 days; romaine; dark green, upright leaves to 10"; uniform and vigorous; mild flavor	33
Prizehead	45–55 days; looseleaf; upright, broad, deeply curled leaves; thick midribs; never bitter; medium-slow to bolt	WA
Red Sails	48 days; looseleaf; deep bronze leaves surround nice center head; attractive as well as nutritious; AAS	WA
Ruby	53 days; looseleaf; bright green, frilly, savoyed leaves shaded with intense red; heat resistant; slow to bolt; AAS	WA
Salad Bowl	45 days; looseleaf; light green, deeply lobed leaves; slow to bolt; good for early summer sowing; AAS	WA
Slobolt	45 days; looseleaf; bright green, crumpled leaves; resists bolting in summer; good for early summer sowing	33
Summer Bibb	62 days; butterhead; medium green, soft leaves; extremely heat resistant	19

*Listings correspond to seed companies listed under Sources of Seeds at the back of the book.

Nutritional Value: Romaine and looseleaf lettuce are high in vitamin A, have respectable levels of the B vitamins, and are also sources of vitamin C and calcium.

Choosing Varieties: There are four distinct kinds of lettuce. Leaf lettuce is the hardiest and quickest to mature, in 40 to 50 days. Butterhead types, like BIBB and BOSTON, form loose heads and take longer to mature, roughly 60 to 75 days. Romaine, or cos, takes longer still, about 75 to 85 days. It is more heat-tolerant than true head lettuce. Head lettuce, sometimes called crisphead lettuce, is the slowest to mature, requiring 85 to 95 days. It is also the hardest to grow because it is least tolerant of heat and most likely to be caught in a heat wave due to its long time to maturity, at least on the East Coast. West Coast gardeners have a long, cool winter suited to crisphead types.

MELONS
Cucumis melo

Have you ever eaten a cantaloupe? Probably not unless you've been to Europe or have grown CHARANTAIS. You've been eating muskmelons and calling them cantaloupes, like most Americans.

Muskmelons have netting on the skin and shallow vein tracks (the pumpkinlike ribbed look). The flesh ranges from salmon to green, and is fragrant, or musky. The fruit always slips from the vine when ripe. True cantaloupes' vein tracks are often dark and distinct. The skin is rough and scaly with flecks of corky tissue. The flesh is fragrant and orange. The fruit does not separate from the vine when ripe.

Honeydews, casabas, and crenshaws are sometimes called winter melons because they ripen late in the season and also will keep a month or so if stored properly. They lack a powerful aroma, and the fruits are larger and more oval than muskmelons and cantaloupes. The skin can be smooth or wrinkled, but it is always waxen, not corky. The vines grow large and require a long growing season.

Combined with their low disease tolerance, this makes the winter-melon varieties difficult to grow in most places.

Well-grown muskmelons are loaded with sugar. Musky or fragrant varieties will be perfect at a sugar content of 10 percent. A percentage point or two lower and they will seem flavorless. A milder muskmelon or a honeydew won't taste right with sugar under 13 percent. When the plant is healthy, the days bright, and the nights cool, melons can reach 15 percent sucrose. The sugar is the very last thing that the vine puts into its fruit, building up until the moment the melon separates from the stem. A perfect vine-ripened melon will be much sweeter than one picked "green" for shipping. That is why homegrown muskmelons are the very best you can eat.

Soil Preparation: Muskmelons grow well in a wide range of soils, but they do best in soils that are loose and hold a lot of moisture. While about 80 percent of the root system is concentrated in the top 2 to 10 inches of soil, some of the roots will go 4 to 5 feet deep if they can. The plants do very poorly on compacted soils or soils that don't drain well. Muskmelons require a very tight pH range, between 6.0 and 6.8, and don't tolerate acidity. If the ground can produce good crops of beets, peas, spinach, broccoli, or onions, chances are good the pH is right for muskmelons.

For fertility, work a generous amount of manure into the soil at least two weeks prior to your transplanting date. Use 1 to 2 pounds of fresh cow, horse, or hog manure per square foot. The organic matter in the manure will also make the soil more porous and absorbent—exactly what melons like. Compost does the same thing. It will also help buffer excess soil acidity and provide longer-term fertility. Thoroughly dig or till these materials into the top 6 to 12 inches of soil.

How Much to Plant:

A rough guideline is 10 to 15 feet of row per person, yielding an average of 7 to 11 melons.

Planting:

Plant at least two kinds of melons with different ripening periods. Muskmelons tend to set the maximum number of fruits that the leaves can support all at once. For direct-seeding in the garden, the recommended planting time is two weeks after the last frost date. That's when it's safe to transplant melon seedlings, too.

Traditionally, melons are grown in hills spaced 3 to 5 feet apart in long beds usually 5 feet wide. When direct-seeding a large crop, the hill method saves time in soil preparation and planting. Instead of tilling and manuring the entire area, you need only prepare hills by digging a bushel-basket-sized pit, working in manure, and filling it back in. Then you plant six to eight seeds per hill, and later thin to three or four plants, depending on the space you've allowed for each vine to spread.

That works, but in most gardens equidistant spacing in beds 4 or 5 feet wide gives better results. Plants grown in hills compete with each other more than plants in long, wide beds do. Equidistant spacings also shade out weeds faster when mulches aren't being used, and capture sunlight more efficiently.

Using two varieties that grow large vines, Mike Zahara, a vegetable crops specialist at the University of California, tried several spacings to see which gives the best yield. He found 18 inches between plants to be ideal. He also found that each plant needed to grow about 6 square feet of leaf area in order to produce sweet melons. An 18-by-18-inch spacing is much closer than usual, but each vine soon overlaps with its neighbors in all directions, eventually spanning a circle about 4 feet across. The ground is quickly covered. You'll get about one more melon per plant using a wider spacing, but the total yield will be less because there are fewer plants.

Once you've prepared good soil and chosen the best varieties, starting plants extra early is the most effective way to create larger, healthier vines by the time the diseases become active. Sometimes all the fruit may ripen before the plants are infected.

Muskmelon seed doesn't germinate well in soil below 80°F. The plant's roots spread quickly and deeply, so the soil should be thoroughly warmed. The vines grow best with daytime temperatures in the 80s, and they can perform well in temperatures over 100°F. Unused seed is good for up to five years.

Handling Seedlings:

If you live in a short-season area, give your melons a head start by growing transplants. But you can't hold muskmelons in pots long without interfering with growth. Plan on raising them in pots for only two weeks after they sprout. Add another three days for germination (at 80°F soil temperature), and you should be planting muskmelon seeds in the garden about 17 or 18 days after sowing in pots. If you are going to plant into black plastic in the garden, start the seeds a week earlier. Transplant covers give another week's lead.

Even though the seedlings won't be in pots long, use large pots so the roots are never restricted. Three- or 4-inch plastic or clay pots (peat pots may trap roots and dry too fast) are ideal. An inexpensive potting mix is two parts screened compost to one part vermiculite. Make this blend in 4-gallon batches. Each batch gets about a cup of bonemeal. Nearly every seed you plant will sprout, but start a few extras in case some seeds are bad.

Muskmelon seed germinates surprisingly well in dryish soil. Sow the seed about a half-inch deep. One watering should be all you need till the seed is up—don't overwater the pots. The seeds need heat. If it's sunny, you can get 80°F soil temperatures inside a cold frame quite easily in mid-spring. When the sun goes down, bring the pots indoors to keep their soil warm. If the days are cloudy, use bottom heat. After the seedlings emerge, they can stay in the cold frame around the clock unless frost threatens. The soil in the pots will warm rapidly once the sun is up. Feed the seedlings once a week with a weak solution of fish emulsion or manure tea. When the plants have two true leaves (or when the first roots show at the bottom of the pot), they are ready to go into the garden.

Growing Guidelines: Black plastic mulch keeps the soil 3 inches under the surface an average of 5 degrees warmer than unmulched ground—day and night, clear weather or cloudy, amounting to good growing weather a week earlier than normal. On a bright day, the soil will be around 10 degrees warmer than bare ground. After a night of losing heat, it will cool to within a couple of degrees of unmulched ground. On sunless days, the mulched ground won't accumulate any extra heat.

Clear plastic tunnels or row covers have much the same effect: a week's jump on the growing season over black plastic

alone. The clear plastic covers have slits that eliminate the need for venting on sunny days. Under the row covers on a bright 75°F day, the melon vines will be basking at around 88°F. On a cloudy day, there may be almost no temperature difference. At night there's no difference between inside the covers and outside, either, until the dew point is reached. When the plastic fogs up with condensation, the slitted covers can offer 3 to 4 degrees of protection from frost. Without slits, polyethylene tunnels give 5 to 7 degrees of frost protection.

Both of these techniques are useful for getting the first planting of muskmelons off to a good start on the disease season anywhere the temperature consistently drops below the ideal for starting melons—even in the South. They work best where it's sunny, and will do little to help you in cloudy weather. Plants can grow under the covers for up to six weeks, or until it's time to let bees in for pollination. If you can use only one of the techniques, the black plastic is the best choice. It's cheaper and easier to install, and it doesn't have to be removed until the season's over. Weed control without mulch under the clear covers would be cumbersome.

Watch for blossoms. Where the leaves join the stem along the main shoot and along the larger side shoots, the first flower buds form. These will all be male. The melon-producing flowers appear a week or so later, on the secondary side shoots and on any primary side shoots that are forming then. Ordinarily, many of these blossoms will set, but only a few melons will mature. The others will develop to hen's egg size, then shrivel as the vine reabsorbs most of the nutrients.

Muskmelon vines cannot be handled as casually as other plants. They are much more easily damaged then cucumbers, for example. As the vines approach the edges of the bed, gently turn them back toward the center. If you just flop them over, the leaves will have a tough time righting themselves. This peculiarity of muskmelons is another reason why mulch of some kind is so important—it eliminates the need for cultivation.

Keys to Top Yields: Muskmelons are one of the biggest gambles in gardening, but several techniques can help bring in a dependable crop of top-notch melons. Researchers have found that muskmelon transplants produced not only earlier but one-third more fruit than the same variety grown by direct seeding. Drs. Brent Loy and Otho Wells, plant scientists at the University of New Hampshire, have been studying the effects of transplanting, black plastic mulch, and clear plastic row covers on muskmelons in New Hampshire. Forcing the melons with these techniques often produces earlier yields, and always produces a yield increase, ordinarily 20 to 50 percent. In several seasons the advantage from black plastic mulch and clear row covers has been two to three times greater than that achieved by transplanting alone.

The point in starting early is to force the plants to grow rapidly from the moment you start them—using every trick to create tropical conditions. The leaf area of the plant at fruit set determines how many melons will develop. Big plants can carry more melons, and starting the plants early, providing perfect conditions for growth, makes big plants. But poor timing can cause all your efforts to backfire. If you start the plants so early that the soil is cool at transplanting, they'll just sit there until the soil

warms. The slowdown in the plant's rate of growth translates to smaller plants at flowering and fruit set, and thus, fewer melons.

The plants always need plenty of water, but especially as the fruit develops. Three Israeli scientists set up an experiment in which drip irrigation was used to keep a heavy, arid soil fully supplied with water during various growth stages of the plant. Providing high soil moisture during the seedling to flowering period, and during the flowering to 3-inch fruit period, had no effect on yield. But plants irrigated during the last period—that is, until ripening—produced 45 percent higher yields on the average over the four years of experimentation (because the fruits were bigger). Irrigation also stretched out the harvest. There was no effect on sugar content in this experiment. If you feed your plants with manure tea, do it around fruit set and again two weeks later.

Harvesting and Storing: Thirty-five to 45 days after pollination (depending on the variety), the first muskmelons will begin to ripen. You can usually smell a ripe melon before you see it. On many varieties the skin color begins to turn yellow, though a few stay greenish behind the netting. The best test for ripeness is to lift the fruit gently and look for a crack at the stem. Push the stem gently with your thumb. If it separates, the fruit is ripe. If the stem appears reluctant to separate, check again the next day. After the fruit separates (slips) from the vine the sugars actually begin to decline, so pick all melons promptly and refrigerate any you won't eat within a few hours. Melons will keep for about a week in a refrigerator. The ideal storage temperature is 45°F. Dip the melons into 135°F water for 30 seconds, and they won't mold. A good harvest will continue for ten days to two weeks per variety.

Pests and Diseases:

About flowering time the two worst pests, cucumber beetles and melon aphids, often show up. Cucumber beetles spread bacterial wilt disease when they feed. Bacteria multiply inside the plant's veins. After a while the veins clog, causing runners to wilt and eventually die. The beetles often gather on seedlings of late melon plantings and can destroy them within a few days. It is hard to control the beetles with rotenone or other botanic poisons, because more fly in to replace the ones you kill.

You can make traps for cucumber beetles out of thinnings of all sorts of cucurbits. It seems the beetles much prefer a pile of wilting, damaged leaves to fresh ones. Make neat stacks of five or six leaves each around the garden. The beetles will feed on and breed among them prodigiously. Carefully collect the traps in the cool of the morning and destroy the sleepy beetles.

Melon aphids not only feed heavily on the vines, they also spread cucumber mosaic, another serious disease. The first sign of melon aphids is leaves that are cupped downwards. Under the leaves you'll find a colony of small dark aphids. This insect is especially destructive where cotton plants can serve as an alternate host. Though many predatory insects devour aphids, they may still get out of hand; the best control is an insecticidal

MELONS

Variety	Description	Sources*
Big Daddy	88 days; muskmelon; large fruits to 8 pounds; thick, light orange flesh; good flavor and aroma	12
Burpee Early Hybrid Crenshaw	90 days; oval fruits to 14 pounds; pointed at stem; green skin; salmon pink flesh; skin yellow-green when ripe	5
Burpee Hybrid	82 days; muskmelon; vigorous; heavy netting; orange flesh	5
Bush Star	88 days; compact bush; oval fruits to 2 pounds; salmon flesh; powdery mildew resistant; excellent for small spaces	11, 37
Charantais	75–90 days; cantaloupe; very long vines; scaly skin; easily bruised; extremely fragrant when ripe; orange flesh	33
Crenshaw Casaba	110–125 days; smooth, pear-shaped fruits; thin, yellow-tan skin; salmon flesh; sweet; susceptible to powdery mildew	22

MELONS—*Continued*

Variety	Description	Sources*
Edisto	90 days; high in sugar; resistant to powdery and downy mildew; especially suited to the South	8
Golden Beauty Casaba	110–125 days; large, vigorous; needs cool weather before harvest; globular; white, sweet flesh; susceptible to mildew	27
Hale's Best	90 days; small, round fruits with heavy netting; salmon flesh; high quality; susceptible to mildew	8
Hale's Best Jumbo	88 days; large, round fruits with heavy netting; salmon-orange flesh	38
Harvest Queen	95 days; medium-sized, oval fruits with sparse netting; orange flesh; resistant to fusarium wilt	8
Hearts of Gold	85–90 days; small to medium fruits; green netted rind; orange flesh is sweet and juicy	38
Honeydew	110–125 days; heavy, round to oval melon with creamy white skin; no ribbing; sweet green flesh; will not slip stem	5
Honey Drip	90–110 days; Honeydew type; silvery, smooth skin; green, fragrant flesh; will not slip stem	24
Limelight	96 days; Honeydew type; large melons to 7½ pounds; thick, juicy, sweet flesh; fruits slip from vine when ripe	5
Persian	105–120 days; vigorous vine, but subject to mildew; large melon with dark green, netted skin; orange, sweet flesh	27
Rocky Sweet	80 days; vigorous, prolific vines; globe-shaped fruits to 4 pounds; thick, green, sweet flesh	16
Short 'N Sweet	70 days; compact, nonvining; melons have netted skin, orange flesh; good for small gardens	24
Sweet and Early	75 days; 6 to 8 fruits per plant; round to oval with corky netting; salmon flesh; resistant to mildew	39

*Listings correspond to seed companies listed under Sources of Seeds at the back of the book.

soap solution delivered in a forceful spray.

"Disease is the most common cause of blandness in melons," says Dr. Henry Munger, a horticulturist at Cornell University, "and many attack during the ripening period. As it ripens, the fruit makes a heavy demand on the plant for sugar. I think the plant becomes more susceptible because it is working hard then. What looks like an insignificant amount of powdery mildew to our eyes can result in flavorless melons."

Diseases tap into the sugar flow from the leaves to fuel their own growth and reproduction. There's less for the fruit, and the plant must burn more sugars to maintain health. Downy and powdery mildew also block light from the leaves, reducing sugar production. Eventually leaves or whole runners die. The quality of melons is more and more vulnerable in the last days of ripening.

Disease resistance and tolerance are the primary qualities to look for in any melon that fits into your frost-free season. Resistance means that the melon can ward off attack. Tolerance means the plant usually remains vigorous even after infection. There's a muskmelon that's at least tolerant to every common disease, and some are strongly resistant to several.

Nutritional Value: Muskmelons are rich in vitamin A. They also contain the B vitamins, vitamin C, iron, calcium, and phosphorus. Winter melons supply vitamins C and A.

OKRA
(Lady's finger)
Abelmoschus esculentus

Okra is one of the oldest cultivated food crops. The edible portion of the plant is the long, pointed seed pod, which is best picked when green and used as a vegetable dish, often rolled in corn-meal and fried, or added to soups, stews, casseroles, and curries. Okra is also a major ingredient of gumbo, a very popular Creole dish. The mucilaginous texture of the pods often comes as a surprise to first-time okra eaters, but it is valued as a thickener for gumbos, soups, stews, and catsup. An easy way to avoid releasing the mucilaginous material from the pods is to cook them with their caps on.

Okra is not difficult to grow, given the proper conditions. It is a good yielder in the garden, producing pods over a long period of time. Standard-sized plants grow to a height of 4 to 7 feet, and dwarf strains measure 2 to 4 feet tall. The red-and-yellow blossoms are very attractive, resembling ornamental hibiscus, and they add a bright spot of color to punctuate the predominant green of the garden.

Okra is a warm-weather crop, growing best when average temperatures are between 70 and 85°F. However, since it matures so quickly (first harvest is two months from seeding), it may be grown in any area that offers ten weeks of warm and sunny weather. The plants do poorly in cool, damp, or cloudy regions. Okra is very susceptible to frost damage.

Soil Preparation: Any soil that is well drained and rich in nutrients will support okra. The recommended pH range is 6.0 to 8.0. In the spring, after the last frost, till the soil to a depth of 8 inches and incorporate copious amounts of finished compost or well-rotted manure. If okra follows early peas, it will make good use of the nitrogen stored in the soil by the pea nodules.

How Much to Plant: A rough guideline is three to five plants per person.

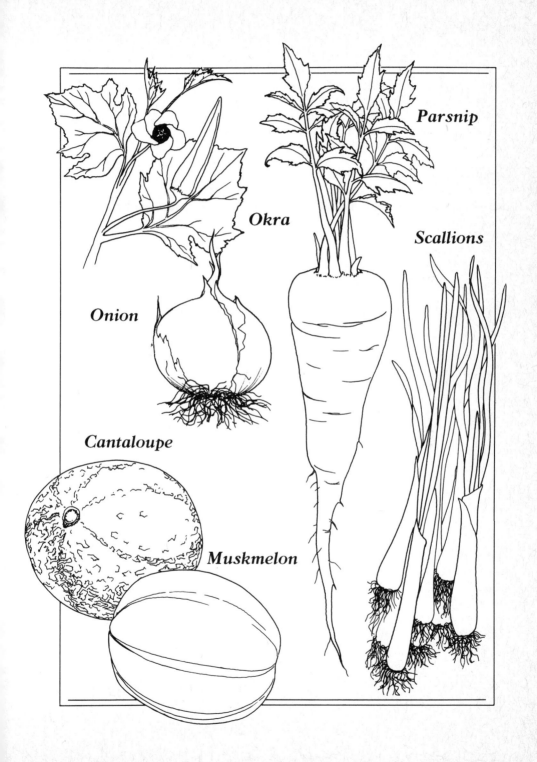

Okra

Parsnip

Scallions

Onion

Cantaloupe

Muskmelon

Planting: Okra is direct-seeded on the frost-free date only after the soil temperature has reached 60°F. Soak seed overnight to hasten germination, both indoors and out. Space conventional rows 48 to 72 inches apart for large varieties, 24 to 48 inches for dwarf varieties. Sow seed every 3 inches in rows. Growing bed spacing is 18 inches. Set seed ½ inch deep in heavy soils, 1 inch deep in lighter soils. Unused seed is good for five years.

Handling Seedlings: In very short-season regions, plants may be started indoors six to eight weeks before transplanting time, which is three to four weeks after the frost-free date. Use individual containers for transplants so roots are not disturbed. Set seedlings every 14 inches in rows for tall varieties, and every 10 inches for dwarf varieties.

Growing Guidelines: After the seedlings are 3 inches high, thin tall varieties to stand 14 inches apart in rows, or 10 inches for dwarf varieties. Okra is a heavy feeder and a quick grower, so give it nitrogen-rich supplementary feedings. Side-dress with manure or compost, or water with solutions of fish emulsion or manure tea every three weeks.

Plants should be mulched to a depth of 4 inches. If compost is put on top of a hay mulch, the compost will act as a long-lasting top-dressing, and no nutrient-rich watering or side-dressing is needed. If no mulch is used, keep the soil loose by frequent cultivation. Water plants only if the soil becomes very dry.

OKRA

Variety	Description	Sources*
Annie Oakley	50 days; hybrid; spineless; productive; long, slender pods	14
Blondy	48 days; dwarf "white" variety; productive; plants to 3' high, 2 ' wide; pods best when 3" long; good in small areas	14
Clemson Spineless	55–60 days; popular variety; plants to 5' tall; pods to 9" long; recommended for short-season, hot-summer areas; AAS	38
Dwarf Green Long Pod	50 days; dwarf plants to 2½'; pods are 7" long; early, high yielder	14
Emerald Green Velvet	55 days; prolific yields; plants to 7' tall; pods to 9" long; widely adaptable, but recommended for short-season areas	14

*Listings correspond to seed companies listed under Sources of Seeds at the back of the book.

To contain rampant growth, prune a few branches and leaves below each pod you have harvested.

Harvesting and Storing: Pods begin to form in about two months. For use as a green vegetable, pick them when they are no more than 2 or 3 inches long and still soft. They will reach this stage in only five days after the flowers fade. If pods are allowed to grow much longer, they become fibrous and unfit for green use, and if they are allowed to mature on the plant, no more young pods will be produced. For a continuous harvest up until frost, pick pods at least every third day. Cut the pods from the branches rather than tug at them to avoid disturbing the roots.

Some people are quite sensitive to contact with okra plants. To avoid the burning itch, wear a long-sleeved shirt and gloves. Waiting until the dew has dried completely can also make picking painless.

Okra is best when used immediately after harvesting. If fresh pods will be held for more than a day before being used, sprinkle them lightly with water and spread in a single layer in a cool place. When stored in a closed container, fresh pods tend to generate heat.

Pests and Diseases: Okra may be attacked by corn earworms, green stinkbugs, and imported cabbageworms. In hot-summer regions, Southern blight may be a problem. See Cabbage and Corn for insect controls.

Nutritional Value: Okra is a good source of calcium and fiber, and also offers some vitamin A.

ONIONS AND SCALLIONS
Allium cepa

Whether you want to grow onions all year or just one perfect crop, you must first choose the right growing method. Most home gardeners grow onions from dry sets because success is virtually assured. Come harvest, there are baskets of papery-skinned beauties. However, onions grown from sets sometimes bolt before harvest, making the bulbs tough and subject to rot. Additionally, they are thick-necked and can be hard to cure sufficiently to last through storage without going bad.

Other gardeners grow their onions from seed sown right in the garden. One immediate advantage of this method is the wide variety of seeds available. Also, these onions store better than those grown from sets. But the crop must be planted quite early to get onions of a good size, so it is subject to some tough weather and early losses.

It is also possible to grow onions from transplants—seedlings either bought at the garden center or started indoors. Many gardeners find that transplants offer the best of both worlds. You can start seeds in January, indoors or in a cold frame, and put fair-sized plants outdoors by April. The only tricky part of this process is hardening-off the transplants so they survive those first few days outside.

Soil Preparation: Regardless of which technique you choose, to achieve success you need good, well-drained soil with a pH of 6.0 to 6.5. If your soil is too acidic, the pH can be raised with an application of dolomite. Light soil is preferable to heavy. Clay soils can constrict the growth of onion bulbs and retain excessive amounts of water. Therefore, if your soil is heavy, lighten and fertilize it with humus and manure. Sandy soil can produce solid, heavy onions, provided it has been richly fertilized. A heavy application of fresh, raw manure can be used if it is spread on the land in the fall for spring planting. However, an application of well-rotted manure, uniformly applied and plowed into the soil, is the best treatment.

How Much to Plant:
A rough guideline is 40 plants per person.

Planting:
Select your sets early, while they are firm and still dormant. Divide them into two groups, those larger than a dime and those smaller. Use the smaller bulbs, because these will give you magnificent onions at harvest. The larger set bulbs are not as good as the small ones because they are at a later stage of maturity and therefore likely to bolt (form a flower stem). But you can plant them for green onions. By pulling them young, you'll harvest them before they have a chance to bolt.

Plant these larger culls so close they almost touch, in rows 12 to 14 inches apart. Once the plants are about 4 inches tall, hill the soil around them and they'll grow a longer, edible white stem. When the plants are about 6 inches high, start pulling and eating.

For mature, full-term onions from sets, plant each of the smaller bulbs 1 inch deep, 2 inches apart, in rows from 11 to 14 inches wide. They should mature in about 100 days.

If you want to grow your own onion sets, plant a large quantity of seed in a small fertile area. Because of crowding, the bulbs will stay small. Seeds that produce good set bulbs include YELLOW EBENEZER, STUTTGARTER, and GOLDEN MOSQUE. Begin in April by working a small area, about 100 inches square for 50 sets. The spot you choose should receive full sun, have rich soil with a pH of 6.4, and be well worked with organic matter. Plant the seeds closely—almost touching—in a wide band. Then, cover them with 1/2 inch of soil. Do not attempt to thin them.

Plan to harvest in August. If the summer is rainy, bend the plants over just prior to harvest, so moisture doesn't funnel into the heart of the small onion bulb. After the sets have been removed from the soil, spread them (tops down) on dry ground for about ten days to cure. Protect them from rain. Pick over the bulbs, discarding those with thick necks—these will not keep. When the tops are limp and the small necks are thoroughly dry, remove the tops. Store the sets at 35°F in a dry place with good ventilation.

Growing from Seed:
One package of seed sown outdoors can produce scallions, large bulbs, sets, or bolting plants, depending on the time of year it is planted. Seeds germinate best at 60 to 65°F, but temperatures anywhere from 50 to 75°F will do.

Plant seeds outdoors as early as the ground can be worked. Set them 3/4 to 1 inch deep, with one to five seeds per inch. When they begin growing, you will have to thin the rows. To produce large keeping onions, thin the plants to 3 inches apart. For green onions or little boiling onions, thin them 1/2 inch to 1 inch apart. From sowing to harvest, onions from seed take 130 to 150 days. Unused seed is good for one to two years.

Handling Seedlings:
If you want to produce blockbuster onions from seed, you will have to start them indoors

and move them to the garden early in the season. The size of the onion you pull depends a great deal on the length of the day. Onions start to bulb when they get from 11 to 16 hours of daylight a day, depending on their type. Japanese varieties, which start to bulb when days are just 11 or 12 hours long, can produce mature onions as early as May. If the plants are very small when the critical daylength is reached, they will bulb nevertheless, producing little onions. So if you want softball-sized onions, the plants must be large when they approach the critical daylength. That size is most successfully reached by planting sets, or by planting seeds indoors in late January. To start onions indoors, sow seeds thinly, 10 to 12 to an inch, about $\frac{1}{2}$ inch deep, in rows about 4 inches apart.

To make the move outdoors without killing the young plants, you must first harden them by withholding water and exposing them to night temperatures only slightly above freezing for seven to ten days. Discard the very small plants.

Plant transplants every 4 to 5 inches, in rows 12 to 24 inches apart. Set the plants 1 to $1\frac{1}{2}$ inches deep. Water after transplanting, but be sure the soil drains well. The plants will mature in midsummer, earlier than sets. By growing both transplants and sets, you can extend your harvest.

Growing Guidelines:

Water your plants deeply about once a week during active growing. Once they have bulbed, stop watering. Bulbing will begin when the critical day length is reached, provided temperatures are not too low. In the first stage of bulbing, the plant stops growing leaves and begins putting nutrients into its bulb. Next, the plant stops producing roots. Finally, the entire plant goes into a state of rest. Soon the leaf sheaths just above the bulb weaken.

When the leaves are grown, they will often produce flowering heads or a swelling package of little bulblets. Pull or snip these off as they appear, to keep the onion's energy moving to the root bulb.

Once the plants are set out, be sure to weed your onion patch. Onions compete very poorly with other plants, and will sometimes give up entirely if weeds smother them. Take special care to pull weeds during May and June, when their growth is most vigorous, and keep after them on a regular basis for the rest of the season. Some people find an onion hoe useful in keeping the patch weed-free. It is a wedge-shaped instrument that provides shallow soil penetration. Because onion roots are near the surface, cultivate carefully.

Japanese varieties make their early growth in the fall, lie dormant through the winter, and resume growth in the spring. In the North, these seeds can be sown in late August (mid-September in the South), and survive till spring if they have reached 6 to 8 inches in height by the end of October. If you want to over-winter a crop, sow the seeds at the correct time for your location, 1 inch apart in well-drained soil. Keep the plot weeded during fall and spring. In cold-winter areas, prevent the plants from heaving during thaws by pressing soil firmly around their bases. Wait until spring to thin the plants, then thin to 2 inches apart.

Harvesting and Storing:

You will know the bulbs are ripe when the tops of the plants begin to fall over. When half the plants have toppled, pull a rake (teeth up) over the rest. Allow the onions to stay in the field for a few days before digging

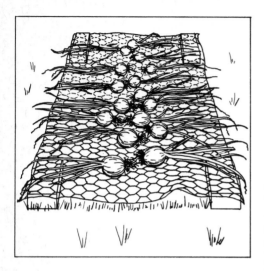

Curing onions. Spread mature, freshly harvested onions on mesh to cure outdoors. Bricks keep onions off the ground for faster, even curing.

them up. But don't leave them in the field indefinitely or their leaves will rot at the neck and they won't store well.

When you harvest the onions, take only those you will eat immediately into the house. Those to be stored must first be cured. Leave them outdoors in the shade for about a week, allowing the tops, and especially the necks, to dry completely. If the neck does not dry, it will provide a moist surface where rot can get a foothold and ruin the crop. When handling onions, be sure not to bruise them; bruises will also allow entry to organisms. Keep the papery "wrappers" intact, because they contain an enzyme that naturally inhibits sprouting during storage.

After a few days of curing, the onion tops should look withered and dry. At this point, you can braid the tops so the onions form attractive clusters that can be stored in an attic or another dry, cool spot. If you prefer, the tops can be cut off 1 to 1½ inches above the bulbs and the bulbs stored in mesh bags, to hang from rafters. Or make trays from 1-inch turkey wire, and store onions in them in double layers. If you cut the onion tops and find plant juices still running in them, use these bulbs immediately and return the rest outdoors for additional curing.

Some types of onion are simply too soft to store well. Bermuda onions and the sweet Spanish kind, for example, have large soft interiors, thick necks that don't dry well, and thin skins. They will either sprout or rot within 30 days. For good keepers, make sure you plant varieties that are listed as storing onions.

Humidity—or, more accurately, the lack of it—is another major factor in onion storage. High humidity leads to root growth and rot. Moreover, the larger your onions, the more likely they are to spoil. Sprouting, which also leads to rot, is most frequently caused by warm temperatures. Therefore, the ideal spot to store onions is cool and dry.

Pests and Diseases: If the seedlings suddenly turn limp and pale and then keel over, look for onion maggots. The adult maggots—small, gray-black flies about ½ inch long—live only two to four weeks. The female lays her eggs on young onion leaves or the neck of the plant. Occasionally, she will lay eggs on soil near the plant. Each female can lay hundreds of eggs, which hatch in two or three days. The creamy white offspring are only ⅓ inch long. One maggot can destroy more than 20 seedlings in its short life. The maggot enters the base of the onion plant to feed on the tissues. When grown, it leaves the plant to enter the soil as a chestnut-brown pupa. Control these pests by moving the onion patch to a new location every year. The maggots, with a taste only for onions, will simply die away on the off years. You can also plant Japanese bunching onions, a variety resistant to maggots.

Diseases that can threaten your crop include smut, downy mildew, tip burn, leaf blight or blast, fusarium basal rot, pink root, and of course, neck rot. Onion smut usually shows up as a swelling or hardening of the leaves just above the neck. Eventually, this swelling bursts open, spilling black powdery spores over the plant. This disease attacks the entire plant. Onion smut is most troublesome where onions have been planted in the same spot over a period of years. The best way to avoid the disease is to shift the crop around. Should the disease invade

your garden, yank out the plants and burn or otherwise permanently dispose of them. Do not add them to your compost pile.

Downy mildew tends to show up in midseason, especially when the weather has been warm and humid. You'll notice your plants developing a soft, violet covering. There is little to be done for downy mildew—except to pray for a series of clear, dry days. Another disease, tip burn, is caused from high concentrations of ozone, usually the result of thunderstorms. The leaves of the plant will look brown and withered.

Fusarium basal rot, another in the list of potential problems, is controlled by planting only fusarium-resistant types of onion. Pink root attacks weakened plants. It can be avoided, like many other

ONIONS

Variety	Description	Sources*
Autumn Spice	95–100 days; a long-day onion good for northern areas; also a good keeper	10, 39
Downing Yellow Globe	112 days; medium-sized globe onion; suited to north-central states; excellent keeper	15
Early Yellow Globe	95–100 days; early, heavy yields; mild flavor; good keeper	15
Express Yellow	250 days; can be sown in fall where temperatures don't fall below 5°F; harvest June and July	36
Fiesta	110 days; medium to large globe shape; firm, pungent flesh; stores well	33
Garnet	100 days; medium to large globe; firm and pungent; good keeper	3
Golden Mosque	105 days; nonsprouting quality plus earliness; supreme variety for sets; good for pickling	33

(continued)

ONIONS—*Continued*

Variety	Description	Sources*
Northern Oak	108 days; popular, large onion; tolerant to fusarium and some strains of pink root; stores well	33
Southport Red Globe	110 days; round, medium-sized bulb; purple-red skin; pink-tinged flesh; excellent keeper	15
Southport White Globe	110 days; medium to large round globe; fairly mild flavor; not as good a keeper as Southport Red Globe	WA
Spartan Gem	100 days; long-day variety; medium to large globe; firm and pungent; good keeper	5
Spartan Sleeper	110 days; long-day variety; globe-shape; a good keeper that won't sprout readily in storage	33
Stuttgarter	120 days; long-day variety; medium-large, flat onion; yellow-brown skin; good in sandy soils; excellent keeper	33, 39
Sweet Sandwich	112 days; vigorous; up to 5" across; sweet and crisp; keeps 6 to 8 months without becoming hot and pungent	36
Wethersfield	103 days; large, flattened, red onion also used for sets; white, soft, pungent flesh; good keeper	23
Yellow Ebenezer	100–140 days; high yields; excellent for scallions and sets; mild and sweet; remains firm; good keeper	12, 24
Yellow Globe	98–112 days; long-day variety; medium-sized bulbs; good for cool-climate areas; all-purpose onion with good flavor	16
Yellow Globe Danvers	110 days; a long-day variety; heavy producer; entirely free of thick necks; good keeper	WA

Bunching Onions (Scallions)

Variety	Description	Sources*
Beltsville Bunching	65 days; good for fall or spring planting; crisp, white shanks; good as scallions; resists bolting	33
Evergreen White Bunching	65–120 days; long, silvery-white stems; stalks divide from base and will not bulb; good as scallions	WA
Southport White Bunching	65–110 days; slow-bulbing strain of Southport White Globe; grows quickly; good as scallions	13

*Listings correspond to seed companies listed under Sources of Seeds at the back of the book.

problems, by digging a new spot in the garden for onions each year.

Neck rot is a storage problem, rather than a growing problem. It is caused by a botrytis fungus. White varieties are most susceptible to this rot, so be careful to choose a good storing variety if you are planting in quantity. It also is necessary to cure the onions so the neck tissue is completely dry before putting them away.

Nutritional Value: Onions supply a fair amount of protein, and are rich in calcium and vitamin B$_2$.

Choosing Varieties: The latest, most exciting development in onions is the availability of new oriental varieties that can be set out at the end of summer, spend the winter in the garden, and reach maturity in late spring. While fall planting is traditional in the Sunbelt states, it is an exciting new opportunity for Northern gardeners. These varieties can be planted where winters get quite cold. Seeds of at least one variety—EXPRESS YELLOW—are commercially available.

PARSNIPS
Pastinaca sativa

Although it is not one of the more popular vegetables today, devotees of parsnips insist that few dishes are better than parsnips, sliced and steamed, served with butter. Their sweet, nutty flavor can also enhance soups and stews. Parsnips can be prepared in the same manner as carrots.

The parsnip is a biennial, but is treated as an annual like most root crops. It is grown for its long, slender, white roots. The most frost-resistant of all vege-

tables, parsnips can be left in the garden over winter, even in the coldest climates. The parsnip requires a long growing season, and any inconvenience this may present to the gardener in terms of tying up garden space is offset by the fact that it stores so well in the ground and is available throughout the winter for fresh, tasty eating—a time when fresh, crispy vegetables are rare. It is indeed a winter vegetable and its flavor is enhanced by light frosts that change its starches to sugars.

Parsnips require a growing season of 80 to 120 days, and are generally grown in regions with autumn or winter frosts, which promote the sweetest taste and crispiest texture.

Soil Preparation: Like other long-rooted crops, parsnips need a deep, rich, well-drained and well-aerated soil. Sandy loams are ideal, but parsnips may be grown in any average loam if the soil is loosened before planting. Heavy clays will not produce good crops. Prepare the soil to a depth of 12 to 18 inches before planting, removing any rocks or other debris. Incorporate plenty of compost or well-rotted manure, but avoid using fresh manure before planting, since it will cause roots to fork. Work in a potassium-rich fertilizer like wood ashes or greensand. Recommended pH is 6.0 to 6.8.

How Much to Plant: A rough guideline is 25 plants per person.

Planting: Parsnips can be started using seeds or transplants. In mild-winter areas with temperatures that seldom dip below freezing, sow seed in late fall and winter for a spring crop. In areas with cold winters and freezing temperatures,

PARSNIPS

Variety	Description	Sources*
All American	120 days; dependable producer; 12" roots with good texture, small core	12
Harris Model	100–120 days; popular variety; 10–12" roots; smooth, white flesh; does not discolor quickly after harvest	13, 15
Hollow Crown	95–105 days; heavy yielder; 12" tapering roots; standard, old favorite	5, 38

*Listings correspond to seed companies listed under Sources of Seeds at the back of the book.

sow seed as soon as the ground can be worked in spring, two to four weeks before the last frost, or get a head start with transplants.

For direct-sown seed, the soil temperature for best germination is 50 to 70° F. Seed is very slow to germinate and should be soaked in water for several hours or overnight before planting. Sow seed thickly, $1/2$ inch deep, and cover the furrows with vermiculite or a mix of leaf mold and sand, since the seed has trouble coming up through crusted soil. Mix in radish seed to act as a planting marker. Keep the furrows moist to hasten germination. Conventional rows should be spaced 18 inches apart. Wide-row planting is suitable. Spacing for growing beds is 6 inches. Unused seed is good for one to two years.

Handling Seedlings:

Start seeds indoors in individual containers four to six weeks before setting out, which can be done from four weeks before to four weeks after the frost-free date. Set seedlings every 4 to 6 inches in conventional rows, and use the spacing given above for raised beds.

Growing Guidelines:

When the radishes have been harvested and the parsnip seedlings are about 1 inch tall, thin them to stand 4 to 6 inches apart in the conventional rows and wide rows. Keep weeds down during this period, and mulch between the rows when the radishes are harvested. Although parsnips are not particularly heavy feeders, a mid-season side-dressing of wood ashes or compost will hasten roots along to maturity. Keep parsnips well watered.

Harvesting and Storing:

The parsnip's flavor is greatly improved by a few hard frosts, and it should not be harvested before being touched by frost. Parsnips may be left in the ground over winter and dug up as needed. The only requirement is a thick hay mulch to facilitate digging in areas where the ground freezes hard. The roots may be harvested in early spring, as the ground begins to thaw, even if no protection was given over the winter, but make sure to harvest them before new growth begins in the spring, since they will become woody, limp, and tasteless after that. They may also be dug just before the ground freezes hard in the fall and stored over the winter in a cool (32 to 40°F), moist storage area.

Pests and Diseases:
Parsnips are seldom bothered.

Nutritional Value:
Besides being tasty, parsnips are also quite nutritious, providing vitamins B_1, B_2, and C, as well as potassium.

PEANUTS
(Earth nut, goober, goober pea, ground nut)
Arachis hypogaea

Although the peanut is an important food and livestock crop in many tropical and semitropical areas of the world, this plant is more often grown as a novelty in the home garden.

The plants grow from 1 to 2 feet tall, and are either of erect or creeping habit. Limited-space gardeners should look for erect-growing or bush varieties.

Peanuts are a very tender, long-season crop; they can be grown successfully in any area that offers 120 frost-free days, as long as the climate is warm and sunny. Peanuts need a long period of warm nights to develop properly.

Soil Preparation:
Peanuts will grow and yield on poor soil, but yields will be improved by adding compost rich in phosphorus and potassium, or by adding bonemeal and wood ashes. The peanut, a legume, takes its own nitrogen from the air and stores it in the soil. Thus there is no need to add nitrogen to the soil, since an excess will result in too much top growth and poor seed develop-

ment. The soil should be well drained, light (a sandy loam is ideal), and on the acid side (a pH of 5.0 to 6.0). Work through the soil to make sure all rocks and other debris are out of the growing area. Short-season gardeners should try to provide a south-facing slope in a sheltered area for this warmth-loving crop.

How Much to Plant:
A rough guideline is 16 plants per person.

Planting:
Seed is often sown directly into the garden on the frost-free date. It may be planted either in or out of the pod. If the pod shell is thin, it is best to plant pods without shelling them. If not, then the seeds should be removed very carefully; if the red skin of the seed is torn, germination will not occur. Seeds are subject to rot, especially in heavy, cool, or damp soils. Soil temperature should be at least 60°F before planting. Although peanuts are a legume, it is generally not recommended to treat them with bacterial inoculant before planting. Unused seed is good for five years.

Space conventional rows $2\frac{1}{2}$ to 3 feet apart, and plant the seeds every 4 to 6 inches along the rows. The spacing in growing beds is 18 inches. Peanuts may also be planted in hills, like squash, four seeds or pods to the hill, the hills spaced 18 inches apart. In cool weather or in heavier soils, seeds are planted $1\frac{1}{2}$ inches deep; in long-season areas and in very light soils, seeds are planted at least 4 inches deep.

Handling Seedlings:
In areas with short seasons, gardeners sometimes gamble on earlier outdoor planting dates or start plants indoors. Sow seeds in individual containers that will allow transplanting without disturbing the roots. Peanuts

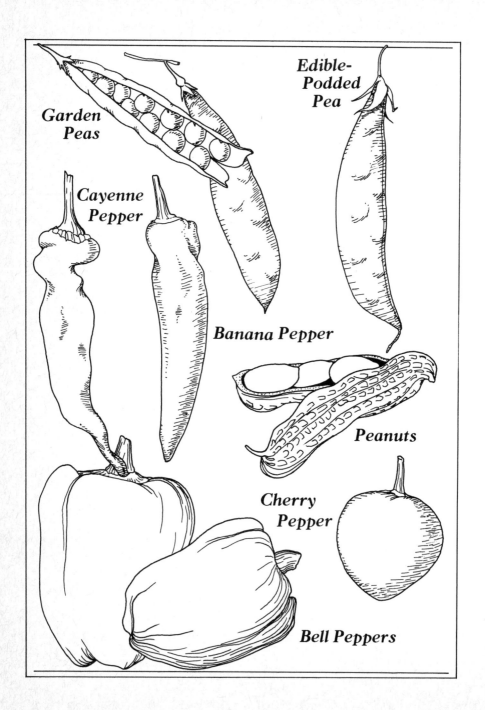

Garden Peas

Edible-Podded Pea

Cayenne Pepper

Banana Pepper

Peanuts

Cherry Pepper

Bell Peppers

do not transplant easily, and any damage to the roots will set back growth. Start seeds four to six weeks before the frost-free date, at which time they can be set out in the garden.

Growing Guidelines:

After seedlings have been up for two weeks, thin them to stand 10 to 12 inches apart in rows. Thin the hills so the sturdiest three seedlings remain. Supply only enough moisture to keep the soil from drying out until a mulch is applied. Cultivate shallowly to eliminate weeds, being careful not to disturb the peanut roots.

The plant will produce two kinds of flowers: relatively large and showy blossoms on the upper portions, and inconspicuous ones at the base of the plant on the ends of runners (called pegs). It is the inconspicuous flowers that are important, for they contain ovaries that will develop into peanuts. The runners will grow laterally for a short distance, then dip down and bury themselves in the soil, each to produce an underground seed pod. To hasten the burying process, hill up loose-textured soil around the base of the plant once it reaches 2 inches in height, thereby enabling the runners to make soil contact in a shorter time. It is important to keep the soil surface loose, so the runners can work their way into the soil.

After the runners have implanted themselves, add a thick mulch on top of them, and around plants. The mulch, in addition to serving the usual purposes, will encourage the peanuts to develop close to the soil surface, which makes harvesting easier. After the mulch has been applied, the crop will need no more care for the rest of the season.

Harvesting and Storing:

In gardens with longer seasons, peanuts are traditionally harvested before the first autumn frosts arrive, when the seeds have filled out the pods, the pods' veins have begun to darken, and the foliage has yellowed. In shorter-season areas, the crop may be left in the ground past the first light frosts if the pods have not fully matured. Even after the tops have died down, the nuts will continue to mature for several weeks. Keep testing to see when peanuts have matured.

If the plants have been properly mulched, they may be pulled up by hand with ease. Most of the peanuts will adhere to the roots, and the others may be recovered by probing in the ground. If the peanuts have formed more deeply in the ground, use a spade to dig them up.

There are two ways to cure peanuts. The traditional practice calls for the entire plant to be hung in a warm, dry location with good ventilation. The other, perhaps more convenient, practice is to remove the pods and dry them on screens or trays, also in a warm, dry place. Whichever method is used, the curing period is at least one month, or longer if conditions are not ideal. Save some of the largest pods for planting the following season's crop.

After curing, the peanuts may be eaten raw or roasted. To roast them, place the pods in a 350° F oven for 20 minutes. Be careful not to scorch them.

Pests and Diseases:

There are no serious pests or diseases of peanuts when they are grown in the home garden.

Nutritional Value:

The "nut," actually a seed, is both a tasty snack and a solid nutritional package offering good amounts of vitamins B and E, healthful oils (3:1 ratio of unsaturated to saturated fatty acids), and up to 30 percent protein.

PEANUTS

Variety	Description	Sources*
Early Spanish	100 days; small, flavorful nuts; most dependable variety for short-season areas	12, 16, 33
Jumbo Virginia	120 days; productive; 1 to 2 large nuts per pod; rich flavor; vines spread 3½' across	5
Spanish	110 days; 2 or 3 small, sweet nuts per pod; early, heavy bearer; dwarf bushes	5, 24
Valencia Tennessee Red	120 days; 2 to 5 large, sweet nuts per pod; Spanish type; well adapted for warm, long-season areas	24

*Listings correspond to seed companies listed under Sources of Seeds at the back of the book.

PEAS

Pisum sativum

Peas symbolize spring to vegetable gardeners the way crocuses do to flower gardeners. Pea planting has a firm date in local lore that's as deeply rooted as the spring equinox, and practiced gardeners push their peas into finger-numbing earth—with good reason. When the peas come in, they bring an intense sweetness to the spring table that rivals the sweet corn, melons, and peaches of summer.

But you must plant them early to get full crops. Most gardeners can't quite believe just how early that is. Peas never do well in warm weather. The plants stop growing, leaves wilt, and fruiting stops. Even if the plants are well watered, the symptoms continue.

Soil Preparation: One of the most important factors in growing healthy, productive pea vines is soil drainage. A study conducted in Oxfordshire, England, found that waterlogging for as little as 24 hours reduced pod weight by 18 percent. After four days of waterlogging, 90 percent of the leaves had died. Peas have a low tolerance for oxygen deficiencies in their root zones, and waterlogging can cut oxygen levels in the soil by 90 percent in only a few days. Soggy soil also interferes with the plant's uptake of nitrogen. The study found that young plants survived some waterlogging, but older plants, especially those in the flowering stage, did not.

Lots of organic matter and a deeply worked soil are the best insurance against waterlogging. If your soil is heavy clay, lighten it with generous additions of leaves, grass clippings, peat or compost. Raised beds can also improve drainage. And since you're less likely to be walking on the soil in beds, they can eliminate another common pea problem: soil compaction. Compressing the soil around pea plants robs them of oxygen much the same as waterlogging does. Tests in western Oregon, an area of mild, wet winters, found that the survival rate of winter-grown peas was significantly higher when raised beds were used.

Peas (and their nitrogen-fixing bacteria) like a pH of 6.0 to 7.0, and can't tolerate highly acidic soil.

How Much to Plant: A rough guideline is 40 plants per person.

Planting: Peas are grown during the winter in the South and on the West Coast, where they're called English peas to differentiate them from cowpeas. In most of the rest of the country, they are a spring and sometimes a fall crop. Peas can be planted as soon as the ground thaws in the spring. They will germinate in soil that's only 40°F and can survive temperatures down to 19°F, so a few frosts and freezes don't harm them a bit.

Staggering plantings every ten days will give you a continuous harvest throughout early summer. You can also plant peas with different maturing times on the same day for a longer harvest later on. The latter method has its advantages, as it gets all the plants into the ground when temperatures are still cool, and because some varieties will do better than others in any year.

The spot you pick to plant your peas should be well drained and sunny, but it needn't be highly fertile. Peas and other legumes get most of their nitrogen from the atmosphere. This nitrogen fixation is the result of tiny bacteria, called *Rhizobia,* which form nodules on the roots. The bacteria change atmospheric nitrogen into a form that can be used by the plants. Only very early, before the nodules have formed, do peas need a nitrogen boost. Working in compost just before planting is a good way to do this. Never use fresh manure with peas. The excess nitrogen it contains will produce lush, leafy plants with very few pods on them, and will stifle natural nitrogen-fixation.

If peas have never been grown in your soil before, the seeds may have to be inoculated with nitrogen-fixing bacteria before planting. Roll wet seeds in the fine, black inoculant powder immediately before planting. One packet of pea inoculant is usually enough for a pound of seed. Once your soil has been inoculated, the bacteria will live there for many years. There's no need to inoculate seeds again.

Since peas are among the hardiest of vegetables and don't transplant well, there's nothing to be gained by starting plants indoors. Just put the seeds out in the garden as soon as the ground can be worked. Soaking them in water for 24 hours beforehand will help to loosen the tough seed coat and speed germination. Plant seeds 2 inches deep in heavy or warm soil and about 1 inch deep in sandy or cool soil. Peas don't mind a little crowding. Bush varieties can be scattered over a bed about 1 inch apart and later thinned to 2 or 3 inches. Plant seeds of climbing varieties in two parallel rows 6 inches apart, with one plant every 2 inches. Unused seed is good for three years.

Growing Guidelines: After the seedlings are up, drive stakes between the rows and staple on wire or plastic mesh. Ideally the mesh should be large enough to pull a fistful of peas through. It makes picking much easier. The supports should be at least as high as your variety is supposed to grow, otherwise the plants will climb up and over, and you'll end up with a tangled mess. Anchor the end posts securely or the weight of vines and pods will pull down the trellis.

Trellising peas. Put your tomato cages to work early by planting peas 3 inches apart around the outside of each cage.

Once seedlings have sprouted, you shouldn't need to water until the onset of flowering. Peas are quite drought-tolerant, and need only about an inch of rain every two weeks until they start flowering. Mulching will help keep the roots cool and conserve moisture. Numerous tests have shown that watering during the early stages of growth has little effect on the plants. Even when the leaves show signs of wilting, the plants continue to grow. It's only when the first blossoms appear that peas need extra water. Once they flower, give the plants an inch of water a week until the pods are filled. Drip irrigation will help keep the leaves dry, which in turn will check the spread of diseases.

Since peas are planted early in the season, weeds are usually not a big problem. By the time most of them appear, the peas are already strong enough to compete on their own. Any weeding should be undertaken with care because stem and root tissues are quite fragile. Cultivate shallowly and not too close to the plants—better to let a few weeds grow than to risk damaging fragile roots. Mulching is the best way to control weeds.

Harvesting and Storing:

Most pea varieties take about 65 days to begin bearing. About three weeks after the plants begin to blossom, the first peas (low on the plants) should be ready for picking. Keep a close eye on the pods during the ripening stage so that the peas don't overmature, lose their sweetness, and turn starchy. Start picking when the pods are well filled and have turned light green. Snow peas should be harvested when the pods are about 2 inches long and the peas inside are only the size of BBs. Fifteen feet of vining pea row should yield about 5 pounds of peas a week for several weeks.

To keep peas producing, pick every day. Hold the upper stem with one hand and pinch the pod with the other. It's always best to pick them a few minutes before they end up on the table. As with sweet corn, the sugar in peas begins turning to starch within a few hours after being picked, and the peas lose their sweetness.

If you find yourself inundated with peas and pea-freezing, try leaving the excess to dry on the vine. When the peas are ripe, the vines will begin to die away, and the pods will turn hard and brown. As they begin to split open, harvest them. To finish the drying and kill any insect eggs, place the peas in a pan in a 120°F oven for three hours. Then store them in an airtight container. Dried peas are excellent in soups.

Pests and Diseases: Hungry birds are about the worst enemy of young pea plants. They can quickly ruin the planting. If birds give you a hard time, cover the emerging plants with a cage of chicken wire. By the time the plants have outgrown the cages, the birds will have plenty of alternate food sources and should no longer be a problem.

One of the insect pests that causes the most damage is the pea aphid. This green, soft-bodied insect sucks plant juices, causing leaves to droop. Two or three generations of aphids may be born in a single season, leading to a population explosion. The insects can be controlled with an insecticidal soap spray.

Despite their tiny size, thrips can cause a lot of damage to plants. In addition to killing leaves with their rasping/sucking action, these black or dark brown insects spread disease. You can generally find them on the undersides of leaves in the driest part of the season. Soap sprays will also control thrips. Use rotenone for particularly bad infestations.

The pea weevil often causes headaches for Northwest gardeners. The adult beetle lays eggs on pea pods. The small larvae, which are white with a brown head, burrow through the pod and into peas. Plants can be dusted with rotenone at blossom time to keep the adults away.

Peas are susceptible to a variety of diseases, but they can be kept in check if resistant varieties are planted and rotated yearly. Fusarium wilt, also known as pea wilt, causes yellowed leaves and wilted plants. This soilborne disease enters the plant through the roots and can kill plants. Resistant varieties include EARLY FROSTY, THOMAS LAXTON, GREEN ARROW, and SPARKLE.

Wet spring weather can cause problems with powdery mildew. At first the leaves, stems, and pods become covered with a white, powdery mold. Later, black specks appear and the plants become stunted or die. Overhead watering can spread this disease and should be avoided.

Root rot affects underground stems and roots and will kill plants. It is caused by overwatering. If you rotate your pea patch, always keeping it in well-drained soil, root rot shouldn't be a problem.

Other Problems: Peas are somewhat sensitive to deficiencies of phosphorus and potash. Leaves may take on a purplish discoloration or become dry and curled at the edges. An application of wood ashes, which contain both nutrients, at a rate of 5 to 10 pounds per 100 square feet, should take care of this problem. The ashes will also help to raise your soil's pH if it's too acidic.

Nutritional Value: Peas are a good source of protein, and offer significant amounts of vitamins A and C.

Choosing Varieties: Pea seeds can be either wrinkled or smooth. The smooth-seeded varieties are hardiest, and are often grown commercially. However, they're usually not the tastiest. Home gardeners should stick to the wrinkled-seeded types, which produce much

PEAS

Variety	Description	Sources*
Alaska	55 days; early; good for short-season areas; resistant to fusarium wilt; good fresh or dried	WA
Alderman	70–75 days; tall variety; needs staking; oval, curved pods; dark green peas; good for canning or freezing	12, 33, 38
Burpeeana	63 days; early, very prolific; vines to 24"; 8 to 10 peas per pod; peas retain color when cooked; good for freezing	5
Early Frosty	60–68 days; vines to 30" long; high yields; wilt resistant; good garden variety; good for freezing	37
Freezonian	63 days; short, vigorous vines; resistant to fusarium wilt; pods hold 7 to 8 peas; excellent for freezing; AAS	WA
Frosty	60–67 days; strong, vigorous vines to 28"; high yields; resistant to fusarium wilt; pods hold 7 to 9 peas; sweet flavor	13
Green Arrow	70 days; strong vines to 28"; high yields; resistant to downy mildew, fusarium wilt; pods held high on plant	WA
Little Marvel	58–64 days; vigorous, bushy, dwarf plant; heavy yields; dependable; long, 6" pods; good fresh or frozen	5, 38
Snappy	63 days; vigorous, productive snap pea; 6' vines need support; powdery mildew resistant; fleshy pods	5
Sparkle	55–60 days; compact vines to 18"; high yields; wilt resistant; concentrated crop of 3" pods; good for freezing	15, 19
Sugar Ann	56 days; short-vine snap pea; no support needed; pods to 2½"; AAS	15
Sugar Snap	70 days; vines, to 6' or more, need staking; dwarf varieties available; pods, peas edible at all stages; freeze well	WA
Thomas Laxton	62 days; short vines; heavy yields; very resistant to fusarium wilt; good for freezing	WA
Wando	68 days; heavy producer; short vines; pods to 3½"; withstands hot, dry spells	15

*Listings correspond to seed companies listed under Sources of Seeds at the back of the book.

sweeter peas. You'll also have to choose between dwarf and climbing varieties. Dwarf or bush varieties require less trellising (although they should have some support), but they produce smaller and fewer pods per plant. Climbing varieties bear over a longer period, and the peas hold their sweetness longer. But you must build trellises or supports for them to climb on, or end up with an impenetrable mass of plants.

Snow peas, which often turn up in oriental dishes, are eaten pod and all when the peas are still small and immature. Another edible-podded type, the popular SUGAR SNAP pea, an All-America Gold Medal winner a few years back, offers both full-sized peas and a sweet, edible pod. Now there are several new dwarf varieties in this class. Edible-podded peas are grown the same way as other types. However, many gardeners like to grow shelling peas as a spring crop for freezing and save the edible-podded varieties for eating fresh as a fall crop.

PEPPERS
Capsicum annuum
var. *annuum*

Bell peppers are not difficult to grow, but they can be contrary when it comes to setting fruit through the hot summer months. In most of the country, bell peppers will set an early crop of fruit, then simply stop producing through July and August. By September, the bushes are beginning to set fruit again, but the rapidly cooling nights overtake them before the crop matures. They go down with the first frosts, along with the gardener's expectations.

In certain favored areas, such as the Gulf Coast and coastal California, gardeners don't have this problem. Their peppers set fruit right through the summer months as long as they're picked regularly. They have no secret technique, but they do have the right climate. With some care, it's possible for growers in most of the United States to reproduce such favorable conditions and keep the crop coming.

Soil Preparation: Prepare your pepper patch in the fall by tilling under at least 150 pounds of manure per 1,000 square feet of area. Peppers like a loose, humusy, well-drained and rich soil. Although peppers aren't particularly acid-sensitive, growing well in a pH range from 5.5 to 6.8, acidic soil should be sweetened into the middle of this range with ground dolomite. Dolomite is also useful in remedying magnesium deficiency, a condition which peppers won't tolerate.

How Much to Plant: A rough guideline is two or three plants per person.

Planting: Plant seedlings 14 inches apart in the row, with 18 inches between rows. This produces a dense canopy of leaves which holds water vapor under the plants and prevents sunlight from drying the mulch excessively.

Growing from Seed: Don't attempt to grow peppers from seed unless you have a greenhouse or hotbed with good exposure to sunlight. Pepper seedlings don't grow satisfactorily under artificial lights or on windowsills, and transplants can be readily purchased from a local greenhouse.

Pepper seed remains viable for two to four years. Minimum germination of fresh seed is 55 percent. Therefore, sow twice as much seed as you need. A packet of nonhybrid seeds yields 50 to 70 plants, a hybrid packet about 25 to 35 plants. Sow seed $\frac{1}{4}$ to $\frac{1}{2}$ inch deep in a loose, well-drained potting mix of one-half compost and one-half peat or vermiculite. Sow seed in flats in rows 2 to 3 inches apart, with six to ten seeds per inch of row. The seed can be germinated in the dark, but should be moved into full sunlight as soon as the seedlings start to emerge. Keep the soil only slightly moist, increasing the moisture content after the seedlings have completely emerged.

Pepper seeds will not germinate if the soil is 55° F or lower. At 60° F, germination takes about 25 days. The optimum temperature is 75 to 80° F. In this range, most pepper varieties germinate in seven or eight days. However, if you can maintain 68° F or higher, you should notice germination within two weeks of sowing.

When the seed leaves (cotyledons) are fully expanded, or when the first true leaf appears, carefully prick out the young seedlings and plant them in their permanent transplant-growing flat or containers. When pricking out young seedlings, always hold them by the leaves and not the stem. Space seedlings 2 to 3 inches apart in flats, or plant single seedlings in 2- to 3-inch peat pots.

Handling Seedlings: Some growers have tried pruning peppers to increase yields, but scientists have found that pruning or stunting in any form reduces yields. For that reason, young seedlings should be transplanted into soil that has warmed to at least 60° F. If you're buying plants, don't buy any with flowers or fruit on them or, once transplanted, the seedlings will have to deal with fruit

production when they should be concentrating on establishing roots. Stunting and permanently reduced harvests can result.

It takes seven to ten weeks from sowing to produce dark green, stocky (4- to 6-inch-tall) transplants. Keep your seedlings in full sun, water regularly and evenly without soaking the flats, and maintain a growing temperature of 65 to 80° F daytime (optimum is 75°) and 60 to 70° F nighttime. Fertilize the plants weekly with a dilute fish emulsion. If you are a smoker, wash your hands thoroughly and don't smoke while handling the plants, or you may infect the peppers with tobacco mosaic virus.

Growing Guidelines: "Peppers are native to the moist tropics of South America," says Dr. James F. Gauss, a horticulturist at the University of Illinois. "They will not tolerate cool (below 60° F at night), hot (above 80° during the day and 70° at night), or dry conditions. The ideal growing temperature range for green peppers is considered to be 70 to 80° F during the day and 60 to 70° at night. Flower buds and blossoms will drop rapidly if temperatures fall very far out of these ranges, if soil moisture is depleted or atmospheric conditions are hot, dry, and windy."

Even under ideal conditions, the large-fruited bell peppers will drop many of their flowers after several fruits have started to form on the plant, so don't allow June-ripening peppers to stay on the plants to full size. Pick them young and often to prepare the plant for fruit set during the very hot months to follow.

What can be done if you live in an area where midsummer heat can drag on for weeks in the upper 80s or low 90s? Four techniques can help: daily watering during dry spells, close spacing, a little shade in the most brutal heat, and the use of early varieties.

Hot, dry days may cause peppers to transpire too much water, even when there's enough in the soil. The result is flower, bud, and fruit drop. The trick is to supply moisture in such a way that the air around the peppers stays humid—and that's where mulch comes in. Grass clippings make the best mulch for peppers in most of the United States because they hold considerable amounts of water, and the shaggy surface of the clippings allows water to evaporate and filter up through the pepper foliage. The effect is similar to setting a house plant on a tray of wet pebbles to keep the air humid. Use clippings thickly—about 6 inches deep, starting an inch or two from the stem and extending out to the dripline. Aluminum foil mulch really boosts yields, but is only useful where high humidity prevails. Otherwise, the reflected sunlight would shrivel the plants.

During dry, hot days in July and August, water each plant thoroughly, making sure the surface of the grass-clipping mulch is wet—and do it daily. Of course, if your soil is not well drained, heavy watering can drown the roots, causing rot and eventually killing the plants.

Another technique that helps keep the plants cooler and more moist in hot weather is light shade during the heat of the day. Careful gardening planning can provide the shade automatically if you plant tall-growing vegetables like corn or a trellis of cucumbers or runner beans along the south side of your pepper rows. By mid-August, when the scorching heat subsides, the beans will have finished bearing and can be removed to increase direct sunlight to the peppers. A lath frame also works well. Don't shade peppers completely—they need only light shade from about 11 A.M. to 3 P.M.

Keys to Top Yields:

Daily watering of peppers during dry spells means many water-soluble nutrients will be leached from the top layer of soil. In addition, peppers are heavy feeders of nitrogen, potassium, calcium, and magnesium, with the greatest need coming in the third month of growth—the middle of summer. Supplemental feeding, then, is extremely important for high-yielding plants.

In July, sprinkle a handful of bonemeal around each plant and renew the grass-clipping mulch. Manure tea, fish emulsion, or side-dressings of rotted cow manure should be applied in early August. Don't overload the soil with high-nitrogen fertilizers, as an imbalance of this nutrient can create more bush than fruit. Several waterings with dilute nutrient solutions through August will help feed the plant when it needs it most.

Harvesting and Storing:

Sweet peppers may be picked when immature or full size, in the green or red state, although the vitamin C content is higher when the fruit is red. Hot peppers may be picked at any time for fresh use, and when they have become fully ripe for drying or pickling. Cut the pods rather than pull them from the vines to keep from disturbing the plant's roots. When even light frost is predicted, pick all pods. They will keep for one to two weeks at 50 to 60°F in a moist place.

Both hot and sweet peppers may be frozen without preliminary blanching. Thin-walled hot peppers are easy to dry and can be ground and stored in jars. Cut the whole plant and hang it in an airy place to dry, or harvest the individual pods and string them to hang in the kitchen for both ornamental and culinary purposes. You may also pickle hot peppers for use as condiments.

Pests and Diseases:
Insect pests include aphids, Colorado potato beetles, corn earworms, European corn borers, leafminers, pepper maggots, and tomato hornworms. Diseases include anthracnose, bacterial spot, blossom-end rot, and mosaic. Despite the impressive list of potential enemies, however, garden peppers are not greatly subject to injury by insects or diseases. See Corn, Potatoes, and Tomatoes for insect and disease controls.

Nutritional Value:
Studies show a positive relationship between protein and vitamin C content in the fruit and nutrient levels in the soil—all the more reason for side-dressing and manure teas during midsummer months. Besides being an excellent source of vitamin C, peppers also are noted for vitamin A content.

Choosing Varieties:
Choosing early varieties, especially in the North, is a key to all-summer pepper production. CALIFORNIA WONDER and YOLO WONDER are the standard peppers, but they do best where the climate favors peppers. In most of the country, these varieties often fail to fruit. "The small-fruited early varieties are much more tolerant of hot

PEPPERS

Variety	Description	Sources*
Bell Boy	70 days; bell-type; tobacco mosaic virus resistant; good for the North, but adaptable to cool and hot areas; AAS	WA
Big Bertha	72 days; early bearer; large fruits to over 1 pound; meaty walls; savory flavor	12, 33
California Wonder	68–89 days; early; good choice for the North; blocky, thick-walled fruits; perfect for stuffing	WA
Canape	62 days; early, high yields; good for short-season areas, North; 12 to 15 fruits per plant; mild and sweet	13
Early Bountiful	58–65 days; extremely vigorous; high yields; tobacco mosaic virus resistant; good choice for the North	25
Early Prolific	62 days; produces small bell-type fruits quickly; good for areas with cool, cloudy summers, like Alaska	36
Hungarian Yellow Wax	60–65 days; bushy plants; fruits to 8"; yellow turning red; moderately hot; very good for pickling	12, 24, 33

PEPPERS—*Continued*

Variety	Description	Sources*
Jalapeno	70–80 days; deep green fruits turn red; perhaps the hottest of all North American varieties; good pickled	12, 13
Keystone Resistant Giant	80 days; sturdy bush habit; heavy foliage; good for the southern areas of Oregon	17
Klondike Gold	72 days; hybrid; giant, blocky, golden fruits; thick-walled	33
Lady Bell	72 days; early starter; heavy yields; disease resistant; good for New England area	13
Midway	67–70 days; medium-early pepper; continuous yield; good for Northeast areas of U.S. and Canada	32
Miss Bell	69 days; large yields; tobacco mosaic resistant; tolerant of cool nighttime temperatures	10
New Ace	62 days; short, sturdy bushes; fruits have medium-thick walls; good choice for northern areas; good for freezing	3, 39
Park's Whopper	65 days; compact; vigorous; matures early; produces large crop until frost	24
Staddon Select	64 days; medium to large bell-type; tall, heavy producer; especially suited to northern areas with adverse conditions	WA
Sweet Chocolate	58 days; medium-small fruits with blunt ends; ripen to a rich brown; tolerates cool nights; sweet flavor	15
Yolo Wonder	75 days; large, heavy fruits are solid and blocky; heavy crown set; good protection from sunscald; mosaic resistant	WA

*Listings correspond to seed companies listed under Sources of Seeds at the back of the book.

weather than the large-fruited varieties," according to the USDA. They are also more tolerant of cool weather conditions.

Plant breeders have developed many new hybrids for the North in recent years. BELL BOY, EARLY BOUNTIFUL, and NEW ACE have been acclaimed for earliness and high yields—in fact, the early varieties tend to outyield the standards, even on the latter's home territory. EARLY PROLIFIC produces fruit very quickly, bearing well even in Alaska. It is the first pepper to receive the Award of Merit from England's Royal Horticultural Society, having grown successfully in that country's cold, wet climate. BIG BERTHA is an early bearer with large fruits that rival the standards. CANAPE was introduced into the United States from Japan in 1968 and was one of the first successful hybrids for home gardens in short-season areas.

LADY BELL and PARK'S WHOPPER topped the yield charts in recent variety trials at the University of Connecticut. According to Steve Windham of Mississippi State, "MISS BELL combines large yields of fancy fruits and virus resistance equal to the CALIFORNIA WONDER types, plus it's an early variety with resistance to flower and fruit drop when exposed to low night temperatures." MISS BELL and BELL BOY also outperformed other varieties in trials in northeast Louisiana.

POTATOES
Solanum tuberosum

People who think that all potatoes taste pretty much the same have probably been buying all theirs in the supermarket. That means they've tasted only the four or five varieties that make their way to the supermarket shelves. There are 200 registered varieties of potatoes, with their varying textures, tastes, keeping qualities, and colors. And a person can grow a year's supply in just 50 square feet.

Roger A. Kline, vegetable crops specialist with the New York State Cooperative Extension Service, says the gardener can expect to harvest from 2 to 5 pounds of potatoes per plant. That's higher than the expected yield from cucumbers, eggplant, and peppers, and slightly lower than that from tomatoes and squash. But

yields can be significantly higher under the right conditions.

Using French-intensive methods, harvests of 2.5 pounds of potatoes per square foot have been reported. That's about four times more than the national average. Kline figures that the 135 pounds consumed per capita (including chips and French fries) can be raised in 50 square feet. Robert Lobitz, a market gardener from Paynesville, Minnesota, reports that it's not unusual for him to dig 10 pounds of potatoes from a single plant.

Soil Preparation:
Potatoes grow best in loose, sandy loam, but any soil can be made suitable for them. Potatoes are not particularly heavy feeders. In fact, too much nitrogen will encourage excessive vine growth and reduce yields. They need a slow, steady supply of nutrients throughout the growing season, as supplied by a generous application of compost every year. Using compost, it may take up to five years to build the soil up to its maximum capability.

Organic potato grower Robert Lobitz relies on cattle manure, bonemeal, and fish and seaweed emulsion to improve the soil. He spreads well-rotted manure and bonemeal in the spring and plows them under about a week before planting. The fish and seaweed emulsions are sprayed on about every two weeks during the growing season.

It is a common belief that potatoes must be grown in acidic soil. Actually, potatoes grow better in a slightly alkaline soil, but so does the organism that causes scab, probably the most common potato disease. Scab can be minimized by planting resistant varieties and rotating the potato patch.

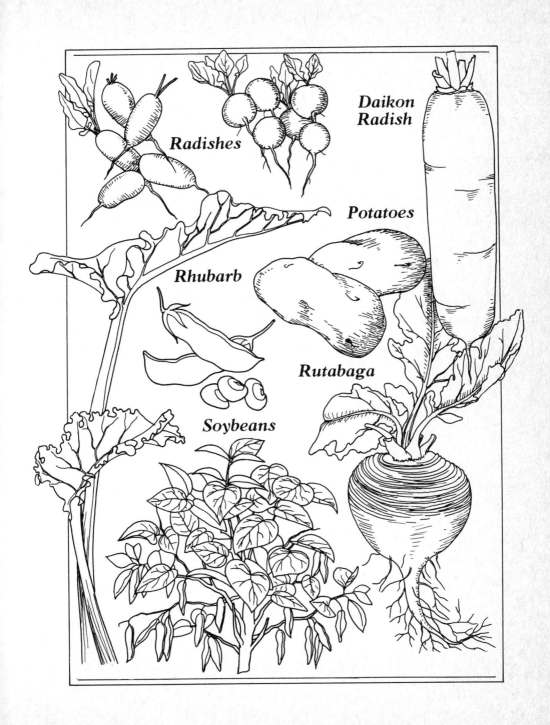

Radishes

Daikon
Radish

Potatoes

Rhubarb

Rutabaga

Soybeans

How Much to Plant: A rough guideline is 4 to 6 plants of early potatoes and 10 to 15 plants of late potatoes per person.

Planting: Potatoes are started not from seed, but from mature potatoes with "eyes" which sprout when planted. The seed potatoes can be planted whole, or cut into small pieces—each with an "eye." Or they can be sprouted before planting time. To presprout seed potatoes, expose them to temperatures between 40 and 50°F to break their dormancy. If the temperature is much higher than that, the tubers will begin to shrivel, which may set back their development. Start this treatment about two weeks before planting time.

Because sprouted potatoes emerge from the soil rapidly—sometimes within a few days—they shouldn't be planted as early as unsprouted ones. Plant about a week or two before the last frost date. They'll catch up with the plants from unsprouted seed potatoes and still reach maturity about two weeks earlier.

Unsprouted potatoes are normally planted early, at about the same time as peas—four to six weeks before the last spring frost. As long as the plants are less than 6 inches tall, they'll survive a frost pretty well. But if they're over 6 inches, a frost may set them back considerably or kill them.

As the sprouts emerge, mound soil or mulch around them so that only the top few inches are left uncovered. Hilling should be continued for three to four weeks until the mound is about a foot high.

Growing Guidelines: The development of the potato occurs in four phases. The first is marked by the vegeta-tive growth of the canopy, and can last from 30 to 70 days depending on variety, weather, and time of planting. During this phase, the primary growth takes place along the main shoot and the leaves emerging from it.

During the second growth phase, tubers begin to form. This development is usually marked by, but not dependent on, flower bud formation. Adequate moisture is critical during this period. "Potatoes can use a lot of moisture when they're setting," says Robert Lobitz. "The ground is just full of hair roots." Cut back on water once they start flowering.

Blossoming usually marks the start of the third phase: tuber growth. Too much water during this period can cause the tubers to grow too rapidly, causing hollow-heart. This is the time when the gardener can start harvesting new potatoes by reaching under the plant and carefully pulling out the largest tubers.

The final growth phase is maturation, when the leaves begin to die back and tuber growth slows. There is a significant increase of the dry weight of the tubers during this period.

Keys to Top Yields: Robert Lobitz says that since he started planting whole, sprouted seed potatoes, yields have doubled for most varieties. The tubers may turn out a bit smaller than those from cut seed potatoes, but the plants set much more heavily. He plants potatoes with two to four sprouts. If they have any more, he breaks them off. They are planted about 4 inches deep and 12 to 14 inches apart in rows spaced about 3 feet apart.

Organic gardening researcher and author John Jeavons of Mendocino County, California, uses the same technique. "It's really important that the eyes have started to sprout," he says. "Otherwise, they'll just sit in the ground for a month." In Jeavons's raised beds, he plants potatoes about 9 inches apart. Besides increasing yields, close spacing of potatoes effectively suppresses weeds, according to researchers at Cornell University. Rapid early growth also curtails the growth of weeds.

Harvesting and Storing:

When the vines have died back about halfway, the main harvest can begin. The tubers are usually dug with a fork, but some gardeners just pull them up by the vine. Tubers should be dried in a protected location for a few hours before storage. Potatoes store best at a temperature around 40°F. Any colder and the sugar content increases, giving them an off-taste. If it's warmer, they begin to sprout. Keep them in the dark to prevent greening, when the skin changes color and the potato becomes inedible.

Pests and Diseases:

The Colorado potato beetle is probably the most famous potato pest. "The best thing gardeners can do is pick them off," says Dr. J. D. Hare, an entomologist with the Connecticut Agricultural Experiment Station. Dr. Robert Metcalf, an entomologist with the University of Illinois, agrees and calls handpicking "the most underrated method an organic gardener can use."

The adult Colorado potato beetles emerge from the ground when the soil temperature reaches 54 to 56°F. They climb the plant and eat for about a week before mating. Destroying them early will reduce subsequent populations. A thick mulch will discourage the beetles from climbing the plant. Leafhoppers

may also appear early in the season, feeding on the leaves and sapping the vitality of the plants. But they seldom do enough damage to kill the plant or even reduce yields significantly.

Flea beetles also feed on the leaves of young plants. Because they emerge from the soil in the spring, frequent cultivation can help keep the population down. Fall plowing and crop rotation are other effective control measures.

Aphids are a problem on potatoes throughout the country, particularly since some species transmit the virus which causes potato leaf roll. Insecticidal soap sprays are effective. Even a strong stream of water can be used to dislodge aphids from the plants.

Potato scab is an organism that thrives in slightly alkaline soil. Since potatoes prefer their soil a little alkaline, the best way to control scab is to plant resistant varieties and to rotate the potatoes with other crops.

Nutritional Value:

Potatoes are a source of protein, B vitamins, vitamin C, magnesium, potassium, iron, calcium, and sulfur.

Choosing Varieties:

A favorite early variety is the old standby IRISH COBBLER. It's a white variety that grows well in heavy soils, has a good flavor for boiling, and is fairly reliable. For an early red variety, try NORLAND. It's suited to small gardens because the plants don't get too big, but can yield harvests of as much as 25 pounds from a 10-foot row. They're also good for gardeners who don't have really rich soil. However, like most early varieties, they don't store well.

KENNEBEC is at the top of the list for reliability. This midseason white will pro-

POTATOES

Variety	Description	Sources*
All Blue	90–120 days; good yields; potatoes have blue skins and blue flesh; good flavor; a novelty	12
Bake King	115 days; midseason variety; good yields of oval to oblong tubers; good for baking	12
Butte	110–120 days; uniform russet baker; high yields; excellent disease resistance	12
Early Gem	110 days; early, good yields; medium-long tubers; scab resistant; best in sandy, loamy soils	23
Explorer	90–120 days; true seed potato; sows, germinates, and transplants like peppers or tomatoes; yields uncertain; variable size	WA
Irish Cobbler	100 days; early; high yields; round to oblong white potatoes; widely adaptable	WA
Kennebec	115 days; vigorous and hardy; high yields; adapts well to all climates	9, 20
Norland	115 days; hardy; excellent yields; plants remain small; resistant to scab; good for northern areas	23
Red Pontiac	115 days; heavy yields well into midseason; oblong potatoes; does well in heavier soils; good winter keeper	5
Russet Burbank	120 days; late; heavy brown russet skin; white flesh; excellent for baking	23, 24
Viking	115 days; new potatoes can be harvested 70 days after planting, larger roots later; drought resistant	12

*Listings correspond to seed companies listed under Sources of Seeds at the back of the book.

duce a heavy yield year after year. VIKING is also a consistent producer of big potatoes.

The best baking varieties are the russet types. RUSSET BURBANK is the most popular, but it won't grow well in sandy soil. EARLY GEM is a good choice for these conditions. Most of the russets grow best in the western half of the country, but BAKE KING is a variety that was developed in New York to meet eastern requirements. BUTTE is a recent introduction that is particularly high in vitamin C and protein.

For novelty and flavor, try a variety with colored skin and flesh like ALL

BLUE. Most of the colored potatoes are more difficult to raise and don't yield as well, but their flavor makes them worth trying. In fact, the flavor of all varieties increases when they're grown organically. In two European studies, potatoes raised organically scored higher in taste tests than chemically grown potatoes.

RADISHES
Raphanus sativus

With a little planning and some shopping around in seed catalogs, you can plant varieties that will keep you in radishes throughout the entire year. Start with the tangy, fast-growing varieties early in the spring, and follow those with a summer type that will do well in hotter weather. Then, late in the season, plant some winter keepers that you can store until planting time next year.

Soil Preparation: Radishes grow well in just about any soil type, although a sandy loam is ideal. Plant radishes in ground that was manured for a previous crop; fresh manure will produce lush top growth and skimpy roots.

How Much to Plant: A rough guideline is 35 plants per person.

Planting: Quick, early radishes will be at their best only if they're grown in cool temperatures. Hot weather, particularly as the roots are maturing, will almost always turn them pithy or woody and very hot. Time your plantings so that the radishes will mature before temperatures rise into the 80s.

Spring radishes can go into the garden as soon as the soil can be worked. Since all you plant will mature at the same time, try staggering plantings by a week or so for a steady, manageable supply. Summer varieties can be sown from late spring to midsummer. Winter types should be planted no later than August 20 in most areas.

Plant eight or ten seeds per foot in rows at least 9 inches apart, or use them to mark rows of other crops. One seed packet should sow about 35 feet of row. Avoid sprinkling seeds thickly in the furrow, because the thinning that will be required later on will disturb the roots of the plants you leave. A planting depth of $1/2$ inch is optimum. Unused seed is good for five years.

Growing Guidelines: Give seedlings a steady supply of water when the plants are about an inch high. Radishes grown without moisture stress are crisp and mild, but with too little water they become woody and hot. Alternate drying and wetting encourages cracking.

Harvesting and Storing: Pull spring and summer varieties as soon as they mature, or any time after the roots begin to swell. All the fast-growing radishes start to decline in quality soon after they've matured. Within two days they'll be next to worthless if left in the ground. It's best to time your planting so that you can use the radishes as they mature. When you find yourself with too many, harvest the mature ones, cut off the tops, and store them in the refrigerator.

Winter radishes, for storage, mature in late September or early October. They'll take frosts without any damage, so you can leave them right in the ground until the hard freezes come. Then simply cut off the tops and store the roots in boxes of damp sand.

Most of the volatile oils that make

the roots hot are concentrated in the skin and outer layer of flesh, so if you end up with a harvest that's too spicy for your taste, peeling them will help.

Pests and Diseases:
Root maggots sometimes tunnel into the radishes, ruining the crop. Don't plant where a member of the cabbage family has grown in the past three years. If maggots are a continual problem, cover young plants with cheesecloth to discourage adult flies from laying their eggs in the soil.

Flea beetles can pester radishes. Set yellow-orange boards coated with Tanglefoot into the soil every 10 feet.

Most radishes grow so rapidly that disease is seldom a problem.

Nutritional Value:
Radishes are a good source of vitamin C and fiber.

Choosing Varieties:
Very short-season types are in and out of the ground before you know it. The fastest-maturing variety is SAXA, ready to eat in 18 days. It's a red, marble-sized radish that is good for popping into salads. Because it grows so fast, it stays crisp and relatively mild. CHERRY BELLE is a larger round radish that tastes much the same and matures in about 22 days. It stores well in the refrigerator. Larger still is CHAMPION, which grows to silver-dollar size in about 27 days. A 1957 All-America winner, it's still popular. CHAMPION can be planted earlier than other spring types and grows large without becoming soft and spongy.

There are several carrot-shaped early radishes that grow 5 to 6 inches long in about the same time as the smaller, round types. Because they grow more than twice as long as round radishes, these varieties need deep, loose soil. Prepare the ground as you would for carrots.

Radishes are the most popular of all vegetables with the Japanese, who are far ahead of us in breeding versatile cultivars. While nearly all American radishes bolt or become harsh in the summer's heat, there are several varieties from Japan, such as SUMMER CROSS, that can be grown successfully through the hot months. Compared to the crisper spring radishes, these daikons may seem somewhat less snappy, but their mild flavor and large size make them ideal for stir-frying, pickling, and steaming.

Winter radishes grow big—up to 2 feet long, weighing several pounds or more. They're also usually harder and more fibrous than earlier varieties, a trait that makes them less appealing for eating fresh, but which gives them their long storage life. Try cooking them as you would turnips or parsnips, or dice them into a wok with other vegetables.

BLACK SPANISH (60 days) is an excellent winter radish. Shaped like a turnip, with black skin and translucent white flesh, it will keep wrapped in plastic in the refrigerator for five months or more. It's a very pungent radish and a bit on the hard side, but among the most flavorful of the winter types.

CHINA ROSE (55 days) is a smaller, oval winter radish that has light pink skin and grows to about 5 inches in length. Another intriguing Chinese variety is GREEN SKIN & RED FLESH. The name aptly describes this fat, round radish that can weigh in at more than a pound.

Of the mild, long daikon types, CHINESE WHITE CELESTIAL, WINTER KING MIYAKE, and the strong-flavored MIYASHIGE are favorites. If you really like radishes, try SAKURAJIMA, a turnip-shaped variety. This monster can grow to a size of 50 pounds in warm climates. You've got to give it lots of room at planting time and wait 70 days for it to mature. (You can use that time to figure out what to do with 50 pounds of radish!)

For something even more unusual, plant some MUNCHEN BIER radishes. A mainstay in Munich beer halls, where they are served sliced raw, this long white radish matures in about 45 days. The spicy, succulent seedpods are also relished. To try them, let the plants flow-

RADISHES

Variety	Description	Sources*
All Season	45 days; white and tapered; best at 12½" long; slow to bolt; good keeper; resists pithiness	5
Black Spanish	60 days; large, turnip-shaped; deep black skin; white, pungent flesh; excellent for winter storage	WA
Champion	20–28 days; sow spring or fall; round, bright red roots; grows large, but not pithy; good keeper; AAS	WA
Cherry Belle	20–30 days; sow all summer long; long, roundish, bright cherry red; resists pithiness; good keeper; AAS	WA
China Rose	55 days; winter radish; rose-colored skin and flesh; excellent keeper without losing quality	8, 38
Chinese White Celestial	60 days; winter variety; cylindrical, stump-rooted; solid, crisp, white flesh; excellent keeper; good for pickling	21
French Breakfast	23 days; oblong and blunt; rose-scarlet in color; mildy pungent, white flesh	WA
Green Skin and Red Flesh	55–60 days; fall or winter harvest; green skin with reddish purple flesh; can grow to 1½ pounds; good raw or pickled	34
Long Scarlet	25–30 days; long, tapered, deep red roots; crisp, tender, white flesh; good for bunching	12
Miyashige	50–78 days; stump-rooted, to 15"; roots to 6 pounds; crisp, pure white flesh; good for keeping, pickling	15
Munchen Bier	45–67 days; long, white roots; masses of thick, tender, juicy, stringless pods atop 24" stems; sweet flavor; good in salads, steamed	36
Sakurajima	60–150 days; slow growing; roots to 14"; can grow to 65 pounds in Florida; pure white, tender flesh	21, 40

(continued)

RADISHES—*Continued*

Variety	Description	Sources*
Saxa	18–25 days; plant spring or fall; very small, deep red globes; pure white flesh; holds well in good conditions	8
Summer Cross	45 days; roots to 15"; rose-scarlet root; mildly pungent, white flesh	13
White and Long	55 days; Chinese summer radish; white roots to 12" long; good for tropical areas; tolerates summer heat	34
White Icicle	28 days; long, slender root; white flesh; crisp and tender, mild and sweet	WA
Winter King Miyake	50–60 days; vigorous and productive; hardy; sow summer or fall; roots to 20"; resists pithiness; pure white flesh	34

*Listings correspond to seed companies listed under Sources of Seeds at the back of the book.

er. If grown for pods, the roots should not be harvested; they'll be tough and woody.

RHUBARB
(Pieplant)
Rheum rhaponticum

Rhubarb's leaf stem, properly called a petiole, is the only edible portion of the plant. Both roots and leaves are toxic to humans and should never be eaten. The petiole which supports the large round leaf is pink, red, or reddish green, and thick and fleshy. The taste is slightly acid and serves an interesting foil to the palate when sweetened and added to other cooked fruits. It is commonly prepared in sauces, pies, and jams. The stems are also pulverized and fermented with sweetener to make an interesting homemade wine.

Rhubarb is not a suitable plant for a small garden. It is a long-lived perennial that grows large and rangy. It needs a well-prepared site where it will remain for many years. Although it occupies the garden all season long, its useful harvest period is eight to ten weeks at most. But in larger gardens, rhubarb certainly deserves a spot, for it produces its delicious leaf stems with little attention from the gardener once it is established.

Rhubarb favors cool weather. The upper half of North America is more favorable than the lower half. Areas where the mean temperature in summer is above 75°F and in winter is above 40°F are not suitable. Areas where winter dormancy is brought on by temperatures that freeze the crown are most desirable. In some areas with mild winters, the plant will remain dormant in the summer and leaf out in winter.

Soil Preparation: Rhubarb will do well in a wide range of soil types, although well-drained sandy loams are preferable. Whatever the soil type, good drainage is critical. Dig a trench, and lay aside the good topsoil. Make it 18 inches wide and 2 to 3 feet deep—the deeper the better. Discard the subsoil and fill in the trench with well-rotted manure and rich compost. At this point, add a shovelful of bonemeal and two shovels of granite dust per plant. Mix these thoroughly into the organic material. Other long-term phosphorus and potassium fertilizers such as rock phosphate and greensand can be substituted for the bonemeal and granite dust. Pack down the organic material to within 12 inches of the top of the trench and fill in with topsoil. Short-cuts can be made, of course, but these directions are for a rhubarb bed constructed for use over a long period of time. Soil pH can range from 5.0 to 6.8.

How Much to Plant: A rough guideline is two or three plants per person.

Planting: Rhubarb is best started in the home garden from crowns that are purchased or donated by a fellow gardener. Crowns can be planted as early as possible in spring, before their dormancy has broken, or in fall before the ground freezes hard.

The plants in an established bed should be divided and replanted every five years to keep them from crowding each other and producing slender, inferior stalks. Divide plants that are at least three years old and dormant, either in early spring or fall. Dig the crowns and split them so that at least two large buds or "eyes" remain on each piece; leave as much root on each piece as possible.

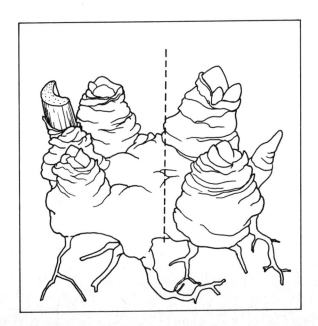

Dividing a rhubarb crown. Dig up the dormant crown in the fall or early spring. Cut off top growth and any sections of the crown that are rotten or shriveled. Cut the healthy crown into pieces with at least two "eyes" or buds.

Roughly four to six pieces can be split from each crown. Do not allow these divisions to dry out before planting.

In the prepared bed, plant crown divisions 3 feet apart in rows set 4 feet apart. Bury the crowns 2 to 3 inches deep, then firm the soil.

Growing Guidelines: Keep the bed free of weeds, moist, and in good, workable condition. Rhubarb leaf and stem production will fall off sharply when the roots become dry. Mulch with straw or hay when plants are 4 inches tall, and side-dress with manure through the summer and fall months. After the leaves die down and the ground has frozen, cover the bed with a deep layer of manure, leaf mold, or compost.

Keys to Top Yields: Allow the leaves and stems to mature without cutting the first year; from the strength stored in the roots, more growth will be produced the following year. Remove seed heads as they appear in order to redirect energy into the roots and leaves.

Season Extending: To extend the harvest, rhubarb roots can be forced to produce shoots over the winter.

Harvesting and Storing: Do not harvest any stalks the first year. The second year, take only a few. Full harvesting begins in the spring of the third year, when the stalks are 12 to 24 inches long and the leaves are fully developed, but before the stems become tough. Pull the stems from the crown with a sideways twisting motion. Harvesting can continue for eight to ten weeks, but always leave at least half the plant intact. Too heavy a harvest one year will undercut the next season's production.

After harvest, rhubarb cuttings can be stored in the refrigerator for two to three weeks without losing quality.

RHUBARB

Variety	Description	Sources*
Cherry Red	good producer; cherry red outside stalk; greenish inside; very tart and juicy; good for mild-winter areas	24
Chipman's Canada Red	heavy stalks; bright red inside and out; very sweet and juicy; remains red when cooked; seldom goes to seed	12
Flare	good producer; stalks vary in color from red to green; balance between sweet and tart taste	12
McDonald's Canadian Red	stalks dark red inside and out; reputed to be the sweetest; no need to peel stalks; excellent for sauces and pies	14

*Listings correspond to seed companies listed under Sources of Seeds at the back of the book.

Cooked rhubarb can be frozen and stored for up to a year. Rhubarb is also candied and preserved by canning.

Pests and Diseases: Only the rhubarb curculio causes serious damage. Eliminating wild dock growing in the nearby area helps to prevent infestation of this pest because wild dock is, along with rhubarb, a host to the larvae.

Nutritional Value: Rhubarb stems are a good source of vitamin A and potassium, and provide some vitamin C as well.

RUTABAGAS
(Canadian turnip, swede, Swedish turnip, cabbage)
Brassica napus,
Napobrassica Group

The biennial rutabaga, thought to be a cross between a turnip and a cabbage, is relished for the dense flesh of its bulbous root, which may grow to weigh as much as 6 or 7 pounds. There are both white- and yellow-fleshed varieties.

Although the taste of the rutabaga is similar to that of the related turnip, the rutabaga takes about a month longer to mature and is primarily a fall crop, with much better storage characteristics. In the kitchen, rutabaga roots are used much like turnips, usually steamed and mashed or served whole as a vegetable dish, or added to soups and stews. The roots can also be cut raw into slivers and served with a dip. The strong-flavored greens may be used as a potherb.

Rutabagas are not difficult to grow, provided they are given ample moisture and cool nights as they approach maturity. A hot autumn may destroy the quality of the root, as may a deficiency of potas-

sium or boron. Only one planting is usually made in a season.

Rutabagas do best in medium- and short-season areas where they are planted in late spring or summer so that the roots may mature in cool autumn weather. Best root development is made in temperatures averaging from 60 to 65°F. Planted in the spring or in hot climates, the tops will grow rankly, producing small and pithy roots. This hardy crop tolerates frost well, but when roots freeze, taste and texture are altered.

Soil Preparation: Rutabagas thrive in medium-heavy soils, including the heavier sandy loams, although they may be grown in lighter soils if ample nutrients and moisture are provided. The soil should be well limed (the ideal pH is 6.5 to 7.2), rich in organic matter and nutrients, but not overly rich in nitrogen, which will force top growth to the detriment of the root. Prepare the soil to a depth of 10 inches and incorporate plenty of aged compost and some wood ashes for extra potassium.

How Much to Plant: A rough guideline is 10 to 13 plants per person.

Planting: Sow seed directly in the garden 15 weeks before the first expected frost. Space seed $\frac{1}{2}$ inch apart in conventional rows set 18 inches apart. Growing bed spacing is 9 inches. Rutabagas may also be grown in wide rows. Cover the seed with $\frac{1}{2}$ inch of soil and do not tamp the soil too firmly after planting. Unused seed is good for four years.

Growing Guidelines: As soon as seeds have germinated, thin the seedlings to stand 1 inch apart in rows. In two weeks, thin again to 8 inches apart. Mulch the rows deeply after the second

RUTABAGAS

Variety	Description	Sources*
American Purple Top Yellow	85–90 days; standard variety; globe-shaped roots with purple tops; flesh is sweet and smooth textured	12
Laurentian	90 days; globe-shaped roots with purple tops; perhaps the most dependable of all varieties	15

*Listings correspond to seed companies listed under Sources of Seeds at the back of the book.

thinning to keep the soil cool and moist through the growing season. Rutabagas need no further attention until harvest time.

Harvesting and Storing:

Rutabagas may be harvested anytime they are large enough to be of use. They are at their best when 3 to 5 inches around and no longer than 5 to 7 inches. Most gardeners wait to harvest until after the first sharp autumn frost, which improves both the taste and texture of the roots. It's important, however, not to let the roots freeze, for this will shorten their storage life and alter their flavor unpleasantly. They keep for five to six months in good shape, provided they are stored in cool (32 to 40° F) and moist conditions. They can be stored right in the garden, covered with a deep mulch to keep the ground from freezing, and harvested as needed. If any roots remain in place until the spring, they will sprout new growth which can be used as a potherb.

Pests and Diseases:

See Cabbage. Rutabagas are bothered far less than cabbage.

Nutritional Value:

The smooth, waxy, blue-green tops are a rich source of vitamins A, C, and E, and the roots themselves contain plenty of vitamin A and calcium.

SOYBEANS
Glycine max

Traditionally used as a green manure crop or livestock feed, it has not been until the last several decades that Westerners have discovered the soybean's great value in human nutrition.

The plants grow from 12 inches to more than 24 inches tall and most are bushy, although some have an indeterminate habit. These legumes produce pods usually containing three to four seeds, in shades of yellow, brown, black, or in various combinations of these colors. The seeds are about the size of navy beans.

Soybeans have a rich nutty flavor all their own. The home gardener can fully appreciate their versatility and good taste by using them as a fresh vegetable or as dried beans. The green shell beans can be steamed as a vegetable dish, chilled for use in salads, roasted like peanuts, or added to soups, stews, and chili. The dry beans are also used for soups and stews, and in addition can be ground into flour, or processed into soy milk, tofu, or tempeh.

Most soybeans require a long and hot growing season, with temperatures averaging between 70 and 80°F. There are some varieties, however, that mature in as little as 70 days, affording gardeners in all areas the opportunity to grow this crop. Soybeans are slightly more cold-tolerant than other beans, but are still susceptible to frost damage.

Soil Preparation:

The soil should be light, well drained, well limed, and not too rich in nutrients—especially nitrogen, which will impede the production of pods and seeds. Even clay soils will support good crops, as long as they are not waterlogged for long periods. Choose the sunniest area of the garden. Prepare the soil to average fineness, and do not add compost unless the soil is very deficient in nutrients. Soybeans, which are legumes, will add nitrogen to the soil for crops that follow. The recommended pH is 6.5 to 7.0.

How Much to Plant:

A rough guideline is 37 plants per person.

Planting:

Soybeans are generally direct-seeded. Soak the seeds overnight to hasten germination, and inoculate them before planting. There are inoculants specifically suited to soybeans, but these may not be readily obtainable; in lieu of soybean inoculant, one suited for peas and beans can be used. Plant the seeds only when the soil has warmed up thoroughly to an optimum germinating temperature of 65 to 70°F, about a week after the frost-free date. The planting area can be warmed up by covering it with black plastic for two weeks before planting. Remove the plastic when planting. Plant the beans 1½ inches deep in moist soils, or 3 to 4 inches deep in dry, warm soils (generally in hot climates). Space seeds 1½ inches apart in conventional rows set 30 inches apart. Soybeans are suitable for planting in wide rows. Raised bed spacing is 9 inches. Unused seed is good for three years.

Growing Guidelines:

After the plants are 2 to 3 inches tall, thin them to 4 inches apart in rows and apply a mulch. Avoid working among plants when the leaves are wet, since leaves are easily broken then, and disease can be spread. Keep the soil evenly moist, especially after flowers have opened, until pods have set.

Harvesting and Storing:

For use as a green shell bean, pick when the seeds are mature, or nearly mature, but before the pods and foliage have begun to wither. To make hulling easier, steam the pods for ten minutes; then drain them, break them in half crosswise, and squeeze out the beans. At this stage, soybeans may be eaten fresh, or they may be canned or frozen.

For storage as dry beans, harvest when the pods are dry but the plant stems are still green. Waiting longer than this may give the pods time to shatter, resulting in loss of the seeds. Store soybeans in airtight containers in a cool (32 to 40°F), dry location.

Pests and Diseases:

Soybeans are subject to attack from both, although none are usually serious. Potential insect pests include cutworms, grasshoppers,

SOYBEANS

Variety	Description	Sources*
Altona	90–100 days; reliable producer; good for northern areas; beans are bright yellow when mature	15
Early Green Bush	85 days; bushy plants grow to 16″ tall; a midseason variety	33
Extra Early Green	70 days; short-season variety; produces many tender, very tasty beans	38
Fiskeby V	91 days; bushy plants to 18″; suited for northern gardens; an especially high-protein variety	33
Frostbeater	75 days; reliable, heavy producer; does well in northern gardens; bright green beans with robust flavor	5
Kanrich	100–115 days; heavy yields; plants to 24″; long-season type; recommended for warm climates only; good canned or frozen	8, 21

*Listings correspond to seed companies listed under Sources of Seeds at the back of the book.

Japanese beetles, leafhoppers, Mexican bean beetles, and white grubs. The fuzzy leaves of the plant seem to drive insects to more succulent garden plants. Diseases include bacterial blight (in cool, rainy weather), bacterial pustule, and downy mildew. See Beans for insect and disease controls.

Nutritional Value: Soybeans are protein powerhouses, containing 40 percent of that nutrient. They are a favorite meat substitute among vegetarians.

SPINACH
Spinacia oleracea

Spinach is usually thought of as a spring crop, but in most areas, it does best when sown in the fall and overwintered. See the details on this method under the heading of Planting. Spinach is a spring tonic, excellent with carrot juice, great in salads. Unfortunately, it is often abused by cooking.

Soil Preparation: Spinach fares best in a fertile soil with plenty of moisture and good tilth. Light, sandy soils with little organic matter will yield spindly, light-green spinach of poor quality. Like most leafy green vegetables, spinach needs lots of nitrogen for rapid growth, so your soil should be well fertilized. Work in 1½ pounds of fresh manure per square foot at least six weeks before planting.

Spinach likes slightly acidic conditions—between pH 6.0 and 6.5. If the

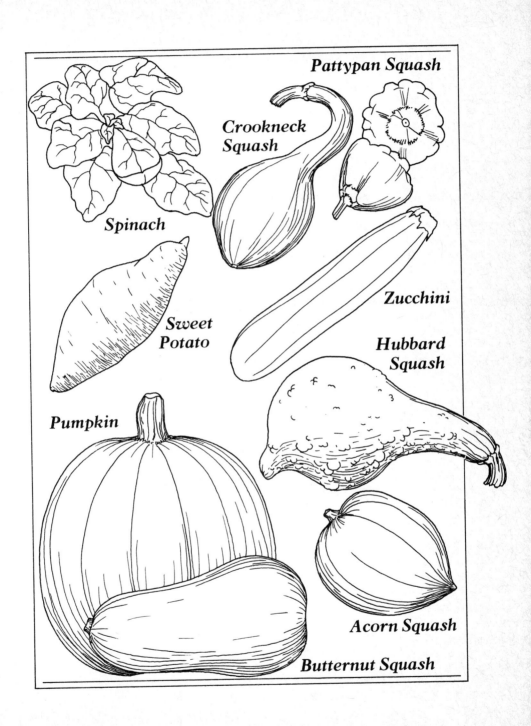

Pattypan Squash

Crookneck
Squash

Spinach

Sweet
Potato

Zucchini

Hubbard
Squash

Pumpkin

Acorn Squash

Butternut Squash

pH is over 6.7, spinach will be one of the first plants to show a manganese deficiency, since manganese gets locked up in alkaline soil. Look for speckled yellow leaves that curl upwards.

How Much to Plant: Since spinach does not produce abundant greens, you'll need a lot of plants. A rough guideline is 30 plants per person.

Planting: You can plant spinach in the spring, fall, and winter with some knowledge of varieties and advance planning that includes fall soil preparation, protective devices, and planting two or more varieties for extended harvests. Your scheme will take advantage of spinach's fast-maturing nature. Direct-seeded, it is in and out of the ground in eight weeks or less, making it perfect for succession plantings. It will even germinate in near-freezing ground, although germination is best at 60°F. In the North, the early crop can be harvested in plenty of time for late sowings of corn, beans, and all fall crops. As a late crop, it can follow corn, beans, cabbage, and onions.

Since spinach can germinate in very cold soil, you should plan to plant it just as soon as the ground thaws and dries enough to work. The previous autumn, manure the soil and work the ground. Be ready as the time approaches and watch the weather. In the spring, a missed day can mean a missed week or more because rains are frequent and the ground takes a long time to dry in cool weather. Plant super-early varieties like INDIAN SUMMER or COLD-RESISTANT SAVOY. Advance your planting time two to four weeks by covering an autumn-prepared bed with a cold-frame sash or a plastic tunnel in the spring. The ground will soon warm enough to plant.

After soaking the seeds in water for 24 hours to soften their coats, sow them ½ inch deep, about 2 inches apart. Seeds should germinate in about a week. Although it is possible to transplant spinach seedlings raised indoors, they do not take the move very well and usually suffer shock. Always try to direct-seed your crops into rich soil. Unused seed is good for one to two years.

Getting a good, even stand from a late-summer planting can be a problem. In hot soil, many of the seeds won't germinate. At soil temperatures above 70°F, the germination rate drops below 50 percent. Freeze the seeds for a few days, then moisten and hold them in the refrigerator a few more days to start the germination process. The soil is likely to be dry, so wet the ground thoroughly, and when it dries enough to work, prepare a seedbed. After you plant the seed, cover the rows with boards to keep the sun off the soil. But be sure to remove the boards as soon as the seed germinates. Where heat and sun are severe problems, you might try starting the plants in a cool place in individual containers, then transplanting them once they're up and growing.

In solar structures, like attached greenhouses and solar cold frames, spinach is an excellent crop to plant in February so it will mature at the end of March. Eileen Weinsteiger, a researcher on the solar growing project at the Rodale Research Center, says, "We've found that MONNOPA does very well in solar structures." Be ready to ventilate solar structures devoted to spinach when the daytime high temperatures pass 80°F.

Growing Guidelines: When the young plants show two good-sized leaves, thin them to stand 4 to 6 inches apart. Thin conscientiously: if spinach growth is stunted or checked by over-crowding, the plant tends to run to seed more rapidly. And it's important to keep the soil moist but not soggy. If the soil dries out, the plants will bolt faster, too. Give your spinach a dose of fish emulsion or manure tea when the plants show four leaves each. Since spinach does not compete well with weeds, cultivate shallowly and don't disturb the fine root system. Mulch early in the season to keep the soil cool and moist.

A heavy feeder, spinach has a deep taproot with an extensive, fibrous system branching out from it. Whether you plant the crop in rows or beds, make sure your soil is cultivated at least 1 foot deep. Growing spinach in double-dug beds is an excellent idea.

The faster spinach is grown, the better it will taste. If the temperature suddenly jumps into the danger zone when the days are starting to lengthen, cover your plants with shade cloth to nurse them through the hot spell. It may not keep plants from bolting, but it may promote longer and better growth. "We did a test last summer with temperatures in the 80s and found that 40 to 45 percent shade netting did not work," explains John Jeavons, an organic gardening researcher and author in northern California. "The crop just sat there and looked at us—it didn't grow. But when we put on a 55 percent netting, the spinach grew 4 inches more in a week."

Keys to Top Yields:

According to popular wisdom, hot weather, plain and simple, is what causes spinach to send up a seed stem that branches out and forms a 2- to 3-foot-high flower stalk covered with small, bitter leaves. Hot weather *does* make the seed stalk grow fast. But the real switch that turns your spinach from the succulent leaf-producing stage to the flowering stage is longer daylight hours. And the longest days of the season come very early in summer—in some regions right after the last frost.

The best advice if you plan to grow large, buttery leaves is to sow seed very early so that the plants are producing before the longest days arrive. To avoid bolting, time your plantings so that the crop can mature while the days are short and the weather is cool.

Season Extending:

Plant a very hardy variety like BLOOMSDALE LONG-STANDING or WINTER BLOOMSDALE in the late summer or fall. You want the plants to get up and growing, but not necessarily to develop leaves of harvestable size. (If leaves do get that big, eat them, because they'll almost certainly become winter damaged.) In cold-winter areas, cover the plants with a 2-foot mulch of straw soon after the ground freezes. Polyethylene tunnels aren't suitable since they will sag badly under a snow load. Once the ground has frozen, the leaves should not be exposed to sunlight, or they can become badly dehydrated. When the ground begins thawing in the spring, uncover the spinach. You'll begin picking a month or two ahead of a crop from an early spring sowing, especially if you've overwintered them in an open cold frame under deep mulch, then put the glass on the frame after the mulch is removed.

Anywhere the winter is reasonably mild, like the Deep South and coastal California, the best spinach crops come in the fall and spring. Southerners, too, can adapt the overwintering technique to their spinach beds. If a brief period of freezing weather sets in, mulch the plants heavily or cover them with glass or polyethylene, and the spinach plants' productivity will increase. Be sure to remove the covering when the air temperature under it approaches 80°F, or you'll encourage bolting.

Harvesting and Storing:

Spinach is ready to eat six to eight weeks after planting. Each plant should have six leaves 7 to 8 inches long before you start to harvest.

By carefully harvesting the outer leaves of the fall crop, you'll be able to extend the productive life of each plant, says Dr. Raymond E. Webb, chief of the Vegetable Laboratory of the Horticultural Science Institute at the USDA research facility in Beltsville, Maryland.

"When each plant gets to be 6 inches tall, make the first harvest by cutting large leaves around the youngest leaves, leaving at least a 2-inch growing point in the middle of the plant," he says. The leaves should be about as big as your hand when you cut them. Make certain you pick only from the outside, taking care not to denude the plant completely. "During the following spring, you should be able to get at least three good additional cuttings from each plant, harvesting the leaves as you did during the previous fall," Dr. Webb explains.

You can also harvest the entire plant by cutting the taproot just below ground level with a sharp knife. Always harvest the largest plants first, giving the smaller ones time to catch up. At the first signs of bolting, cut all the plants at once. Spinach can be eaten fresh, canned, or frozen.

Pests and Diseases:

By growing spinach during the cool parts of the year, your crop will be virtually free of pests and diseases. Besides forcing plants to seed prematurely, high humidity and warm temperatures encourage foliar diseases. The two most common are downy mildew (or blue mold) and cucumber mosaic virus (or yellows). If such diseases are a problem, turn to resistant varieties like MELODY, HYBRID NO. 7, and VIRGINIA SAVOY. The cabbage looper, spotted cucumber beetle, beet leafminer, and beet leafhopper are the major insect pests. Treat the cabbage looper with *Bacillus thuringiensis* (Bt). Handpick the other insects and spray with purchased insecticidal soap or homemade soap sprays. In cases of dense infestation, dust with rotenone. For leafminers, promptly remove all affected leaves to prevent the population of parent flies from increasing.

Nutritional Value:

Cup for cup, spinach has one of the highest amounts of vitamins A and B_2 of any common vegetable. It also contains very high amounts of iron, calcium, and protein.

Choosing Varieties:

There are two main types of spinach, the crinkled-leaf and the smooth-leaf. Commercial canners like the smooth-leaf type because the dirt washes off easily. Gardeners, on the other hand, most often choose the chewier crinkled-leaf varieties. The most popular among home gardeners is the savoy type, which has very crumpled leaves.

"I haven't found a better hybrid spinach than MELODY [a semi-SAVOY All American Selection winner]," says George Park, Jr., of the Geo. W. Park Seed Company, Greenwood, South Carolina. He sells 50 percent more of MELODY than of any other spinach variety, even though the seed is one-third more expensive. Because the plant is semi-erect, it doesn't lie on the ground and pick up grit. Its leaves are convoluted and sweet, with great texture and taste. Besides sowing MELODY for main spring and fall crops and BLOOMSDALE LONGSTANDING for late spring, early in the season try the very fast INDIAN SUMMER, some COLD-RESISTANT SAVOY for cold-ground sowing, and some WINTER BLOOMSDALE for overwintering under mulch.

SPINACH

Variety	Description	Sources*
America	50 days; heavy yields; dark green leaves; slow to bolt; good for spring planting; AAS	WA
Bloomsdale Longstanding	48 days; vigorous, erect plants; thick, glossy, crumpled leaves; stands well in hot weather	WA
Cold-Resistant Savoy	45 days; super early; tolerant of heat, cold, blight; used for late summer, early autumn harvest; can be wintered over	31, 33
Dark Green Bloomsdale	40–50 days; vigorous, upright plants; large dark green, fleshy, deeply crumpled leaves; resists bolting	37
Hybrid No. 7	40–45 days; erect, upright habit; large, dark green, semi-crumpled leaves; downy mildew resistant; good canned, frozen	WA
Indian Summer	39 days; super early; upright habit; heavy yields; dark green, semi-savoyed leaves; disease resistant	15
Melody	45 days; semi-erect plant; semi-crumpled leaves; resistant to downy mildew, yellows; for spring or fall planting; AAS	5
Monnopa	45 days; arrow-shaped leaves; low oxalate content; very mild; hardy and bolt resistant	36
Virginia Savoy	39–40 days; massive, thick, heavily crumpled leaves; blight and yellows resistant; withstands cold weather; fall crop	3, 8
Winter Bloomsdale	44–50 days; spreading, low-growing; firm, thick, crumpled leaves; hardy; cold tolerant; winters well	5

*Listings correspond to seed companies listed under Sources of Seeds at the back of the book.

SQUASH, SUMMER
Cucurbita pepo
var. *melopepo*

Some simple techniques will give you a perfect squash almost every day from early summer until the first frost. Two healthy squash plants are all you need for a dependable supply, plus an occasional squash to give away, no doubt. You must diligently pick the young squash. And you must keep your plants vigorous, which in most places means warding off the squash vine borer.

Soil Preparation: Though squash prefers a fertile, sandy loam with a pH between 6.0 and 7.5, as long as there's plenty of organic matter where the roots are growing, squash plants don't care what the rest of the garden is like. So rather than amending all the soil in the area where you want to grow squash, just build one fertile hill for every six seeds. Dig out an area 6 inches deep and about 2 feet wide, then mix the soil you've removed with several shovelfuls of aged manure, compost, or leaf mold. Refill the hole, shaping the soil mixture into a mound. Make the hills 4 to 6 feet apart. Don't step on the hill once you've built it, though. Researchers at the University of Georgia found that compressing the soil where squash is growing can reduce yields by up to 58 percent.

How Much to Plant: Two vines will provide a steady—but not overwhelming—harvest that most families will probably find ample.

Planting: Summer squash are happiest when the weather's warm. Mature plants can survive temperatures down to about 30°F, but even a light frost will kill

seedlings. Seeds shouldn't be planted outdoors until the day/night average temperature reaches 50°F. The minimum soil temperature for germination is 60°F; the optimum is 95°F. In cold soil, seeds often fail to germinate and rot. In Palmer, Alaska, tests of a number of zucchini varieties by the USDA showed that only BLACK JACK consistently germinated in cold ground.

Plant six seeds in a circle on top of each of the fertile hills you've made, burying the seeds half an inch deep. They'll germinate in seven to ten days. Later, thin seedlings to the best two in each hill. Unused seed is good for five years.

Handling Seedlings: Start seeds indoors about three weeks before planting time (late April in most parts of the country). Squash roots are very fragile, so be careful when transplanting seedlings. Once outdoors, cloches or hotcaps will protect plants from cold and accelerate growth until hot weather arrives.

Growing Guidelines: Squash need full sun and plenty of water—soil for squash should always be moist. Leaves may wilt dramatically on hot days, even though the plants get adequate water, but they'll revive at night. The plants are heavy feeders. Side-dress with compost, or water with manure tea, at first fruit set. Bush squash are really compact vines, and often grow 6 feet long. About six weeks after germination, the first blossoms appear. Male blossoms are usually the first to show, and always greatly outnumber females. The males are narrow and straight, while the females are smaller and have a tiny fruit at their base.

Squash is usually bee-pollinated. But according to Dr. Frank Parker, a bee biologist with the USDA, indiscriminate use of pesticides and destruction of natural habitats have seriously reduced wild bee populations in this country. He says gardeners and farmers frequently find that their squash plants are not pollinated. The blossoms wilt, and the tiny fruit on the female flower turns black and rots. Unless you see bees actively working on your plants, Dr. Parker advises hand pollination.

The easiest way to pollinate is to pluck a male flower, tear off the petals, and swish the pollen-laden end inside a female flower. You can also transfer the pollen with a paint brush.

Summer squash varieties will cross-pollinate each other, as well as winter squash and many pumpkins. The cross won't affect that year's fruit. But if the seeds are saved, next year's squash will be mongrels. If you grow more than one variety of squash (or pumpkin) in your garden, don't save the seed.

Keys to Top Yields:

There are two good reasons to pick all summer squash before they get too large. First, they taste best when young and tender. But more important for getting a squash a day all season is that it keeps the plants producing. Once the squash mature seed, hormonal changes in the plant send messages that slow down production.

Keeping the vines picked sounds easy, but in fact the job has a way of getting ahead of gardeners. Summer squash can grow an inch or more in a single day. For best production and eating, zucchini, crookneck, and straightneck squash should be picked when they are about an inch in diameter and 4 inches long. Scalloped or pattypan types are at their best when about 2 to 3 inches across.

Harvesting and Storing:

About a week after pollination—or about 50 days from planting—the fruit will be ready to harvest. Squash should be picked while the rind is still soft enough to pierce easily with a fingernail. To avoid damaging the fragile plants, cut the squash at the stem with a sharp knife.

By picking the young squash regularly and preparing for vine borers, you can expect each plant to produce five or six squash—about 2 pounds—every week until frost.

Summer squash, unlike their winter cousins, don't store well. They'll last only a week or so, at best, in cool temperatures.

Pests and Diseases:

The major squash pest is the squash vine borer. One day the vines look healthy, but on the next the plants wilt badly and the leaves turn black at the edges. At this point, the plant is nearly finished. Closer inspection reveals a yellow sawdustlike material called frass at the base of the stems. The inch-long white borers eat the stems and at the same time inject a toxin which causes wilting.

Once the larvae are inside, only an injection of *Bacillus thuringiensis* (Bt) or major surgery will save the plant. Slit the stems to locate and destroy all the borers. Then mound soil over the wound. Damaged plants will often recover, although they may never regain their earlier vigor.

A better approach is to keep the borers from ever burrowing into your plants. The adult borer is an orange and black wasplike moth that lays eggs at the base of the stems in late June or early July. In the South, the moths come twice, in April as well as early summer. Any place that the stem touches the ground is

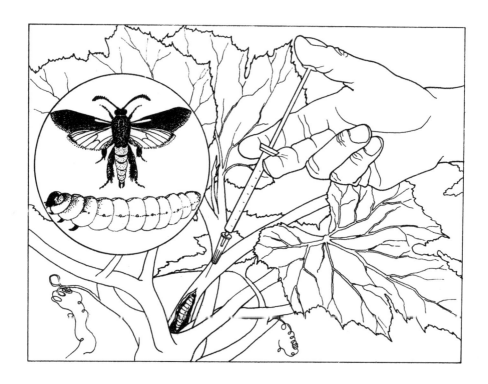

Squash vine borer. Destroy the larvae of this moth by injecting Bt into the center of the stem an inch above the borer hole or 1½ inches from the soil line.

a potential egglaying site. The moth locates the stem by feel. Since the females begin laying at about the time the vines start running, and remain active for a month, check plants regularly for the tiny (¹⁄₂₅-inch) red or orange eggs. They are almost always around the base of the stem or, if you have very light soil, just below the surface. Rub off and destroy as many as you can find. Mark Boudreau, a research assistant at the University of Illinois, recommends dusting the base of the plants with rotenone as soon as the first eggs appear and continuing the treatment every two days for about a week. The rotenone kills the larvae as they begin to chew into the stem.

In two or three days, the larvae hatch and burrow into the plant, where they grow fat on the soft material inside. There may be three or four worms in each tunnel and as many as four tunnels in a plant. In a very short time, the plant will begin to wilt and drop leaves.

Researchers at the University of Illinois have recently devised ways to keep the adults from laying their eggs on squash plants, including wrapping strips of nylon stocking around the stems. Since the adult moths sense the plant by touching it, wrapping an old pair of panty hose around the base and any part of the vine touching the ground can prevent the moths from feeling the stem and laying eggs. The stockings also have the advantage of being elastic enough to stretch as the plant grows.

Because the moths won't dig far into the earth, soil can be mounded on the plant stems. The soil must be piled higher each week, though, to accommodate the plant's growth. Adding a late planting makes sense, too. If seeds are sown in mid-July, the seedlings won't be up until the adults are long gone. About the time your first planting succumbs,

SUMMER SQUASH

Variety	Description	Sources*
Aristocrat	48–53 days; hybrid; popular variety; upright fruits; good-quality zucchini; AAS	23, 24
Benning's Green Tint	54 days; more tender than Patty Pan; pale green, disc-shaped fruits with scalloped edges; best when very small	15, 22
Black Jack	55 days; open, bush-type; smooth, cylindrical, black-green fruits; good for home gardens	33
Burpee Hybrid	50 days; vigorous, bushlike plant; heavy yields; medium-sized fruits with medium green color	5
Early Golden Summer	48–53 days; bush-type; meaty fruits with fine texture; bright yellow fruits change to golden orange when mature	WA
Early Prolific	51 days; bushy plant; very productive; cylindrical fruits to 6"; AAS	WA
Gold Rush	53 days; compact bush; uniform, smooth, cylindrical, deep golden yellow zucchini; AAS	15
Onyx	55 days; very high yields; holds size well; shiny, black-green fruits; freezes well	10
Peter Pan	52 days; semi-bush habit; medium green fruits with large scallops; excellent quality; AAS	33
Scallopini	50 days; compact growth habit; cross between scallop and zucchini types; scalloped, bright green shell; AAS	33
Seneca Prolific	50 days; very early; continuous heavy yield throughout season; tapered, smooth, creamy yellow squash	37

*Listings correspond to seed companies listed under Sources of Seeds at the back of the book.

the second planting will begin to set fruit.

Mosaic viruses, of which there are several, cause problems for squash growers. All types spread rapidly, causing stunted plants and poor fruit set. The diseases are transmitted from plant to plant by aphids, which also damage the plants as they suck juices from leaves and stems.

If aphid populations can be controlled on plants, outbreaks of mosaic virus will be much less common or severe. One of the easiest ways to keep aphids away from plants is to use mulches of aluminum foil and white plastic. It seems that the sun's reflection on the mulch confuses the aphids, which don't land on the plants. Researchers at the Connecticut Agricultural Experiment Station used foil mulch on SENECA PROLIFIC summer squash, and found that the treatment doubled yields in comparison with unmulched plots. The number of aphids that landed on the squash plants were reduced by as much as 98 percent.

Nutritional Value: Summer squash, especially the golden varieties, are good sources of vitamin A.

Choosing Varieties: There are three basic types of summer squash. By far the most popular is zucchini. But some gardeners like to grow the rounded yellow squash with narrow necks that are either straight or slightly curved. Then there are the pattypan squash, which are round and flattened with scalloped edges. Breeders have also developed a cross between the zucchini and pattypan types, called SCALLOPINI. It has the shape of the pattypans with the zucchini's dark-green skin. Summer squash has a bland flavor, and there usually isn't much dif-

ference in taste between types and varieties. The choice of a variety is usually more a matter of color, yield, and disease resistance. Almost all summer squash are bush varieties.

SQUASH, WINTER
Cucurbita maxima, C. mixta,
C. moschata,
C. pepo var. pepo

Winter squash pop up in a kaleidoscopic diversity of colors and shapes, resembling garish drums, day-glo turbans, or The Beach Balls that Came From Outer Space. But if winter squash didn't exist, some enterprising genetic engineer would surely invent it. It's a nutritious vegetable that's remarkably easy to grow, keeps fresh all winter without refrigeration or processing, and can be baked like a sweet potato or made into delicious pies.

Soil Preparation: Squash grows best in a pH range of 6.0 to 7.0. For good squash, you'll need plenty of humus. Thomas Whitaker, a retired USDA plant breeder in California and an authority on squash, says ample organic matter is critical to growing healthy squash. "They're gross feeders, and they need an abundance of nutrients and water at all times because they produce such an enormous mass of vegetation."

Besides its slow release of nutrients, humus has another benefit for squash. Getting a lot of organic matter in the soil means it's going to be better aerated and drained. Dig a big hole for each hill of squash (or a trench, if you plant in rows). A hole 2 feet deep and as wide isn't too large—squash roots can easily spread 3 feet vertically and horizontally. Fill the excavation with whatever rotted organic matter you have—compost, leaf mold, or manure—mixing it with rich topsoil. You can also add a few handfuls of soil conditioners like kelp and bone, blood, or cottonseed meal. Then flood the hole with water before seeding to build up a reservoir of moisture.

How Much to Plant:

A rough guideline is two or three hills or four to six plants of winter squash, and a similar number of pumpkins, per person.

Planting:

In long-season areas (120 days or more), seeds of winter squash are sown directly in the garden one week or more after the frost-free date. In short-season areas, gardeners who wish to get a jump on the season should start seeds indoors (see "Handling Seedlings" below). The minimum soil temperature for germination is 60°F. A black plastic mulch applied two weeks before planting will help warm the soil more quickly. Remove the mulch when planting, and replace it later with an organic mulch. If cloches are used, the planting date may be advanced two to three weeks.

Squash is often planted in hills. Plant vining types in hills spaced 6 to 8 feet apart, six seeds per hill. Bush types require 4 to 5 feet between hills, with six seeds to a hill. Conventional rows may also be used. Space vining types 3 to 4 feet apart in rows set 8 to 12 feet apart. Bush types are set 2 to 3 feet apart in rows spaced 4 to 6 feet apart. Growing bed spacing for summer squash is 36 inches. Plant all seed 1 inch deep. Unused seed is good for five years.

Handling Seedlings:

Start seed indoors four weeks before setting out. Use individual pots so that there is minimal disturbance to the roots during the transplanting process. Set seedlings out three to four weeks after the frost-free date. Use the spacings given under "Planting" as a guide.

Growing Guidelines:

Thin seedlings in hills, leaving the sturdiest two or three to continue growing. Cultivate frequently to destroy all weeds early in the season. Apply a heavy hay mulch around all plants before the vines spread out. Keep the soil evenly moist throughout the season. If your soil is not in good shape, side-dress the plants monthly with aged manure or compost, or water with fish emulsion every three weeks.

Squash is not self-fertilizing, so pollination by bees or other insects is essential. Male and female flowers are distinct, and sometimes appear on separate plants. Male blossoms appear first, about a week before female flowers, and will drop off without producing fruit. Immature fruit that refuses to grow probably has not been fertilized, usually because of adverse weather or a scarcity of insects. Pollination may be carried out easily by using a camel's hair brush to transfer pollen from the male stamen to the female pistil. Female flowers have an enlarged swelling (the ovary) just behind the blossom, and a four-part curved pistil in the center of the blossom; the male flower has no swollen portion behind it, and a single, fat stamen in the center of the blossom.

No matter which squash variety you grow, give the plants full sun. Plant them on the edge of a cornfield (prickly squash vines may help to deter raccoons and the vines can run into the corn, keeping down weeds), but not between corn rows.

Bush varieties are excellent choices for gardeners with small plots, but they set too many fruits, so the quality isn't as high or as consistently good as that of some of the vine types. Fortunately, gardeners can change that. "We've just completed studies," says University of New Hampshire plant scientist Brent Loy, "that show that pruning bush winter squash improved the quality of the fruits. It depends on the plant, of course, but if a gardener has a vigorous plant—something like GOLD NUGGET—and prunes it back to three or four fruits, the quality of these will be much improved. The dry matter will be at least doubled."

Winter squash needs a steady supply of water for uninterrupted growth. If your garden doesn't get an inch of rain weekly, soak each hill with a gallon of water every week, or use furrow or drip irrigation. But don't sprinkle or spray after the plants have a dozen or more true leaves. Moisture on the leaves encourages foliar diseases that are difficult to suppress.

Harvesting and Storing:

All winter squash keep well if cut free of the vine just before a hard frost (or after the vines have died) and cured in a warm spot for 10 to 14 days. Whether field-cured in the sun or cured in a warm room (85 to 90°F), the process encourages hardening of the rind and sealing of minor scratches and blemishes, which are necessary for long storage. The exception is ACORN, which needs no curing and keeps best at 45 to 50°F. Other squash will hold for months (often getting somewhat sweeter with storage) if kept at 55 to 60°F in 60 to 70 percent humidity.

Some gardeners wipe their cured squashes with a mild bleach-and-water solution. Squash breeder Thomas Whitaker agrees that this "helps destroy surface bacteria, but be sure to dry them off well before storing in a cool, well-ventilated place." Stored properly, winter squash will supply months of sweet, vitamin-rich pies, casseroles, soups, and baked squash.

Pests and Diseases:

Cucumber beetles plague cucurbits of all kinds. Striped or spotted, these $1/4$-inch-long pests kill squash by chewing on leaves and stems and by spreading bacterial wilt, a fatal disease carried only by the beetles.

Slitted polyethylene row covers used as season extenders work reasonably well as bug barriers. Reemay and cheesecloth will also stop insects.

Another method is to place a cardboard box, with top and bottom flaps removed, over the squash hill right after planting the seeds. Use boxes that are a foot tall—anything taller will shade the plants too much—and at least 18 inches wide. Then cover the box with an old window screen, making sure it fits snugly. Dirt piled around the edges of the box further seals it off from bugs.

The squash plants grow under this cover until flowers appear or their foliage hits the screen, when the barriers must be removed to permit pollination. But, by this time, the plants will be relatively mature and better able to withstand insect attacks. A barrier will also offer early protection against aphids (which spread viral diseases), squash bugs, and vine borers.

Soilborne squash diseases shouldn't be a severe problem in the garden if good cultural practices are followed. Using ample compost, for instance, promotes plant health, while rotating crops annually limits the buildup of soil pathogens. And something as simple as slipping a board, shingle, or flat rock under the maturing squash can reduce the chances of fusarium rot attacking the fruit.

Nutritional Value: Winter squash is a good source of vitamin A. Pumpkin seeds are the nutritional highlight of these plants, being 30 to 40 percent protein with high levels of vitamins and minerals. Any pumpkin or squash seed is edible and nutritious.

Choosing Varieties: Plant scientist Brent Loy says a high percent of dry matter and a reasonable sugar content characterize the most pleasing squash. Dry, smooth pulp not only makes the best baked squash and pies, but it also has an important influence on flavor. According to Dr. Loy, "If a squash has a high concentration of dry matter, then its overall quality will be better.

"I don't think BUTTERCUP can be beat," says Loy, who's spent 15 years breeding and testing squash. "In terms of taste, flavor, baking quality and dryness, BUTTERCUP comes out tops in our trials at least 90 percent of the time." Neal Holland, a horticulturist at the Fargo, North Dakota, Experiment Station, says the BURGESS strain of BUTTERCUP is the most popular among gardeners and truck farmers. "The fruits are thick and sweet, with a small seed cavity." BURGESS is also well liked for its flavorful dry flesh and good storage qualities.

SWEET MAMA is another short-season BUTTERCUP type, a 75- to 80-day bush hybrid. Spreading only 4 feet, with some resistance to wilt diseases and vine borers, SWEET MAMA yields dark green, 2½-pound, yellow-fleshed fruits.

Color is also worth thinking about when choosing a winter squash. The yellow-orange color of squash flesh, which indicates the presence of carotene, is a key to its nutritional value. Squash vary in their carotene content, however. "BUTTERCUP flesh has a good yellow quality," says Dr. Loy, "more than ACORN, but it's not as high in carotene as BUTTERNUT." A cup of baked BUTTERNUT contains almost as much carotene as a cup of cooked carrots, a particularly rich source. But HUBBARD has only 75 percent as much, and ACORN less than 20 percent. So if carotene content concerns you as much as taste, choose a squash with a distinctly yellow-orange flesh—the darker the orange, the more carotene present. BUTTERNUT, HUBBARD, and GOLDEN DELICIOUS are all excellent choices if you have space for their extensive vines.

A GOLDEN DELICIOUS squash looks like a giant orange persimmon. It's higher in vitamin C content than any other squash, and its sweetish flesh makes excellent "pumpkin" pies. (Pumpkins are varieties of winter squash.) HUBBARD is a traditional favorite, yielding moderately sweet, smooth flesh. But the 10- to 20-pound fruits may be too much for your family. Consider BABY HUBBARD (also known as KITCHENETTE), a semibush variety bearing 5- to 6-pound fruits. BABY BLUE is another small-fruited alternative. Resembling miniature BLUE HUBBARDs, the 5-pound fruits grow on vines that take only half the space of a standard HUBBARD.

BUTTERNUT is a winter classic because it's hardy, borer-resistant, a good keeper, and has orange flesh with outstanding flavor. WALTHAM BUTTERNUT is a particularly good choice, offering uniformly shaped 9-inch-long fruits with dry, sweet flesh. Gardeners with limited space or a short season can try BABY

BUTTERNUT (also known as NEW HAMP-SHIRE BUTTERNUT), which bears 6- to 7-inch, smooth-fleshed fruits, or EARLY BUTTERNUT, an 85-day hybrid semi-bush.

When you're trying to decide which squash to plant, remember that it must mature its fruit during your growing season. While a few winter squash can do double duty, making good eating when young (JERSEY GOLDEN ACORN and HUB-BARD can be eaten like summer squash when several inches long) or storing well when mature, the majority need a full season to develop their best flavor and the hard shell needed for winter storage.

Originally from China, VEGETABLE SPAGHETTI bears 4-pound fruits on sprawling vines easily trained to grow up a trellis. The white fruits gradually turn yellow, a harvest signal. "Most folks pick VEGETABLE SPAGHETTI too early," warns Rob Johnston, Jr., of Johnny's Selected Seeds in Albion, Maine. "Wait until the fruits turn completely yellow before harvesting." After baking or boiling, scoop out the yellow spaghettilike strands and serve as pasta. But don't be misled. While VEGETABLE SPAGHETTI looks like pasta, it tastes like squash.

Pumpkins are the ultimate winter squash. For a large Halloween display pumpkin, choose HOWDEN (or HOW-DEN'S FIELD). At 20 to 25 pounds, this one is a deep orange ball with a ribbed shell. HOWDEN, which matures in 115 days, is generally uniformly round and less likely to develop flat sides—a tendency of larger pumpkins. CONNECTI-CUT FIELD, a longtime favorite, is also in the 25-pound range, red-orange, slightly ribbed, but less perfectly round—it's often flattened at both ends.

Choosing the best pumpkin for pies is more difficult than selecting a good jack-o'-lantern. Pie pumpkins should have flesh that's sweet, dry, and smooth (not stringy). WINTER LUXURY is one of the best pie pumpkins, with sweet, thick, golden yellow flesh. A good keeper, it's also called WINTER QUEEN.

The best all-purpose pumpkin—one that makes excellent pies and handsome jack-o'-laterns—is SMALL SUGAR, also known as NEW ENGLAND PIE, SUGAR PIE, and BOSTON PIE. Its 8-by-10-inch fruits are red-orange, weight 5 to 10 pounds, and have sweet, smooth flesh. A 5-pounder will yield enough puree for two pies.

SMALL SUGAR was a winner in pumpkin-pie taste trials conducted by the Rodale Test Kitchen. Eight varieties were evaluated for top pie qualities—flavor, texture, and color. Other favorites were BLUE HUBBARD and BUTTERNUT. The last two are squash, of course, not traditional pumpkins. The canned pumpkin you find in stores is really almost always winter squash. Researchers at the Rodale Test Kitchen recommend that you experiment, making pumpkin pies from mixtures of SMALL SUGAR and BUTTERNUT or HUBBARD squash. The deep orange of the squash will darken the pale flesh of the pumpkins, while the combination of flavors should produce delectable pies.

Those with small gardens should choose bush or semi-bush pumpkins. CINDERELLA, SPIRIT, JACKPOT, and FUNNY FACE all confine their vines to a 4- to 6-foot spread while producing fruits in the 7- to 15-pound range. Figure on getting two or three pumpkins from each plant. Maine gardener Richard Libby recommends the semi-bush SPIRIT, an All-America Selection. "For production, sweetness, and size—10- to 15-pound pumpkins—it's really one of the better types I've grown," says Libby.

WINTER SQUASH
(INCLUDING PUMPKINS)

Variety	Description	Sources*
Acorn	70–80 days; compact, bushy; fruits to 1½ pounds; 6 to 8 fruits per plant; good for small gardens	5
Alagold	110 days; cylindrical to club-shaped fruits, to 8 pounds; deep, golden, sweet flesh; excellent keeper; resistant to vine borers and pickleworms	14
Baby Blue	95–100 days; early; semi-bush habit; Hubbard type; fruits have light blue skin, yellow-orange flesh; good keeper	9, 12
Baby Butternut	85 days; extra early; fruits to 7"; solid meat with small seed cavity; deep yellow flesh; good baked, boiled, or in pies	9
Baby Hubbard (Kitchenette)	100 days; fruits smaller than standard Hubbard, to 6 pounds; thick, sweet, yellow-orange flesh; good flavor; good keeper	9, 12
Burpee's Butterbush	75 days; bush-type butternut; vines to 4'; 4 to 5 fruits on each; orange-red, delicious flesh; good keeper	5
Buttercup	75–80 days; bush hybrid; turban- or drum-shaped fruits; thick, firm, dry flesh; excellent keeper	WA
Butternut	90–100 days; popular variety from England; dry, sweet, bright orange flesh; borer resistant	WA
Early Butternut	75–85 days; compact, semi-bush; high yields; deep tan skins; good for winter storage	33
Golden Delicious	102 days; large yields; fruits to 6 pounds; thick, golden, sweet flesh; good for storing and freezing	12
Gold Nugget	75–95 days; early, compact, runnerless; buttercup-shaped fruits; dark yellow-orange flesh; good keeper; AAS	WA
Green Hokkaido	98 days; original Japanese variety; not high yielding; rounded fruits; butter-sweet, fiberless flesh	15
Hubbard	110–120 days; large fruits to 15 pounds with blue-gray skin; excellent for baking and freezing; good keeper	WA
Jersey Golden Acorn	90 days; compact, semi-bush plant; fruits to 4½" long, 4" wide; sweet orange flesh; good for containers; AAS	15

(continued)

WINTER SQUASH (INCLUDING PUMPKINS) —*Continued*

Variety	Description	Sources*
Ponca	90 days; extra-early Butternut; small fruits to 8 pounds; dark orange flesh; fine flavor; suited to the North	13, 15
Red Kuri	92 days; Japanese variety; high yields; teardrop-shaped fruits up to 8 pounds; smooth flesh good for pies	15
Sweet Mama	85 days; short vines; high yields; Buttercup type, gray-green fruits; AAS	5
Vegetable Spaghetti	88–100 days; early maturing; oblong, yellow fruits with yellow, spaghettilike flesh	WA
Waltham Butternut	82–85 days; high yields; fruits to 12" long; long, crooked necks; small seed cavity; AAS	5

Pumpkins

Variety	Description	Sources*
Cinderella	95–102 days; compact, bush type; fruits to 10 pounds; good for pies and baking	5
Connecticut Field	100–120 days; fruits to 14" across, 25 pounds; deep orange, hard rind; smooth, somewhat ribbed, sweet flesh	15
Funny Face	90 days; hybrid; to 17 pounds; good carving shape; ideal for short-season areas; nice flesh for making pies	23
Howden (Howden's Field)	115 days; deep, round fruits with extra-thick flesh; ideal shape for carving; good keeper	13
Jack O Lantern	100–115 days; fruits to 9" around; smooth shell is easy to carve; firm, even-textured flesh	WA
Jackpot	100 days; smaller vines; heavy yields; round pumpkins to 10" or more; good for carving	13
Lady Godiva (also Streaker)	110 days; vines to 10' long; grown for hull-less seeds, not flesh; seeds exceptionally high in protein	24

WINTER SQUASH
(INCLUDING PUMPKINS)
—*Continued*

Variety	Description	Sources*
New England Pie (also Small Sugar Pie and Boston Pie)	100–110 days; to 10" around; orange, slightly ribbed skin; fine-grained flesh; a general-use pumpkin	WA
Small Sugar	100 days; standard pie pumpkin; fruits up to 17 pounds; high sugar content; excellent flavor	WA
Spirit	90–100 days; compact hybrid; fruits to 15 pounds; good for short-season areas; excellent for pies, carving; AAS	5
Winter Luxury (also Winter Queen)	110 days; medium sized with closely netted yellow skin; high-quality flesh; excellent keeper	12

*Listings correspond to seed companies listed under Sources of Seeds at the back of the book.

SWEET POTATOES
Ipomoea batatas

Sweet potatoes are not just a Southern vegetable. Roger A. Kline, who works with home gardeners for Cornell University, has found to his surprise that sweet potatoes will grow in northern New York, where the growing season is 100 days. Once you get started growing sweet potatoes, you can sprout your own plants every year from the tubers you've stored over the winter. Sweet potatoes are no more difficult to grow than ordinary potatoes, and they are one of the easiest of all vegetables to store. You don't need root-cellar conditions, only a corner of your home that stays around 55°F from fall to spring.

The kind of sweet potato that comes out of the oven with moist flesh is sometimes called a yam to distinguish it from the kind that bakes dry and is sometimes called a jersey sweet potato. Moist or dry, they're all sweet potatoes.

Soil Preparation: In open soil, sweet potato roots can go 8 feet deep in as little as 40 days. Though commercial growers will not set out a crop on soils less than 4 feet deep, you can get satisfactory yields on most slightly acidic garden soils (a pH from 6.0 to 7.0 is fine), including clay soils, provided they are not wet or underlaid with hardpan less than 18 inches below the surface.

How Much to Plant:
A rough guideline is 10 to 18 plants per person.

Planting:
Sweet potatoes are grown from rooted sprouts (called "slips"). If you have access to untreated tubers, you can grow your own slips. If you can't buy or borrow a few tubers, you will have to buy a bundle of slips from a nursery for your first planting. Nursery slips may look wispy and wilted when they arrive, but most will revive in a few days if you give them plenty of water after transplanting. Don't try supermarket sweet potatoes for sprouting. They're sometimes treated with a chemical that hinders sprouting. Supermarket sweet potatoes are usually long-season varieties, and even if they sprout, they may not yield a crop for Northern gardeners.

For transplanting, a sprout should have at least six nodes. (A node is the swollen section of stem at every leaf.) Max Allison, a researcher at Mississippi State University, says that large sprouts usually have thick stems and enough moisture to survive until new roots form. "You get into trouble with thin, succulent sprouts," he says. "They die much more frequently."

Prepare beds several weeks before the last frost date in your area and cover them with black plastic, leaving an aisle of bare soil between each row to absorb rain. Several weeks after the last frost date, transplant. Warmed by the plastic, the soil gives the slips an early start. Don't transplant too early. Wait until the frost is long gone. You don't really lose two weeks, because the warmer soil boosts plant growth.

In tests at Mississippi State, slips that were buried horizontally 2 to 3 inches deep, with five nodes underground and only their tips aboveground, survived more often than slips planted vertically. What's more, they produced larger crops and more average-sized roots. The sprouts send out roots from the buried nodes, so the photosynthetic materials from the leaves are spread out more. If you like big potatoes, plant slips vertically.

Set your transplants 12 inches apart in the row. Ordinarily, rows are 4 feet apart to allow room for the vines to ramble and for the gardener to stand and weed. But with a relatively compact vine like BUSH PORTO RICO, you could try moving the rows as close together as 2 feet, if you don't mind tiptoeing when you tend the vines. Another way to get tighter spacing is to train the vines up a trellis. The vines have no tendrils, but by weaving them through the trellis from time to time, you can train them upward.

Give your transplants water as soon as they are in the ground. You can expect them to wilt within hours of transplanting, but they will recover, usually within three days or so. Most of the original roots die during this period and are replaced by new ones. The leaves that were buried in transplanting rot harmlessly.

Growing Guidelines:
Though you can expect transplants to grow little or not at all for several weeks while their root systems are growing, be sure to keep them well watered. The sweet potato has a reputation for being drought-resistant, and it will recover from a drought that kills other plants, but it grows best and yields most when given as much water as

other garden vegetables—at least an inch a week (about three gallons per vine).

When the soil is soaked, the vines try to send down roots from their nodes. In the next few days, you must lift the vines occasionally, taking care not to harm them. If you let the vine root anywhere but at its base, it will try to produce sweet potatoes from the new roots, resulting in dozens of undersized potatoes. It's also a good practice to check for unwanted roots and turn the vines each time you hoe weeds.

It's important to keep the young plants well weeded so their roots can grow and spread without competition. Tests have shown that weeding for the first 40 days, when storage roots begin to swell, does more to increase the size of the crop than weeding at any other time. After a month to six weeks of careful hoeing, the vines will spread and shade out weeds.

Can sweet potatoes be mulched? The farther south you live, the more likely the answer is to be yes, though any mulch that cools the soil always reduces yields. In the North, where the season is short, it is important to have the soil warm up early and stay warm through the season. The warmer the soil, the faster the vine grows. One reason most growers plant sweet potatoes in raised beds from 6 to 10 inches high is that the beds warm up earlier in the spring. (Another reason is that the loose soil in the beds lets the sweet potatoes swell without hindrance.)

A straw mulch, about 5 inches deep, will keep the soil as much as 10 degrees cooler than soil under black plastic, too cool for some vines to make a crop. In the North, the cool, short growing season obliges gardeners to use black plastic for a mulch, but it relieves them of the usual pests and diseases of the sweet potato.

Cornell University's Roger Kline says the vines are trouble-free, one reason for their good yields.

Sprouting Roots: Starting at harvest, you should select some of your crop's best roots for next year's sprouting. Pick medium-sized, normally colored, blemish-free roots from healthy vines.

Always check your roots before sprouting by cutting slices from the distal end (the end farthest from the stem) and checking the flesh for an off-color or any whitish flecks larger than a pencil lead. (Before you slice your roots, give them the dunk test. Those that float in water will yield 20 percent larger crops, and have a truer taste, than those that sink.)

Six to eight weeks before the last spring frost in your area, lay your roots on a 3-inch bed of soil in a shallow container. Then add enough soil to bury them an inch deep. Use sand, or a fine potting soil, light enough so you can easily shake it free of the roots that will form on your sprouts. Now put the container in a warm spot—at least 80°F. If you don't have such a spot, use a heating pad. Without heat, your sweet potatoes will just sit. Keep the soil moist, and within two weeks or so the first sprouts will push up, looking for the sun. Move the container to a warm, sunny place.

When it is time for transplanting—about two weeks after the last spring frost, when the soil is about 70°F—some of your sprouts should be 6 to 10 inches tall. Unearth the root and pull or cut off the biggest slips. Don't fret about losing the roots. Your transplants may have meager roots, but if the sprouts are large enough, they should survive. Rebury the tuber to let the smaller slips grow some more. It's better to transplant several times than to take small slips and watch them die in the garden.

Harvesting and Storing:

Harvest can begin any time the crop reaches eating size, but the sweet potato's roots continue to gain size and weight as long as the vine lives. Lovers of large sweet potatoes let their vines grow as late as possible.

Many gardeners harvest immediately after a frost, in the mistaken belief that a frost-blackened vine sends something to the roots that spoils them. In fact, the damage is done when the average daily soil temperature falls below 55°F, which can happen before or after the first frost. The roots lose rot resistance and eating quality. If you have a soil thermometer, use it in the weeks before the first frost to take readings 2 inches below ground level, and harvest when the morning temperature dips below 55°F. If you don't have a soil thermometer, try to harvest on a mild day the week that the first frost usually occurs in your area. In the event that the weatherman offers hope, you can gamble a little and postpone the harvest, but it's better to reap your crop than to risk quality for the sake of a slightly larger yield.

Be gentle when you harvest sweet potatoes. Their skin is extremely thin at harvest, and easily wounded. Don't bruise them with your spading fork, and don't toss them around. Lay the crop in the sun for no more than half an hour, then collect them all for curing.

No matter how carefully you harvest, every root will have at least two wounds, one at each end. Curing encourages the root to close its wounds with a corky layer of cells that seals out disease; it also thickens the skin and makes it waxy. The best conditions for curing are a temperature between 85 and 90°F and a humidity between 80 and 90 percent. Lay the roots in a single layer, and cover them with perforated plastic or newspaper to help keep the humidity high. They'll cure in a week, or in two weeks at room temperature (75°F). If you cure the roots outdoors, shade them from the sun—they get sunscald. If you use an attic or a cold frame for curing, don't leave the roots exposed to night temperatures below 55°F. After curing, put your crop into storage immediately.

Sweet potatoes store best at 55 to 60°F. At cooler temperatures, the roots rot more frequently, and the sound roots that remain lose some of their baking quality. At higher temperatures, there are other problems—the roots tend to sprout, especially during lengthy storage, and they also lose moisture and shrivel.

The best humidity for storing sweet potatoes is between 80 and 90 percent. Most homes have less than 30 percent humidity, and even damp basements tend to dry out in winter. Wrapping each root in newspaper—or another material that will trap some of the moisture released by the roots, but still let them breathe—can raise the humidity next to the root. Also, packing the wrapped roots loosely in a box or basket will raise the humidity around the roots.

Check your stored sweet potatoes from time to time and remove any that are decayed or rotten before the damage can spread. When you take out roots for cooking, discard any with blemished or discolored skins. Tests have shown that such roots often have small quantities of toxins that can cause liver and lung damage to test animals. Bad roots have never been shown to harm people, but it's safest to leave them alone.

SWEET POTATOES

Variety	Description	Sources*
Bush Porto Rico	150 days; high yields; compact growth habit; ideal for small gardens; red-orange flesh; sweet flavor	5
Centennial	90–100 days; vining growth habit; good for short-season areas and South; sweet, moist yellow flesh; keeps well	WA
New Jewell	100 days; vining growth habit; good for short-season areas; moist, sweet flesh; keeps well	23, 24

*Listings correspond to seed companies listed under Sources of Seeds at the back of the book.

Pests and Diseases: In cool regions, flea beetles may cause some problems. In warm areas, pests include nematodes, sweet potato beetles, sweet potato weevils, and wireworms. Sweet potatoes may be affected by black rot, soft rot, soil rot, and stem rot. See Cabbage, Carrots, and Kale for insect and disease controls.

Nutritional Value: Sweet potatoes are rich in vitamins A and C.

SWISS CHARD
(Leaf beet, perpetual spinach, spinach chard)
Beta vulgaris var. *cicla*

Swiss chard and beets share a common plant ancestor, both being derived from the same wild European plant. Swiss chard, however, develops without the thickened, fleshy roots characteristic of beets. Where Swiss chard is short on root development, it compensates by being long on leaf production. The prolific leaf development over the life of a single plant has made it a garden favorite of long standing.

The main advantage of growing Swiss chard is that it can stay in the ground a long time, even during hot weather, yet faithfully keep producing succulent leaves. Swiss chard does well in a variety of soils, tolerates some shade, takes a great deal of heat without bolting, and will allow the gardener to strip leaves from it for as long as two years before it becomes unusable. Certain varieties of Swiss chard are very attractive, worthy of a place in an ornamental garden, with deep green leaves and snowy white midribs, or crimson midribs with red or green leaves.

On soils and in climates where spinach has difficulties, Swiss chard will thrive. It is an excellent culinary substitute for spinach. Swiss chard will tolerate a good deal of frost, and will even keep growing during the warmest part of the season. It can be cropped from late spring to late fall, an unusual growing period for

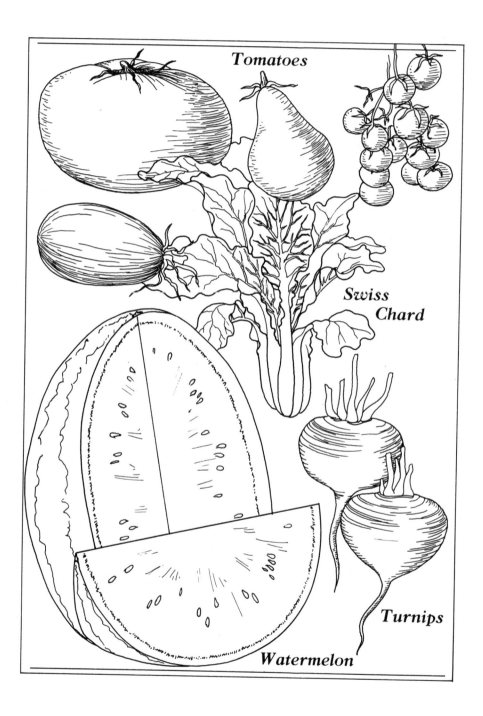

Tomatoes

Swiss
Chard

Turnips

Watermelon

any vegetable. In areas of mild winters, it can winter over in the ground and will sometimes produce a second crop.

Soil Preparation:

For the best Swiss chard, provide a well-drained, fertile soil rich in humus. Fertilize before planting by digging in liberal amounts of well-rotted manure or compost. Swiss chard will tolerate a soil that is slightly acid, with a pH of 6.0 to 6.8.

How Much to Plant:

A rough guideline is three to five plants per person.

Planting:

Direct-seeding is the most common way to start Swiss chard, but transplants can be used for an extra-early crop. Sow seed two to four weeks before the frost-free date. In mild-climate areas, make a late summer planting about ten weeks before the first expected frost for a winter and spring harvest. Sow seed $1/2$ inch deep. The optimum soil temperature for germination is 50 to 85°F. For conventional rows, space seed 3 inches apart in rows set 18 inches apart. The spacing for raised beds is 9 inches. Swiss chard is also suitable for wide-row planting.

Swiss chard, like beets, will sprout more than one plant from a seed. These extra sprouts will have to be pinched out later, while thinning. Unused seed is good for four years.

Handling Seedlings:

Start transplants in individual pots four weeks before planting out, which can be done three to four weeks before the frost-free date. Be careful not to disturb roots while transplanting. Use between-row spacings given above and set seedlings every 9 inches. Use the raised bed spacing above.

Growing Guidelines:

When the seedlings are 5 to 8 inches tall, thin back to 9-inch spacings in the rows. These thinnings can be transplanted if carefully lifted or, if cut, they can be used in the kitchen as tender greens. Swiss chard likes to have moist roots. If the plant undergoes stress from lack of water, it tends to produce seed stalks instead of leaves. Swiss chard normally requires no feeding, but plants grown on poor soils will benefit from a midseason boost of high-nitrogen fertilizer like manure tea or fish emulsion.

Keys to Top Yields:

In dry climates and exceptionally well-drained soils, mulch in warm weather to prevent bolting. If the seed stalk does appear, cut it off quickly to prolong leaf development.

Harvesting and Storing:

Within 40 days from the time of sowing, some leaves will be usable. The most toothsome leaves are those from 6 to 10 inches long. Take a few leaves from the outside of each plant and do not damage the inner leaves. This allows the plant to continue producing. Break off the leaves rather than use a knife, as cutting sometimes causes the plants to bleed. Harvest through the summer and fall as needed, keeping in mind that the older, larger leaves are not as tasty as the young leaves.

Pests and Diseases:

Swiss chard is relatively trouble-free. When plants are small, holes in the leaves may be caused by flea beetles. Aphids, European corn borers, and leafminers sometimes attack the plants. In areas where slugs and snails frequent the garden, they may bother the

SWISS CHARD

Variety	Description	Sources*
Fordhook Giant	50–60 days; reliable crop; grows to 30" tall, 36" wide; dark green, crumpled leaves with thick, white stalks	15
Lucullus	50–60 days; most commonly planted; grows to 20" tall, 30" wide; large, dark green crumpled leaves; broad, white stalks	38
Rhubarb, Chard	55–60 days; grows to 30" tall, 30" wide; dark green, crumpled leaves; deep red stalks; very sweet and tender leaves	5
Ruby Red	60 days; grows to 24" tall; crumpled red leaves; red to white stalks	11

*Listings correspond to seed companies listed under Sources of Seeds at the back of the book.

chard. Possible diseases include blight and downy mildew.

Nutritional Value: Swiss chard is especially high in vitamin C, calcium, and iron. The red-leaved varieties of Swiss chard are also extremely rich in vitamin A.

TOMATOES
Lycopersicon lycopersicum

A century and a half ago, the tomato was practically unknown as a food outside its native America. The Spanish first found the fruit in Mexico. The Indians ate tomatoes, but Europeans were suspicious that the "love apple" was poisonous like its relatives henbane and belladonna. Soon after that, however, they began tasting, then eating them with relish. Now there are several hundred tomato varieties to choose from, including pot plants, giant vines, disease-resistant tomatoes, and quick-maturing types for cold climates.

Soil Preparation: A raised bed prepared in the fall, southern slopes, and dark soils all warm up early in the spring, which benefits tomatoes. You can also cover your tomato plot with clear or black plastic a few weeks before transplanting to warm the soil. Researchers in Alaska gave their tomatoes a head start with wire cylinders wrapped with clear plastic. The soil inside warmed up early, and the young plants grew strong in their shelters. Researchers in Texas got a similar effect by wrapping a 12-inch band of roofing paper around the base of a wire cylinder. Besides warming the soil, the band sheltered the plants from the wind and wind-driven soil.

Before transplanting, prepare your tomato plot with an inch of compost worked into the soil. This will supply enough nitrogen. Too much causes the plant to produce foliage at the expense of flowers and fruit. Once the first fruits have reached walnut-size, side-dress with compost and water occasionally with manure tea.

How Much to Plant:

A rough guideline is three to five plants per person.

Planting:

A week or so before you transplant tomatoes to the garden, take your plants outdoors. Victor Lambeth, a professor of horticulture at the University of Missouri, moves his to a cold frame and removes the glass for part of the day to give them direct sunlight. "If you put plants that grew behind glass, especially those from greenhouses, in the sun without hardening them off like this," he says, "they'll get sunburn and turn white." Put your tomatoes in full sun for a few hours the first day, and gradually work up to a whole day by week's end. Hardening-off helps plants survive borderline frosts that will kill unhardened plants.

Transplant gently. Pick a cloudy day so the roots have an easier job of supplying water to the leaves. Take pains to water daily until the transplants resume rapid growth. Bury part of the stem, as you did in potting the seedlings, to force more roots. Tests in Texas showed that burying the stem horizontally in a shallow trench, so that only the topmost leaves of the plants were aboveground, resulted in higher, earlier yields.

If you plan to transplant before the frost-free date, the plants will need protection on cold days and at night. Plastic tunnels, cloches, hotcaps, and milk jugs all work fine. But it may not be worth the trouble. Cold can damage the plants without killing them, and they may grow and flower poorly all season. The soil must be warm, or the plants will mark time and your early start will be wasted.

Handling Seedlings:

When seed catalogs give a variety's number of days to maturity, they count from transplanting, not from sowing seed. Start tomatoes from seed six weeks before you transplant, and keep your seed-starting soil between 75 and 85°F so your seeds will germinate in a week. If the soil is cooler, transplanting will come later—seeds take two weeks to germinate in 60°F soil. By the way, tomato seedlings can't stand even tiny amounts of natural gas; if yours do poorly or die in your kitchen or on top of your hot-water heater, you might blame a gas leak.

Many gardeners are disappointed by transplants which have flowers or fruit. Early, determinate varieties, transplanted late, sometimes yield only a few poor fruits. Usually, the trouble is not so much the age of the transplants as the size of the container they grow in. The longer you wait to transplant, the bigger the pot you should use. If you start seed six weeks before transplanting, each seedling must be potted in its own 4-inch pot about the time its first true leaf appears. If you start earlier, use a bigger container or be ready to pot up a size in a few weeks.

The tomato six-packs that supermarkets and nurseries sell in the spring usually appear several weeks before transplanting time. While waiting for a home in the ground, the seedlings compete for sun, grow tall, leggy, and rootbound, and often produce flowers. If you buy these plants, purchase them as soon as they appear and repot them immediately.

Trench-planting a leggy tomato. If your transplants are leggy, pinch off all but the top cluster of leaves and bury the plant horizontally. In a few days, the top growth will straighten out and form a sturdy new stem. The buried stem will root.

When you pot or repot a seedling, set it slightly deeper in the soil than it stood before. The buried portion of stem will strike roots. Even a light touch can damage the stem of young seedlings (a plant with only one or two true leaves), so hold them by a seed leaf. Unused seed is good for three years.

Growing Guidelines: You can improve your chances of harvesting tomatoes during hot weather by growing varieties recommended for your area, mulching once the soil warms up in the spring, maintaining a deep mulch through hot weather, and keeping your plants well watered. Don't give up on plants that drop their blossoms during an August or September heat wave. Several years ago 115°F temperatures halted fruiting at Victor Lambeth's experimental plantings at the University of Missouri. "We kept watering," he says, "and kept the plants healthy, and we had a good fall crop. As soon as nights cool

down, you'll get good fruit." Don't expect tomatoes to redden unless the temperature is under 85°F.

A lot of arguing goes on about training tomato plants. One group says that tomatoes yield best when trained to a single upright stem, with all suckers pinched out early. (The tomato sends out a branch, or sucker, from the leaf crotches. A sucker appears shortly after the leaf reaches full size, and it soon rivals the main stem in vigor.) The other group says pinching is wasted time, and the tomato yields best when it is allowed to sucker freely. Both groups are right.

Whether you use a trellis, stakes, or string, pruned tomatoes need little room and can be planted a foot apart or even less. If you want to grow several varieties in a limited space, prune and train your plants. Pruned plants usually bear fruit earlier than unpruned plants, sometimes by as much as two weeks. However, pruned plants demand sturdy supports, and you have to pinch out the suckers

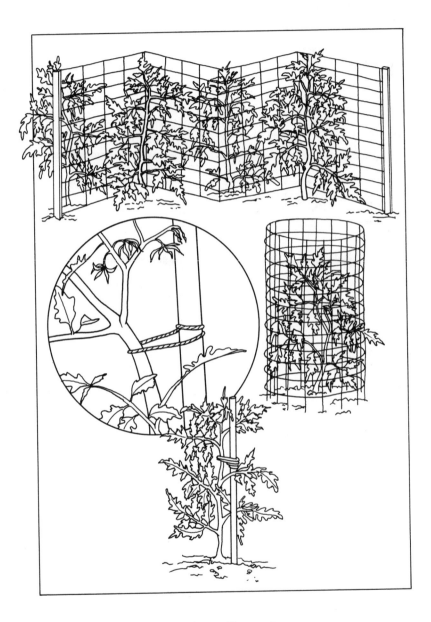

Tomato stakes, trellises, and cages.

and train and tie the main stem every week. Having sparse foliage, the plants don't cast much shade and the fruit can get sunscald—light gray patches of skin that invite disease. You have to top-prune plants when they outgrow their support.

If you pinch suckers, do the job by hand. A 2- or 3-inch sucker will snap off at the base. If the sucker resists, and you need shears to remove it, you're waiting too long. Tobacco mosaic virus, which stunts and yellows tomato plants, will be on your hands if you smoke or if you've been weeding some of the plants besides tobacco that carry the disease, like ground cherry, jimsonweed, catnip, plantain, and horse nettle. If you've been smoking or weeding, wash your hands before you pinch your plants.

Unpruned tomatoes are less work. Some gardeners simply let their plants trail over the ground, but this wastes space, and the fruit and leaves get diseases more readily. A few people tie their unpruned plants to trellises. But most surround their unpruned plants with a wire cylinder—a tomato cage. The kind of reinforcing mesh used in concrete slabs is a common choice. It's cheap, readily available, and has 6-inch openings that allow the gardener to pick large fruit easily. Though it rusts, it will last for years. Farm fencing works, too, and it takes longer to rust.

Wire cylinders need stout anchors or they'll blow over in a storm. When the plant fills a cylinder, it's sometimes hard to see the fruit through the foliage, a problem that is worse when the plant grows over the top of the cage and drapes down the outside. You have to weed a cage by hand, but by midseason, weeds barely survive in the plant's dense shade.

Pruned and unpruned plants yield equal harvests. Before you disagree, be sure you are comparing the two fairly—pounds produced per square foot. It's true that a single unpruned plant will outyield a single pruned plant. There are instances of unpruned plants yielding several hundred tomatoes, while pruned plants will rarely yield 20 pounds of fruit apiece—the average is about 10. And at the University of Maryland, 25 caged, unpruned plants yielded 1,500 pounds of tomatoes, 60 pounds apiece. But the unpruned vine demands more soil and growing space. If you compare plants with equal foliage, the yield is equal, no matter how they grow. You'll have the same yields from unpruned tomatoes planted 24 inches apart in each direction as from pruned plants set 12 inches apart or less.

The tomato flower pollinates itself, provided something jostles it—the wind, a gardener's leg, an insect. In greenhouses, where no wind blows and insects are banned, growers shake their plants every few days. If several windless days becalm your garden, you might gently shake your plants for crop insurance.

Season Extending:

In Alaskan experiments, covering wire tomato cylinders with plastic in the fall stretched the season several weeks. Other methods for saving plants from the first fall frost are often worthwhile. Drape the tomatoes with plastic, paper, even an old blanket. Often a hard freeze that would have killed the plants will be followed by several weeks of balmy weather, and more tomatoes.

Another way to extend the season is to grow tomatoes in a greenhouse, solarium, or large south window. Good vine-ripened tomatoes are far easier to raise indoors in winter. The hardest part is providing a place in intense sunlight that is large enough for several sprawling tomato vines. Tomatoes will grow and fruit well if the temperature can be maintained between 65 and 68°F during the day and 55 to 60°F at night. Choose a variety developed for greenhouse production, and you should be able to pick large, full-red tomatoes.

Harvesting and Storing:

There *is* a way to keep eating home-grown tomatoes after killing frost—pick green tomatoes and ripen them indoors. Vine-ripened tomatoes have about one-third more vitamin C than those ripened indoors. But you might try compensating for that by growing one of the varieties that are especially rich in vitamin C. Small, dark green fruits won't ripen. Light green, nearly mature fruits will ripen in about two weeks at room temperature. They will overheat in sunlight, so keep them off the windowsill. You can prolong ripening by storing the tomatoes at cooler temperatures. Wrap them in newspaper or perforated plastic, or simply spread them on a shelf and cover them all. In the refrigerator at 40°F they last up to six weeks (but won't ripen) when wrapped. Burpee Seed Company now sells a variety, LONGKEEPER, with fruit that takes several months to ripen at room temperatures.

Tomatoes can be canned whole, in sauces, or as paste. In the 1970s there was a spate of illness among people eating home-canned tomatoes, and researchers wondered if new tomato varieties were acidic enough for safe canning. They learned that tomatoes are most acid when they are green, and their pH slowly rises as they ripen. But they found that all varieties are sufficiently acid when picked at perfection. The problem, it seems, comes from overripe fruit.

In one test, 37 out of 107 varieties reached or surpassed a pH of 4.6 when they were overripe, making them unfit to can. (But all of the varieties were safe if picked when ripe.) Picking early is more important than picking a certain kind. Some kinds of tomatoes are more acidic than others; in general, the plum tomatoes are the most acidic.

Outdoors, tomatoes ripen about five or six days after the time their green color fades. Now researchers recommend that you never use overripe tomatoes, that you can by the rules, in boiling-water baths or pressure canners, and that you never taste anything that looks or smells abnormal. Molds can alter the acidity of canned tomatoes enough to permit the development of botulism.

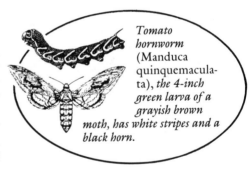

Tomato hornworm (Manduca quinquemaculata), *the 4-inch green larva of a grayish brown moth, has white stripes and a black horn.*

Pests and Diseases:

Insect pests include aphids, cabbage loopers, Colorado potato beetles, corn earworms, cucumber beetles, European corn borers, leafhoppers, nematodes, pepper maggots, potato tuberworms, and tomato hornworms. Tomatoes are subject to anthracnose, bacterial canker, damping-off, early blight, fusarium wilt, late blight, mosaics, psyllid yellows, septoria leaf spot, and verticillium wilt. Resistant varieties and good garden hygiene are the best ways to control disease. (See Growing Guidelines and Choosing Varieties.) Hornworms are often difficult to see—though large (4 inches long), they're the same color as tomato stems. Handpick, use *Bacillus thuringiensis* (Bt), or, if you see white braconid wasp cocoons on their backs, leave them as natural pest controls. Also see Cabbage, Corn, Cucumbers, and Potatoes.

Other Problems: In spite of the short journey that tomato pollen makes, fertilization can be chancy. For a fruit to be full sized and well formed, a pollen grain must connect with each infant seed (the seeds control a fruit's growth). When fertilization is spotty, the seed cavities, or locules, of the tomato grow at different rates, some normally, others slowly or not at all. The result is catfacing—the blossom end of the tomato is divided into lumps and mounds by thin brown lines, which are the dead skins of locules that were surrounded and overgrown by their neighbors. Catfacing is most common in cool spring and fall weather, which hinders fertilization, so be sure you give your plants a sunny, warm location.

Heat also hinders fertilization. When daytime temperatures rise above 90°F or nighttime temperatures top 70°F, many tomato flowers fail to set fruit, and the new flower buds may form poorly and prove to be infertile even if temperatures later cool off.

Teme Hernandez, a professor of vegetable breeding at Louisiana State University, is testing and breeding tomatoes for heat-resistance. He says, "In the tropical and subtropical regions of the South, we have 90 to 120 days of high nighttime temperatures when we can't grow tomatoes commercially." Blossom drop can be heavy. One variety tested by Dr. Hernandez set fruit on nearly 80 percent of its blossoms in the spring. But in the summer it set fruit on only 1 percent of its blossoms.

Large tomatoes of the "beefsteak" type fare badly in the heat. The beefsteaks have many more than the usual three to five locules, thanks to a flower with multiple pistils and multiple ovaries that fuse together to form one tomato, and they demand a lot of pollen. Their characteristic ridges and lumps are due to incomplete pollination, and they are more often catfaced than varieties with a single pistil.

Blossom-end rot—the sunken, dark, leathery region on the blossom end of a tomato which often appears during a dry spell—is caused by a lack of calcium, but even soils rich in calcium don't always prevent trouble. There is evidence that a plant under stress removes calcium from fruits and sends it to shoots. Drought and high water loss from the plant cause too much stress, and will produce rot.

The first two or three clusters to appear are especially prone to develop blossom-end rot. Very little rot appears after these clusters mature, provided the plants have plenty of water. Pick afflicted fruit as soon as the rot is visible—the smaller crop reduces stress on the plant. Determinate plants rarely get blossom-end rot, and heavily pruned plants get it more often than unpruned plants.

Nutritional Value: Tomatoes are a rich source of vitamins A and C, and offer some B_1 as well.

Choosing Varieties: In seed catalogs, a capital letter after the variety name indicates some sort of resistance to pests or diseases: F is for fusarium wilt, V is for verticillium wilt (both are soilborne fungi that yellow, weaken, stunt, or kill tomato plants), and N is for nematodes, tiny wormlike root parasites.

About three-quarters of the common tomato varieties are indeterminate—that is, their main stem and all their suckers continue to grow until frost. Some of these varieties reach 6 feet in a season, others 20 feet or more. With rich soil and a long season, you can expect a taller plant than the nursery says you'll have, so be prepared. Most indeterminate varieties produce a flower cluster every two leaves, and some every other leaf.

About one-quarter of the common tomato varieties are determinate bushy plants. That means the main stem and the suckers produce a specific number of flower clusters each (usually three), and stop growing when their tips turn into flower clusters. Bush tomatoes don't demand nearly as much trellising as the indeterminate types. However, the taller bush varieties, which can reach 3 feet, sprawl more than they stand. Bush determinate tomatoes should not be pruned to a single stem, because a plant without suckers would yield only one to three fruits.

Bush tomatoes have smaller fruit, ranging from cherry tomatoes to half-pounders. In general, their flavor is not as good as that of indeterminate varieties. But they tend to be earlier. Most varieties that bear fruit within $1\frac{1}{2}$ to 2 months of transplanting are bush tomatoes.

TOMATOES

Variety	Description	Sources*
Beefmaster	80 days; indeterminate; very large red fruits to 2 pounds; VFN; tolerates cracking	12, 38
Beefsteak	80–90 days; indeterminate; open-pollinated; large fruits to 12 oz.; somewhat susceptible to blossom drop; meaty flesh	38
Better Boy	72 days; indeterminate; large fruits; somewhat susceptible to blossom drop; adaptable to all climates; VFN	5
Burpee's Big Boy	78 days; indeterminate; dependable, long-term yields; large red fruits to 2 pounds; disease susceptible	5
Burpee's Big Girl	78 days; indeterminate; similar to Big Boy, but with good disease resistance; ample leaf cover prevents sunscald	95
Celebrity	70 days; determinate; exceptional disease resistance; widely adaptable	WA

(continued)

TOMATOES—*Continued*

Variety	Description	Sources*
Coldset	68–74 days; determinate; compact and bushy; seedlings stand well in spring frosts; good in cool soils, cool weather	33
Doublerich	60–90 days; vigorous plant; medium-sized, globe-shaped, bright red fruits; extremely high in vitamin C	4
Early Girl Hybrid	54–62 days; indeterminate; dependable producer; resists cracking; fruits early and late in season	5
Floramerica	75–80 days; determinate; dependable yields; good resistance to most diseases; good in warm climates; AAS	1, 33
Jubilee	72–80 days; indeterminate; non-acid Rutgers type; globe-shaped with orange to yellow flesh	5
Longkeeper	78 days; can be picked partially ripe before frost and kept 6 to 12 weeks in storage; light golden orange when ripe	5
Manalucie	80–90 days; indeterminate; large, vigorous plants; deep scarlet fruits to 8 oz.; resistant to wilt, gray leaf spot	14, 17
Manapal	80 days; indeterminate; large vines form heavy cover; thick-walled red fruits; resists diseases; good in humid areas	8, 22
Marglobe	73 days; determinate; dependable, open-pollinated favorite; vigorous vines; large fruits to 6 oz.	15
Nova	65–75 days; compact growth; early; small, Roma-type fruits; excellent for processing	15
Roma	75 days; determinate; heavy yields; pear-shaped fruits to 2"; VF resistant; a favorite paste tomato	WA
San Marzano	70–90 days; indeterminate; good foliage cover; red, pear-shaped fruits; excellent for paste, sauce, and canning	5, 23
Stakeless	78–80 days; bush-type growth to 24"; fruits held well off ground; wilt resistant; meaty, globe-shaped fruits to 8 oz.	12
Subarctic	62 days; determinate; good potential for heavy yields; compact plants with round fruits to 2½ oz.	15, 33

TOMATOES—*Continued*

Variety	Description	Sources*
Sweet 100	65 days; indeterminate; needs staking; several hundred cherry-sized red fruits per plant, borne in clusters	WA
Toy Boy	55–68 days; determinate plants to 24"; ping-pong-ball-sized fruits set quickly	33
Vendor VF	68–83 days; semi-compact plants; dependable; generally round fruits to 5 oz.; disease resistant; flavorful	15, 33
Yellow Plum	70 days; yellow-skinned; plum-shaped fruits to 2" long; popular for making preserves; also good eaten fresh	13, 23

*Listings correspond to seed companies listed under Sources of Seeds at the back of the book.

TURNIPS

Brassica rapa,
Rapifera Group

Once as widely grown and appreciated as the potato, the turnip is now more misprized than esteemed. It doesn't deserve its bad reputation. A good turnip root is mild and sweet enough to eat raw, though most gardeners cook them. Southern gardeners grow the turnip mainly for its pungent, nutritious leaves. Turnip greens continue to grow long after the first fall frosts, and they are a cut-and-come-again vegetable. And a handful of growers regard the turnip as a gourmet's broccoli. They grow special varieties—called broccoli raab—which send up a large succulent stalk or flower head, picked before its flowers open, either as a spring or fall crop.

Soil Preparation: A deep, open soil rich in organic matter suits turnips best.

Though the plant's edible root goes no deeper than the topsoil, its other roots can reach down 3 to 4 feet in light soil. Not fussy about pH, the turnip will grow well from pH 5.5 to 6.8, which is the usual range for soils rich in organic matter. Let the roots get as big around as a nickel before you give them nitrogen, or you'll get a head of leaves and no turnip.

How Much to Plant: A rough guideline is 30 plants per person.

Planting: There's a simple reason why the best turnip roots are grown in cool weather. The sugar produced during the day accumulates in the roots when nights are cool. But when nights are warm, the leaves use more energy for respiration, and they drain sugar from the roots and soon deplete the store. Missouri truck farmer Bill Schmittel says that warm weather makes the roots bitter. "You have to keep them growing. Anything that slows them up, like heat or not enough water, will hurt their taste," he says.

In the spring, sow the first turnips three or four weeks before the last frost, or as early as you can make a seedbed. The young plants can survive temperatures in the mid-20s. Even this early, the turnip germinates speedily—in 50°F soil, seed will sprout in five days. (In warm soil, seed may sprout overnight.) Space conventional rows 12 to 15 inches apart, and sow three seeds to the row inch. Raised bed spacing is usually 6 inches, but California intensive gardener and author John Jeavons manages with equidistant spacings of 3 inches. Seed can also be broadcast in wide rows. Bury seed lightly with no more than 1/4 inch of soil.

An early planting in cool soil makes a slow start compared to a late planting in warm soil. In tests at the Rodale Research Center, turnips planted in March took ten weeks to produce roots, 2 1/2 weeks longer than turnips planted April 18—which means that the two plantings matured at the same time. So if you choose a fast-growing variety, you can plant an early crop as late as a month after the last frost.

Fall-planted turnips must be sown early enough to reach near-maturity before cold weather sets in. In Missouri, Bill Schmittel plants turnips from August to early September. "Sometimes the late ones don't make it," he says. "But if we get sun and a little good weather after the first frosts in October, there'll be roots." In northern states, an old adage still makes sense: on the 25th of July, sow turnips wet or dry. In the South, the last sowing is usually in October (and the earliest is in February).

Mature turnips respond to cold weather by going to seed, a hazard for early plantings in both spring and fall. When a spring sowing has fair weather and matures rapidly, a late cold spell may cause bolting.

Sow turnips for greens on the same schedule as turnips for roots. The spring harvest comes to an end when the greens turn tough and bitter in warm weather. The fall harvest lasts until temperatures drop into the teens.

Sow turnips for raab in late August and early September. The harvest will start in six weeks and continue a month or more. You can also plant raab turnips late in the fall, overwinter the roots under mulch, and harvest the seedstalks in spring. But don't grow raab as a spring crop because the flowers open too fast. You have to cut while they're young, and the cold slows them down. Unused seed is good for five years.

Growing Guidelines: The leaves of a mature plant occupy an 18-inch circle, but turnips are usually planted quite closely, since the harvests for both roots and greens start when the plants are young. When the first true leaves have appeared, thin plants to one per inch. After these plants have begun to touch each other, thin again to 4 to 6 inches. Use these tender greens in salads. Mulch to preserve moisture and to keep the soil cool once the plants are established. Supply moisture when needed during the short growing season. No supplemental fertilizer is required in good soil.

Harvesting and Storing: The spring harvest is shorter than the fall harvest. Fall roots remain edible until they freeze, weeks after the first frosts. Bill Schmittel says the leaves thaw without much damage after the temperature drops into the 20s. "At about 20°F,

they're killed," he says. "Our rule of thumb is to get the roots up the first time the air temperature falls to 15°F and stays there for 12 hours."

Schmittel stores his crop in bins at 34°F. He doesn't clean the turnips. "The dirt is moist and keeps the humidity high. And the roots don't seem to bruise as easily. When you pull a turnip, just cut the top right at the root—don't leave any green." In cold storage, turnips keep several months provided the temperature is under 40°F and the humidity is high. Avoid warmer storage temperatures— the roots will sprout. If they freeze, the roots will develop pits and watery spots. Turnip roots will also keep in the ground if they are mulched after the tops have died and the soil has turned cold, but they will be more likely to sprout before you get a chance to eat them.

You *can* store turnips in the freezer. First cut them into 1/2-inch cubes, then blanch the cubes in boiling water for 90 seconds before freezing. Or you can preserve your crop by shredding it and making turnip kraut.

For greens, harvest only young turnip leaves that are fully open but not fully grown, and leave the emerging crown leaves for later pickings. Turnip growers often take three cuttings from one planting.

Pests and Diseases:

In the southern half of the country, the turnip's main pest is the turnip aphid. Dry, hot weather is the turnip aphids' signal—they can be scarce one week and devastating the next. In wet weather, fungal diseases keep them in check. If your plants look stunted and you find aphids on the undersides of the leaves, dust with diatomaceous earth or rotenone. You can also dislodge the aphids with a sharp spray of water, but you'll have to repeat the treatment frequently because these aphids can find their way back.

In northern states, turnips are plagued by flea beetles. In fact, in some cabbage fields, turnips are grown to lure the beetles away from the cabbages. Diatomaceous earth and rotenone will check, but not eliminate, flea beetles. You can trap the beetles with yellow-orange water jugs coated with tree Tanglefoot, but the easiest way to protect your crop is to grow it under Reemay.

The best defense against the soilborne diseases (including clubroot, scab, crown gall, and blight) that attack turnips is to rotate your plants around the garden. Allow at least a year to pass before you plant turnips where any other brassica has grown.

Nutritional Value:

Turnip greens have nearly as much vitamin A as spinach, and twice the calcium. They are also high in B vitamins and vitamin C. The roots are mainly a source of vitamin C.

Choosing Varieties:

There are dozens of turnip varieties. The colors range from solid white to gold, and the shapes from round to oval. The old standby is PURPLE TOP WHITE GLOBE— it monopolizes the meager space that supermarkets give to turnips.

Eileen Weinsteiger, a Rodale researcher, has grown several hybrid turnips, among them PRESTO, TOKYO CROSS, and TOKYO MARKET. "I think the hybrids are sweeter than PURPLE TOP," she says. The USDA recently registered its first heirloom turnip. Called the GILFEATHER after the family that kept it, the mild, sweet turnip is prized by gardeners in the area of Brattleboro, Vermont, where it has been grown since it was brought from Ireland in 1863.

TURNIPS

Variety	Description	Sources*
Broccoli Raab	60 days; for summer and early fall greens; loose flower heads and leaves	7, 8, 13
Gilfeather	75 days; best when ½" across; are not pithy when larger; delicate flavor; smooth texture; an exclusive	38
Presto	30–50 days; can be sown progressively from spring to fall; dislikes very hot or cold temperatures; small, uniform roots	13
Purple Top White Globe	55 days; round roots; white with purple tops; tender and firm flesh; high yields; good storer	WA
Seven Top	45–50 days; grown only for greens (roots are woody); greens grow to 16" high; grown as a winter annual in the South	WA
Shogoin	30 days (greens); 70 days (roots); hold up well in hot, dry weather; globe-shaped roots; AAS	WA
Tokyo Cross	35 days; very early; pure white roots to 6" long; hold shape well; good resistance to disease, viruses; AAS	WA
Tokyo Market	50 days; for spring or fall crop; pure white, flattened roots; slow to bolt; mild flavor	21

*Listings correspond to seed companies listed under Sources of Seeds at the back of the book.

The best-known varieties grown for turnip greens are SHOGOIN, which is Japanese, and SEVEN TOP, an old favorite with multiple crowns. Both have woody, unappetizing roots. Growers also cut greens from PURPLE TOP WHITE GLOBE and then harvest the root. In fact, most turnip varieties produce tasty greens.

Broccoli raab has a tender seedstalk with mustardy leaves and a single, broccolilike floret. The edible portion of the seedstalk is the top 6 to 12 inches, which, along with the leaves, can be steamed or eaten raw in salads.

WATERMELONS
Citrullus lanatus

Nothing beats a perfect homegrown watermelon at a summer picnic. And now you can ripen sweet, flavorful melons wherever you live. Techniques vary from grower to grower. Some use plastic mulch or row covers to hurry the harvest. Others rely on extra-early varieties, transplant timing, or special fertilizer and watering programs. Use the methods that suit your season—and appetite—for reliable watermelon production and harvesting.

Soil Preparation: Watermelons prefer a light, fertile, deep loam or sandy soil. Soil should be well drained and have a pH of 5.5 to 6.5. Prepare the soil of the watermelon plot the fall before planting by digging deeply and adding a shovelful of composted manure, a half-cup of bonemeal, a pinch of kelp, and a tablespoon of wood ashes in each planting hole, turning it under to a depth of 6 inches or more so that deep roots may make use of it. If the soil is clay, add half a bucket of course sand to every hill or circle.

How Much to Plant: A rough guideline is 10 to 15 feet of row (five to seven melons) per person.

Planting: When planting seeds directly in the garden, poke them into hills. Hills provide seeds with added warmth to aid germination. Make the hills or circles 13 inches in diameter, then heap up the soil to a depth of 2 or 3 inches. The higher the mound, the warmer it will be, but also the drier it will become in hot weather. Poke eight to ten seeds into each hill and cover with an inch of soil. Unused seed is good for four years.

After the true leaves develop, thin out all but three or four strong plants per hill. When the vines have grown 1 to 2 feet long, thin them to allow only one or two vines per hill.

Spacing of the plants depends on the variety planted and fertility of the soil. Some small varieties adapt to container or circle bed plantings, or to trellising, with slings used for fruit support. Field-grown watermelons, however, require 6 to 12 feet per vine. As vines advance, set them gently back into rows or onto hills.

Handling Seedlings: Transplants don't yield any more heavily than direct-seeded watermelons, but they mature a few days earlier. Start plants in the greenhouse three weeks before the ordinary outdoor planting date. (If the seedlings are any older, transplant shock slows them down.) At Hutchins Farm in Concord, Massachusetts, John Bemis picks more than a ton of watermelons every year. In an area where a spring frost can strike as late as Memorial Day, Bemis starts harvesting by the third week in July.

He used to direct-seed in mid-May, but the emerging plants lost out in the race against weeds. Now Bemis starts all his watermelons in the greenhouse in April. He makes four sowings, one every two weeks. This gives him a steady harvest from July until fall frost, usually late in September.

Bemis starts the watermelons in seedling flats with a soilless mix. He sows two seeds per cell, then thins to one when the true leaves appear. "I think temperature in the greenhouse is critical," Bemis says. "We don't let it drop below 55° F at all, and the closer to 70° F we can keep it, the better the germination." He waters every day because the greenhouse is heated with a woodstove and the air is dry.

The seed should all be up within two weeks. That first sowing stays in

Bemis's greenhouse for another two weeks. During the second week of May, the seedlings are moved out into a cold frame, drenched with a fish emulsion solution, and left there to harden-off for a week or two. He tries to get his first planting out into the field by May 15. First he lays a dark plastic mulch, then sets the plants about 1 foot apart in 6-foot-wide rows. Slitted plastic row covers go on right away and stay on until the first good flush of blossoms appear.

Growing Guidelines:
Melons in plots mulched with black plastic grow much more vigorously and begin running much earlier than those on bare ground. They are ready to pick seven to ten days earlier, and the final yield is about twice as high. If you use plastic mulch, make sure the bed slopes toward the center so that rainwater can drain toward the plants through the planting slits.

Watermelons need plenty of water while they're growing. Water when there's less than $\frac{1}{2}$ inch of rain in any ten-day period. Stop watering once the fruit reaches full size and begins ripening.

Feed melons manure tea every two or three weeks during the season. One gallon covers about ten plants. Give the melons four to five weeks to grow in bare soil, letting the ground heat up, before laying down a thick mulch of organic matter. Before that mulch goes down, top-dress each plant with a shovelful of rotted manure or compost.

In the sandy soils of central Florida, watermelon growers race to ripen their crop before the Fourth of July holiday. Many of them prune their melons by pinching back the main vine. That encourages the growth of side shoots, which set fruit earlier than the main runner. Also, you can pinch out blossoms for earliest production in cooler zones. After a plant forms two or three fruits, pinch out the next cluster of blossoms, and keep on pinching for the next two weeks. If you're facing an early fall, the fruit set on those clusters won't have time to ripen anyway. By preventing their formation, the plant can concentrate all its energy on the first melons. They'll ripen earlier, and they might even be sweeter.

Harvesting and Storing:
To tell whether a watermelon is ripe, first thump it. If you hear a hollow sound, which indicates ripeness, then check the rind to see whether there's a yellow (as opposed to pure white) spot where it's touching the ground, which also indicates ripeness. Then look for a tendril at the joint where the melon stem emerges from the main vine. When that curly tendril withers and turns brown, chances are good that the nearest melon will be ripe. Wait, however, until tendrils on both sides of the stem joint turn brown. That's a sure sign of ripeness.

There's another method of determining ripeness that's almost always a sure-fire success—counting. For every watermelon variety, there's an average number of days from the time the fruit is set until it ripens. That's 27 days for PETITE SWEET and 35 for CRIMSON SWEET. Start counting when a tiny melon appears at the end of a female blossom, and when the correct number of days has passed, it will be ripe. You can use this technique for any variety, once you've figured out the right number of days using trial and error.

Most watermelon is eaten fresh, sliced and served plain or cut into fruit salads. But the flesh will freeze well if

WATERMELONS

Variety	Description	Sources*
Black Diamond	90 days; vigorous vines; large, round melons with dark green skin; red, sweet flesh; seeds stippled black	12
Burpee Fordhook	74 days; early and productive; nearly round melons to 14 pounds; bright red, tasty flesh; hardy in the North	5
Charleston Gray	85 days; vigorous vines; fruits 24" long, to 28 pounds; red flesh; resists anthracnose, fusarium wilt; adaptable	5
Crimson Sweet	80 days; high yields; vigorous vines; round melon to 25 pounds; dark red flesh; resists anthracnose and fusarium wilt; good in the North	5, 8
Dixielee	90–92 days; smooth, light green skin with dark stripes; dark red flesh; resistant to anthracnose and fusarium wilt	14
Petite Sweet	71 days; round melons to 10 pounds; pinkish red flesh with extra-high sugar content; brown seeds	12
Seedless 313	84 days; good yields; vines bear all season; round fruits to 15 pounds; very sweet flesh	11
Sugar Baby	75 days; small melons; round, dark green skin; red, tasty flesh; good variety for the North	15
Sweet Favorite	64 days; vigorous; highly productive; skins have prominent green stripes; flesh has high sugar content	15
Tom Watson	80–95 days; tough, prolific vines; sweet, firm, dark red flesh; does well in the North	22
Top Yield	82 days; melons up to 20 pounds; bright red, juicy flesh; resistant to anthracnose and fusarium wilt	37
Yellow Baby	70 days; small, vigorous vines; oval to round fruits to 10 pounds; yellow flesh with fewer seeds; AAS	5
Yellow Doll	75 days; very productive vines; round melons to 8 pounds; crisp, yellow flesh	38

*Listings correspond to seed companies listed under Sources of Seeds at the back of the book.

packed in a honey-based syrup or sprinkled with lemon juice. Pickled watermelon rind is a regional delicacy.

Pests and Diseases: Though they
might need a little longer growing season, watermelons are easier to grow than
cantaloupes. Cantaloupes are susceptible
to a wide array of diseases, including
powdery mildew and bacterial wilt, while
watermelons are much more resistant to
them. Given a choice, even cucumber
beetles and aphids choose cantaloupe
over watermelon.

Nutritional Value: Watermelons
are valued for fine flavor rather than
nutritional value, which is minimal.

Choosing Varieties: There are
plenty of good watermelons that mature
in 80 days or less. One favorite is YELLOW
DOLL, a round, green-skinned, yellow-
fleshed melon. The taste is extra sweet
and slightly different from red-fleshed
varieties. It's a nice addition to fruit salads.

Even growers with the luxury of a
long season are on the lookout for early
watermelon varieties. "Our season might
be long enough to grow most varieties,"
says Delbert Hemphill, University of
Oregon horticulturist, "but it isn't hot
and sunny enough." When melons
mature late in the fall, they just don't
seem to be as sweet. It could be that
cloudy weather and shorter days reduce
photosynthesis and slow sugar formation. Whatever the reason, gardeners in
the Willamette Valley and other cool
coastal areas of California and the Northwest need short-season varieties. So Dr.
Hemphill planted a trial of 26 watermelon varieties and ranked them not
only for earliness but for size, weight,
shape, color, and flavor as well.

In the race for the earliest melon,
there was a surprise winner—SEEDLESS
313—58 percent of the fruit was harvested by August 29. Runner-up was
SUGAR BABY, the pretest favorite with 53
percent ripe by the same date. SEEDLESS
313 outscored SUGAR BABY (and every
other variety, too) in the taste test as well.
BURPEE FORDHOOK also ranked near the
top of the flavor heap for its exceptional
sweetness. It set some fruit early, too, but
the long period over which it ripens its
fruit is a quality that will make it appealing to most home gardeners.

Dr. Charles Hall, head of the horticulture department of Iowa State University, has been breeding watermelons for
30 years. Admitting his partiality, Dr.
Hall thinks that the best watermelon for
the home gardener is the one he developed years ago, PETITE SWEET. It's a
short-vined plant, requiring about half
the space of conventional watermelons,
and it matures early. "Earlier, in fact,
than most muskmelons," Hall says. It's
sweet, too, and has good disease resistance, which is something many of the
old varieties can't claim.

For a sure, steady harvest, it might
be a good idea to plant a midseason
variety as well. Dr. Hall recommends
CRIMSON SWEET, a melon he introduced
in 1963. Since then, CRIMSON SWEET has
become a favorite from Massachusetts to
California because of its high yield, disease resistance, and top-quality fruit.

SOURCES OF SEEDS

The number beside each company corresponds to numbers which are listed with vegetable varieties in the text. Naturally, other companies may also carry these varieties, but our list is a good place to start when ordering catalogs.

1. American Takii
   301 Natividad Road
   Salinas, CA 93906

2. Allen, Sterling, and Lothrop
   191 U.S. Route 1
   Falmouth, ME 04105

3. Asgrow Seed Company
   1740 East Oak Road
   Vineland, NJ 08360

4. Burgess Seed and Plant Company
   905 Four Seasons Road
   Bloomington, IL 61701

5. W. Atlee Burpee Company
   300 Park Avenue
   Warminster, PA 18991

6. D. V. Burrell Seed Growers Company
   Box 150
   Rocky Ford, CO 81067

7. Comstock, Ferre, and Company
   263 Main Street
   Wethersfield, CT 06109

8. DeGiorgi Company
   P.O. Box 413
   Council Bluffs, IA 51502

9. Farmer Seed and Nursery Company
   818 SW Fourth Street
   Faribault, MN 55021

10. Ferry-Morse Seed Company
    111 Ferry-Morse Way
    Mountain View, CA 94042

11. Henry Field Seed and Nursery
    Shenandoah, IA 51602

12. Gurney's Seed and Nursery Company
    Yankton, SD 57079

13. Joseph Harris Company
    3670 Buffalo Road
    Rochester, NY 14624

14. H. G. Hastings Company
    P.O. Box 4274
    Atlanta, GA 30302

15. Johnny's Selected Seeds
    Albion, ME 04910

16. Jung Seeds and Nursery
    335 South High Street
    Randolph, WI 53957

17. Kilgore Seed Company
    1400 West First Street
    Sanford, FL 32771

18. Orol Ledden & Sons
    P.O. Box 7
    Sewell, NJ 08080

19. Liberty Seed Company
    P.O. Box 806
    New Philadelphia, OH 44663

20. Earl May Seed and Nursery Company
    Shenandoah, IA 52603

21. Nichols Garden Nursery
    1190 North Pacific Highway
    Albany, OR 97321

22. Northrup King Company
    P.O. Box 1827
    Gilroy, CA 95020

23. L. L. Olds Seed Company
    P.O. Box 7790
    Madison, WI 53707

24. George W. Park Seed Company
    P.O. Box 31
    Greenwood, SC 29647

25. W. H. Perron Company, Ltd.
    515 Labelle Boulevard
    Chomedey, Laval
    Quebec, Canada H7V 2T3

26. Pinetree Garden Seeds
    New Gloucester, ME 04260

27. Porter & Son, Seedsmen
    Stephenville, TX 76401

28. Redwood City Seed Company
    P.O. Box 361
    Redwood City, CA 94064

29. The Rocky Mountain Seed Company
    1325 15th Street
    Denver, CO 80217

30. S & H Organic Acres
    P.O. Box 27
    Montgomery Creek, CA 96065

31. Seeds Blum
    Idaho City Stage
    Boise, ID 83706

32. Shepherd's Garden Seeds
    7389 West Zayante Road
    Felton, CA 95018

33. Stokes Seeds
    Box 10
    St. Catharines, Ontario
    Canada L2R 6R6

34. Sunrise Enterprises
    P.O. Box 10058
    Elmwood, CT 06110

35. Territorial Seed Company
    P.O. Box 27
    Lorane, OR 97451

36. Thompson and Morgan
    P.O. Box 100
    Farmingdale, NJ 07727

37. Otis Twilley Seed Company
    P.O. Box 65
    Trevose, PA 19047

38. Vermont Bean Seed Company
    Garden Lane
    Bomoseen, VT 05732

39. Vesey's Seed
    York
    Box 9000
    Charlottetown, Prince Edward Island
    Canada C1A 8K6

40. Dr. Yoo Farm
    P.O. Box 290
    College Park, MD 20740

WA   Widely Available

BIBLIOGRAPHY

Ball, Jeff. *Jeff Ball's 60-Minute Garden.* Emmaus, Pa.: Rodale Press, 1985.

Bartholomew, Mel. *Square Foot Gardening.* Emmaus, Pa.: Rodale Press, 1981.

Bubel, Nancy. *The Seed-Starter's Handbook.* Emmaus, Pa.: Rodale Press, 1978.

Carr, Anna. *Good Neighbors: Companion Planting for Gardeners.* Emmaus, Pa.: Rodale Press, 1985.

———. *Rodale's Color Handbook of Garden Insects.* Emmaus, Pa.: Rodale Press, 1979.

Chan, Peter. *Better Vegetable Gardens the Chinese Way: Peter Chan's Raised Bed System.* Pownal, Vt.: Storey Communications, 1985.

Doscher, Paul, Timothy Fisher, and Kathleen Kolb. *Intensive Gardening Round the Year.* Brattleboro, Vt.: The Stephen Greene Press, 1981.

Hill, Lewis. *Successful Cold-Climate Gardening.* Brattleboro, Vt.: The Stephen Greene Press, 1981.

Hunt, Marjorie B., and Brenda Bortz. *High-Yield Gardening.* Emmaus, Pa.: Rodale Press, 1986.

Jeavons, John. *How to Grow More Vegetables Than You Ever Thought Possible on Less Land Than You Can Imagine.* Rev. ed. Berkeley, Calif.: Ten Speed Press, 1982.

Newcomb, Duane. *Growing Vegetables the Big Yield-Small Space Way.* Los Angeles, Calif.: Jeremy P. Tarcher, 1981.

Raymond, Dick. *Wide-Row Planting: The Productive Miracle.* Charlotte, Vt.: Garden Way Publishing, 1977.

Reilly, Ann. *Park's Success with Seeds.* Greenwood, S.C.: George W. Park Seed Co., 1978.

Staff of *Organic Gardening* magazine. *The Encyclopedia of Organic Gardening.* Emmaus, Pa.: Rodale Press, 1978.

Yepsen, Roger B., Jr., ed. *The Encyclopedia of Natural Insect and Disease Control.* Emmaus, Pa.: Rodale Press, 1984.

INDEX

Page references in *italic* type indicate illustrations;
boldface page references indicate table entries.

Rodale Press, Inc., publishes RODALE'S ORGANIC GARDENING®,
the all-time favorite gardening magazine.
For information on how to order your subscription,
write to RODALE'S ORGANIC GARDENING®, Emmaus, PA 18098.